HOMER ON LIFE AND DEATH

HOMER ON LIFE AND DEATH

JASPER GRIFFIN

CLARENDON PRESS · OXFORD

Oxford University Press, Great Clarendon Street, Oxford OX2 6DP

Oxford New York
Athens Auckland Bangkok Bogota Bombay
Buenos Aires Calcutta Cape Town Dar es Salaam
Delhi Florence Hong Kong Istanbul Karachi
Kuala Lumpur Madras Madrid Melbourne
Mexico City Nairobi Paris Singapore
Taipei Tokyo Toronto Warsaw
and associated companies in
Berlin Ibadan

Oxford is a trade mark of Oxford University Press

Published in the United States by
Oxford University Press Inc., New York

British Library Cataloguing in Publication Data

Griffin, Jasper / Homer on life and death
1. Homer—Criticism and interpretation
2. Life in literature 3. Death in literature
I. Title
883'.01 PA4037
ISBN 0-19-814026-6

9 10 8

Printed in Great Britain
on acid-free paper by
Antony Rowe Ltd, Chippenham

TO THE MEMORY OF
MY BROTHER GEOFFREY, 1940–1962

τὸν μὲν ἄκουρον ἐόντα βάλ' ἀργυρότοξος Ἀπόλλων
νυμφίον

PREFACE

THE desire to write this book arose out of my teaching. Listening to many essays on Homer, I came to feel that the undergraduates who wrote them were being impelled, by the books and articles they read, in the direction of a dryness which did less than justice to the *Iliad* and *Odyssey*. Mycenaean land-tenure, Bronze Age archaeology, the intricacies of formulaic phraseology: these special and technical questions seemed almost to squeeze the poems out. The consequence was that I began to lecture on Homer myself.

I owe many debts to the work of many predecessors and contemporaries. Some personal obligations it is a particular pleasure to record. Mrs. M. Bugge, Mrs. C. Ross, and Mrs. L. Smithson typed the manuscript with accuracy and good humour. My thoughts on Homer have been sharpened by many arguments with my Balliol pupils, who have often made me think again. My colleague Dr. Oliver Lyne read the proofs with a sharp eye, and not only for typographical errors. Professor Hugh Lloyd-Jones, with characteristic generosity, has given me the great benefit of his acute and learned criticism, and also of his stimulus and encouragement. To all of them I should like to express my lively thanks.

Oxford   J. G.
September, 1979

CONTENTS

Preface   vii

Abbreviations   xi

Introduction   xiii

I. Symbolic Scenes and Significant Objects   1

II. Characterization   50

III. Death and the God-like Hero   81

IV. Death, Pathos, and Objectivity   103

V. Gods and Goddesses   144

VI. The Divine Audience and the Religion of the *Iliad*   179

Bibliography   205

Index   212

ABBREVIATIONS

AJP	*American Journal of Philology*
A und A	*Antike und Abendland*
ANET	*Ancient Near Eastern Texts related to the Old Testament*
AOAT	*Alter Orient und Altes Testament*
ARW	*Archiv für Religionswissenschaft*
BICS	*Bulletin of the Institute of Classical Studies, London University*
CAH	*Cambridge Ancient History*
CJ	*Classical Journal*
CQ	*Classical Quarterly*
GRBSt.	*Greek, Roman and Byzantine Studies*
HSCP	*Harvard Studies in Classical Philology*
HZ	*Historische Zeitschrift*
JHS	*Journal of Hellenic Studies*
NJbb.	*Neue Jahrbücher* (the title has been extended in different ways at different times)
Philol.	*Philologus*
REG	*Revue des Études Grecques*
Rh.Mus.	*Rheinisches Museum*
TAPA	*Transactions of the American Philological Association*
WS	*Wiener Studien*
WüJbb.	*Würzburger Jahrbücher*
YCS	*Yale Classical Studies*

In referring to the text of the Homeric poems, Arabic figures mean the *Iliad*, Roman figures the *Odyssey*: thus 7.64 means the sixty-fourth line of the seventh Book of the *Iliad*, but vii.64 the corresponding line of the *Odyssey*.

The translations from Homer are the author's adaptation of the *Iliad* version by Lang, Leaf, and Myers, and the *Odyssey* of Butcher and Lang; and in some cases his own. Translations of the Scholia, never previously translated into English, are by the author.

INTRODUCTION

Nobody who writes on Homer has read everything, ancient and modern, that has been written about the poems. Each of us finds some more suggestive and helpful, some less, among the works of his predecessors. A feature of this book which perhaps deserves comment is the little that is said in it about the formulaic theory of the poems' composition, which since the work of Milman Parry has, in the last forty years, increasingly dominated discussion in English. Impressive as this large body of work has been on its own technical ground, I am perhaps not alone in feeling disappointment at the amount of light it has shed on the poems themselves. I think that it has been made very likely that the *Iliad* and the *Odyssey* represent the end of a tradition of oral poetry. That has some importance, as suggesting a line of explanation for some features of the poems: the repeated lines, the fixed and recurrent epithets, the typical scenes. Negatively, it rules out certain kinds of nineteenth-century analysis, which by pressing on verbal repetitions and minor inconcinnities dissolved the poems into fragments; it also should make us cautious about basing other kinds of argument on such repetitions. It serves, that is to say, as a check upon subjective approaches, but it does not and cannot rule them out in principle.

Even if the poems represent the end of a tradition of oral poetry, that does not tell us how the epics which we have were produced. It has been claimed that 'at a deeper level, all literary criticism of the Homeric poems must be radically altered by the Parry-Lord hypothesis',[1] and even that a new 'oral poetics' must come into existence before we can, without absurdity, presume to tackle the poems at all.[2] But the production of a new 'poetics' has proved difficult, and some recent writing on

---

[1] C. Moulton, *Similes in the Homeric Poems* (1977), 12.

[2] e.g. J. A. Notopoulos in *TAPA* 80 (1951), 1, 'Homeric scholarship must realize that the time has come to lay the foundations of a literary criticism, non-Aristotelian in character and emanating mainly from the physiognomy of oral literature, which differs in style and form from written literature.' Foundations which emanate from physiognomy; the style is new indeed.

formulaic utterances has contributed less to our aesthetic under-
standing than might have been hoped. The late Adam Parry,
in the valuable introduction to his father's collected papers,
wrote, 'To the scholar with literary interests, or to the student
or lover of literature in general, the whole argument may appear
so narrowly technical as to miss somehow the fundamental
issue, which is the poetry of Homer . . .'[3] A too exclusive attention to such questions has also led some scholars to disregard
valuable work done in a different tradition. On the other hand,
the whole conception of oral poetry as in its nature quite different from written poetry is coming to seem less and less tenable.
Ruth Finnegan, in her book *Oral Poetry* (Cambridge, 1977),
shows how the sharp distinction, on which the demand for a
new poetics rests, is eroded by study of the actual material:
'There *is* no clear-cut line between "oral" and "written"
literature' (p. 2), and 'The hope for a precise generalisation
about the nature of oral style of the kind that Magoun, Parry
and others have envisaged is, in my opinion, bound to be dis-
appointed' (p. 130). We shall, I think, have to go on with
aesthetic methods not essentially or radically new, observing
caution and avoiding arguments which are ruled out by an
oral origin for the work, but approaching the epics in a manner
not wholly different from the way in which the Greeks themselves approached them.

The ancient world has, in fact, proved a much more fertile
source of illumination than modern Yugoslavia. First, the vast
mass of Greek commentaries on Homer has proved to contain,
along with much unrewarding material, many acute and suggestive points, and of these I have made more extensive use
than most recent writers. Besides their intrinsic interest, they
have a certain value as a check on our own views: if we find
support for them in the work of the ancient commentators,
then that tends to show that they are so far not anachronistic,
that they made sense at least in later antiquity.

[3] In Milman Parry, *The Making of Homeric Verse* (1971), *l.* On the Yugoslav
material, salubrious reservations in F. Dirlmeier, *Das serbokroatische Heldenlied und
Homer, SB Heidelberg*, 1971; see also A. Dihle, *Homer-Probleme* (1970), 49 ff. 'For all
the proliferation of comparative studies, Homer remains a very special case', is the
judicious conclusion of J. B. Hainsworth, *JHS* 90 (1970), 98. 'The ruling theory of
the day (oral poetry) explains only half', says B. C. Fenik, *Homer, Tradition and
Invention* (1978), 90; perhaps still a generous estimate.

Second, the ancient literature of the Near East has produced parallels. It seems pretty clear that Homer and Hesiod were influenced from Eastern sources:[4] such influence made itself felt both before and after the 'dark age' of isolation from the Levant, which recent scholarship has tended to regard as a shorter break than used to be thought.[5] On the level of myth, the stories of Uranus, Cronos, and Zeus, familiar to the poets, derive from Hurrian and Hittite sources; the conception, vital to the poems and alien to later Greek religion, of all the gods as meeting together on Olympus, resembles the picture we find in the literatures of Mesopotamia and Ugarit. The Old Testament, too, has proved a more rewarding source of comparative material than seems to be usual. It is something of a paradox that the existence of the large, valuable, and convenient book, *Ancient Near Eastern Texts related to the Old Testament*, edited by J. R. Pritchard (third edition, 1969), has tended to lead Greek scholars to quote from it and consequently to omit the Old Testament itself, a collection of writings which is influenced by other Near Eastern cultures,[6] and so not less relevant than the others; besides containing works of higher literary quality and interest. It has seemed particularly interesting on the question of the reality and seriousness of Homeric religion.

There are also a certain number of parallels with Germanic and Irish literature. The aim here, as with the Eastern material, is to bring out, by comparison and contrast, the specifically Homeric character. Motifs and conceptions which are at home in related or adjacent literatures must undergo a characteristic transformation, to become adapted to the unique atmosphere of the Homeric poems. By such comparisons it is possible to gain an insight into that atmosphere.

---

[4] e.g. T. B. L. Webster, *From Mycenae to Homer* (2nd edn., 1964); P. Walcot, *Hesiod and the Near East* (1966); A. Lesky, *Gesammelte Schriften*, 356, 400; F. Heubeck, *Die homerische Frage* (1974), 167 ff.; and recent works of W. Burkert: 'Von Amenophis II zur Bogenprobe des Odysseus', *Grazer Beiträge*, 1 (1973), 69–78; 'Rešep-Figuren', ibid., 4 (1976) 51–80; *Griechische Religion der archaischen und klassischen Epoche* (1977), esp. pp. 282 ff.; 'Das hunderttorige Theben und die Datierung der Ilias', *WS* 10 (1978), 5–21.

L. A. Stella, *Tradizione micenea e poesia dell' Iliade* (1978) also deals with this question.

[5] A. M. Snodgrass, *The Dark Age of Greece* (1971), 238 and 246, argues that Greece was really cut off from the East for less than a century, between 'the extreme outer limits of 1025 and 950 BC'.

[6] See for instance *The Cambridge History of the Bible*, I (1970), 68 ff.

Lastly, I have been able to find much that is congenial and useful in the work of recent German writers on Homer. There are signs that in Germany the oral theory is at last catching on; we in turn, I think, have tended to neglect a body of work from which we have much to learn.

In an area in which the question of authorship and origin has so often dominated discussion, even to the point of eclipsing the poems themselves, it may seem almost provocative that I often talk of 'the poet' or even of 'Homer'. In part this is a form of shorthand: I want to discuss the poems, not to express on every occasion a view on their creation. But it also reflects my belief, which I hope this book will explain and justify, that the *Iliad* is a unity in a deeper sense than is sometimes allowed, embodying a clear and unique vision of the world, of heroism, and of life and death. If that is granted, then it is hard to imagine such a vision as anything but that, essentially, of one man; and it may be felt that we cannot separate from the greatest Greek epic poem the name which antiquity regarded as that of its greatest epic poet. The *Odyssey*, too, has a characteristic atmosphere of its own, which I have tried to define in contrast with the *Iliad*; and it seems natural to regard that poem also, despite the difficulties of its second half, as shaped by one coherent and powerful imagination.

I

SYMBOLIC SCENES AND SIGNIFICANT OBJECTS

The magic meaning of many objects is often closely connected with their symbolic significance . . . it is often an impossibility distinctly to divide the magic and symbolic significance.[1]

THE poet of the *Iliad* created a poem larger in scale than the ordinary epics of his time, and he organized and unified it on a different principle.[2] Instead of a straightforward narrative of an obviously significant event— the war of the gods and the Titans, the whole Theban War, the Capture of Troy—he took a theme which commenced in the middle of the war and ended before its conclusion. The wrath of Achilles and its consequences are made to represent the whole story. In Books 2–4 we see a repetition of the beginning of the war, with the first advance of the Achaeans,[3] the duel of Paris and Menelaus, and the sin of Pandarus which outrages the gods and dooms Troy again.[4] The death of Hector is made to stand for the fall of Troy itself; he alone defended Troy (6.403), and at his death 'it was most like the fall of the city, as if all lofty Troy were ablaze from top to bottom' (22.410 ff.). Such a conception, sophisticated and far from obvious, naturally implied that the poet would create and emphasize incidents which had a further significance for the poem

[1] F. J. M. de Waele, *The Magic Staff or Rod* (1927), 23.

[2] On Homer and the Cycle see my 'The Epic Cycle and the Uniqueness of Homer', *JHS* 97 (1977). The 'digressions' in the *Iliad* are paradigmatic and highly relevant: N. Austin in *GRBSt.* 7 (1966), 295–312.

[3] It is evident from 2.780 ff. with the use of a goddess to announce the Achaean coming, from her words (2.796), 'You are talking as you used to in time of peace, but war is upon us, unavoidable . . . I have never seen such an army . . .', that what we have is, in some sense, the *first* Achaean onset. The light-hearted challenge issued by Paris, 3 *init.*, also implies that he has not had ten years' experience of the Achaeans in war.

[4] H. Fränkel, *Wege und Formen*, 3; Codino, *Introduzione*, 52 ff. Adam Parry, *YCS* 20 (1966), 193, speaks of 'a succession of scenes comprehensively evaluating the human situation'.

than their mere matter of fact happening. The death of Hector is a case in which he has made this significance explicit, and that is important; it confirms that such ideas are not over-subtle and inappropriate to the criticism of an oral epic, but on the contrary were clearly entertained by Homer himself. But more often he does not express the significance of such events in this way, leaving it to his audience to understand it. I take an example which, though not spelt out explicitly, must have such significance.

When Hector was killed, Andromache was at home, fulfilling her wifely duties, as Hector had told her when they parted— 'Go home and attend to your own work, your weaving at the loom, and give orders to the servants to get on with their work; as for war, that shall be men's concern, and mine above all.' Obediently she was weaving and ordering a hot bath for her husband on his return; disturbed by the shrieks from the wall, she rushed up and saw Hector dead, dragged behind Achilles' chariot. She swooned, and as she did so, 'far from her head she threw the bright ribbons . . . and the head-dress which golden Aphrodite had given her on the day when Hector of the shining helmet took her as a bride from the house of her father Eetion'. This is obviously not a mere fact; Andromache, whom we have just seen happy at her wifely work, has lost her husband and her marriage, and she casts down the head-dress which became hers on her wedding day, a vivid symbol of her loss.[5] As Schadewaldt points out, the pathetic touch at the end of her lament is of the same sort: 'Now worms will eat you . . . when

---

[5] 'Go home', 6.490; Andromache at work, 22.440; her head-dress, 22.468. W. Schadewaldt, *Von Homers Welt und Werk*,[4] 331, on 'unwillkürliche Symbole'. I do not agree with M. N. Nagler, *Spontaneity and Tradition* (1974), 49 that what is symbolized here is 'that feeling of sexual violation so remorselessly developed in the Trojan plays of Euripides'. The fact that old Hecuba, too, throws off her veil, 22.406, certainly does not support this gratuitous notion, which Homer is careful to exclude from what he says about Andromache's destiny, cf. 6.454 ff. and 24.727 ff. 'It means it was a love match, and the bride was beautiful', says M. M. Willcock of the head-dress given by Aphrodite, *BICS* 17 (1970), 50; I prefer the comment of the scholiast, *ΣT* in 468: εἰς μνήμην ἄγει τῆς παλαιᾶς εὐδαιμονίας ὅπως τῇ μεταβολῇ αὐξήσῃ τὸν οἶκτον, 'he reminds us of her former happiness, so that by means of the change he may increase the pathos.' Compare the perceptive comment, *ΣT* in 22.500 on the name Astyanax: τὸ ἀπὸ τῆς εὐδαιμονίας αὐτῷ συμβὰν ὄνομα λέγουσα πλέον οἰκτίζεται . καὶ ἐπαναλαμβάνει αὐτό, 'She achieves a more pathetic effect by speaking the name given to him from his prosperity; and she repeats it' (sc. at 506).

the dogs are sated with your flesh, lying naked; while in your house there lie many fine clothes, the work of women's hands. But now I will burn them all—not to benefit you at all, for you will not lie in them, but to glorify you in the sight of the people of Troy' (22.508–14). The well-kept clothes stand for the good housewife and her care of her husband. Now, though she has lovingly looked after his clothes, he is naked, exposed to carrion beasts, and the garments which were the embodiment of her love have lost their meaning and can go into the fire.

We must observe here how deftly Homer makes a point. In practice early Greeks did believe that the purpose of burning the clothes of the dead was to give them to the dead man to wear in the other world—the same natural conception as led them to give him a sword, or his favourite dog, or his servants, or food.[6] Homer, anxious as he always is to underline the absolute separation of the world of the dead from that of the living, will have none of this. Hector will derive no benefit from the burning of his clothes, and purely psychological motives replace superstition. Andromache shows the richness of Hector's household and the completeness with which her own life is destroyed; the Trojans admire, and the act is one of heroic glory.[7]

The examples I have chosen are of course fairly evident to any sensitive reader. In such scenes we see a gesture or a tableau which brings out fully the implications and importance of events, and we observe the poet using simple acts or physical objects (a head-dress, a man's clothes) to convey the emotional significance. This technique is in fact pervasive, not only in the *Iliad* but also, in a rather different way, in the *Odyssey*. I shall first exemplify and discuss it, and then go on to some of its connections and implications.

Clothing lends itself very well to being used in this way. At the beginning of *Iliad* 3, as the two armies approach for the first time in the poem, Paris 'stepped out as champion in front of the Trojan ranks, wearing a panther skin over his shoulders,

[6] The *locus classicus* is Herodotus 5.92, 2, the burning of clothes for the dead wife of Periander, who complained that she was cold and naked in the next world; cf. E. F. Bruck, *Totenteil und Seelgerät*, 28, E. Weiss, *Gr. Privatrecht*, i, 146.

[7] In the same way human sacrifice to the dead Patroclus is presented by Homer as an act of purely secular revenge, 18.336, 21.27, 23.22, 175; the victims are pathetic (21.27 ff. and ΣT in 21.31), Achilles passionate in anger.

and his bow and sword . . .'. He challenges the Achaean chiefs. Menelaus accepts with delight—and at the sight of him Paris is intimidated and slinks back into the ranks; 'as when a traveller is confronted by a serpent . . . so did Paris, beautiful as a god, start back in fear from the son of Atreus.' Before the appearance of Paris, two immediately preceding passages have made the same point. At the end of Book 2 the poet introduced the Carian leader Nastes among the Trojan allies, 'who went to war wearing gold like a girl, the fool; that did not ward off grim death, but he was slain by fleet-footed Achilles in the river, and he took his gold.'[8] The death of Nastes is not actually mentioned in Book 21, but this single allusion characterizes him with deadly finality. Then the armies are described (3.1–9). The Trojans advance with screams and cries like those of birds, but the Achaeans 'in silence, breathing prowess, resolved to stand by each other'. The passages reinforce each other. Trojans are seen, as soon as they appear in the poem, as gorgeous, frivolous, noisy; Achaeans, by contrast, are serious and grim. This contrast will be carried throughout the poem, as the scholiast observes: 'He characterizes the two armies and does not depart from the representation all through the poem.'[9] Trojans propose duels, Achaeans win them (Books 3, 7). Trojans are gorgeously dressed: Euphorbus, slain by Menelaus, 'stains with blood his tresses like the Graces, and the love-locks he wore plaited in silver and gold' (17.51). Their gait, even, marks them as what they are—the boaster Othryoneus is hit 'as he stepped high';[10] Polydorus 'in his folly was showing off the swiftness of his feet, racing between the front ranks, until he lost his life' at

---

[8] Paris steps out, 3.15; he slinks back, 3.33; Nastes, 2.872; cf. in the *Nibelungenlied*, a dashing young Hun, 'dressed out in his finery like a young wife of the nobility'. He is at once killed by Volker, who 'thrust his spear clean through that gorgeously turned-out Hun' (p. 234, Penguin trans.). Such warriors exist only to be slain by proper heroes. A similar contrast is made between the French finery and the English 'warriors for the working day' in *Henry V*.

[9] ΣT in 3.2 ἄμφω δὲ τὰς στρατιὰς διατυποῖ καὶ μέχρι τέλους οὐκ ἐξίσταται τοῦ ἤθους. Cf., for instance, G. Finsler, *Homer*, 1.142, W. H. Friedrich, *Verwundung und Tod in der Ilias*, 21.

[10] Euphorbus, 17.51; Othryoneus, 13.371; καὶ βάλεν ὕψι βιβάντα τυχών, with Σb οἰκεῖον τῷ ὑψηλόφρονι καὶ τὸ βάδισμα;, 'even his gait is appropriate to his arrogance.' Deiphobus, too (13.156), 'strides along, full of pride, stepping lightly on his feet and advancing under his shield'. Contrast the gait of Ajax (7.212): 'with a grim smile on his face he advanced with great strides', and Σ ad loc.: 'The movement of his body shows the courage of his heart.'

Achilles' hands. Asius calls Zeus a liar, Othryoneus promises to drive the Achaeans way from Troy single-handed, Hector hopes to kill Achilles: 'If Achilles really has risen up from the ships, so much the worse for him; I shall not run away from him—no, I shall stand and face him, and either win great glory or be beaten . . .'[11] Paris, having challenged Menelaus, must be shamed by his brother into fighting and then be rescued by a goddess; Hector, after his stirring boast, will be unable to face Achilles and run for his life.

This pattern is vital to the *Iliad*, it is no mere Greek chauvinism. The Achaeans win the war because their discipline is better, as we are told explicitly; their silence and obedience to their commanders go with this. The Trojans lose because they are the sort of people they are—glamorous, reckless, frivolous, undisciplined. And the archetypal Trojan is Paris. He can fight well when he feels like it, but often he will not; he goes out to war at the beginning of Book 3 wearing a leopard skin, and so he has to change into proper armour before he can fight— and we are to supply the reason: because he looked glamorous in it. Hector reproaches him with his excessive good looks, his music, and his seduction of women, and Paris replies that 'the gifts of golden Aphrodite are not to be despised.'[12] This is the Paris who is whisked away from the battlefield by the goddess, and who, while Menelaus searches for him to kill him, is waiting for Helen, at home in his bedroom—'radiant with beauty and dressed in gorgeous apparel. No one would think he had just come from fighting, but rather that he was going to a dance, or had just done dancing and sat down to rest.'[13]

Now, Paris it was who doomed Troy by choosing Aphrodite and the life of pleasure;[14] and since Paris is the archetypal Trojan, the sin of Paris is one in which Troy is inextricably implicated. They may 'hate him like death' (3.454), but they cannot get clear, just as Helen now hates and wishes to be rid

[11] Eustathius, 1144.30, rightly points to the echo in 18.305 of 18.278, τῷ δ' ἄλγιον αἴ κ' ἐθέλῃσιν. He calls it an ἀστεισμός, a piece of wit. Polydorus, 20.410; Asius, 12.164; Othryoneus, 13.367; Hector, 18.305.
[12] Achaean discipline, 17.364; obedience, 3 *init.*, 4.430; Paris, 6.520; Hector reproaches Paris, 3.54. Those who find fault with Hector in the poem may call him 'too good looking', 17.142; even Hector, admirable as he is in some ways, is still a Trojan.
[13] 3.392–4. A good discussion in W. F. Otto, *The Homeric Gods*, 96 ff.
[14] K. Reinhardt, *Das Parisurteil* = *Tradition und Geist*, 16–36.

of him, but still finds herself forced to go on sleeping with him (3.395–420). In Book 3 the poet shows us Paris in contrast with Hector, and both of them in their relation with Helen in Book 6. In the latter book he shows us also the contrast between the false marriage of Paris and Helen, and the true marriage of Hector and Andromache: on the one side a liaison based on pleasure, guilty and sterile, in which Helen wishes Paris dead; on the other the loving parents of a child, where Andromache tells Hector he is the one thing in her life, and he speaks of love and duty. These scenes are all representative. This, we see, is how these people always were, this is the meaning and underlying pattern of events. We see what Paris is doing to Troy, what Hector is, and what his death will mean. The ancient commentators remark regularly on Homer's 'graphic' power, his skill at producing memorable visual scenes,[15] and certainly this is a characteristic of Homeric writing which strikes the audience at once; but these scenes are more than simply vivid. Again we observe that physical objects are used by the poet to achieve his effects of significance.

When Hector comes to call Paris back to the fighting, he meets in turn the three women who love him, his mother, Helen, and his wife; each of them tries to get him to stay with her and not go back to the battle.[16] Hecuba, a true mother, offers to fetch him a drink; Helen invites him to sit down and talk with her. Andromache urges him to stay with her on the wall, or his own reckless courage will leave her a widow and her child an orphan. All three represent the same temptation, in nicely calculated variety and crescendo: the temptation to turn his back on the terrible world of fighting and death, and linger in the delightful company of loving women and their plausible justifications. The drink offered by Hecuba, the chair set by Helen—these embody the attractiveness of yielding to feminine persuasion and turning away from heroism. But we see from

[15] Thus ΣT on 6.405, γραφικῶς, 'like a picture': Eustath. 655.52 on 6.467 ὡς ἐν γραφικῇ ὄψει, 'as if painted in a picture': ΣT on 22.80, Hecuba on the wall, κινητικὸν καὶ γραφικὸν τὸ σχῆμα, 'the scene is moving and pictorial' etc., E. Bethe comments on the scenes in Book 6: 'Dieser Dichter hat mehr gewollt, als nur erzählen ... Alles, was diese Menschen tun und sagen, ihr Gang, ihre Tracht, ihr Haus ... ist Ausdruck ihres Wesens' (Homer, 1,236). Cf. also C. A. Trypanis, The Homeric Epics (1977), 66.

[16] Schadewaldt, Von Homers Welt und Werk,[4] 212 ff. Hecuba, 6. 258; Helen, 6.354; Andromache, 6.431.

Helen's contempt for Paris and Andromache's love for Hector that what a woman really wants in a man is the strength to resist her and go out among the flying spears.

Andromache brings her child to watch Hector; we have seen that his presence marks the union of his parents as different from that of Paris and Helen. He is too young to speak, but by being there he gives the dialogue its colouring, from Andromache's opening words, 'Have pity on your baby son and on me ...' to Hector's doomed prayer that his son may be a greater warrior than his father; and above all in that touching moment when Hector goes to take the baby, who is frightened by his father's grim helmet.[17] The father puts off the helmet, and the parents smile at each other across the child. This enables them to feel in harmony again and is immediately recognizable as human,[18] but we must also see more in it. The function of armour is to terrify, a point I shall make at length, but not to terrify one's own children, so that from one point of view we can see Homer here turning a regular and constant feature of heroic verse into something human and unexpected; and, more specifically, putting to a new use the regular formulaic title—'Hector of the flashing helmet', κορυθαίολος. From another, we see that the Hector who carries out a man's task of defending his wife and child must, in doing so, become alien and terrifying to his own son,[19] as all things are changed from what they were 'beforetime, in peace, before the sons of the Achaeans came'.

Another significant moment has been devised by the poet in the encounter between Hector and Paris. Leaving his mother, 'Hector beloved by Zeus came into Paris' house. In his hand he held his spear, eleven cubits in length, and before him shone the brazen point of the spear, and round the spear ran a golden ring. He found Paris in his bedroom busy with his splendid armour, his shield and breastplate, and polishing his curved bow, while Argive Helen sat among her maidservants and gave

[17] 'Have pity', 6.408; Hector's prayer, 6.476. On this scene, H. Herter in *Grazer Beiträge*, 1 (1973), 157 ff.

[18] Σb in 6.468, λαβὼν τοῦτο ἐκ τοῦ βίου ὁ ποιητὴς ἄκρως περιεγένετο τῆς μιμήσεως, 'the poet took this from life.'

[19] J. M. Redfield, *Nature and Culture in the Iliad*, 123. Interesting reservations on κορυθαίολος : J. B. Hainsworth in *Homer: Tradition and Invention*, ed. B. C. Fenik (1978), 47.

them instructions for their work' (6.318–324). The scene is
again a symbolic one.[20] Hector's coming is preceded by the
gleam of his great spear—the true warrior comes; he finds
Paris not in a respectable part of the house but in his boudoir
among the female servants, among whom he is showing off his
weapons and putting an even greater shine on them. The nature
of the two men is brought out clearly. The scholiasts, with their
sharp eye for such points, saw all this: 'As an example and in-
citement to Paris Hector appears in a martial light, giving advance notice of his coming by means of his spear,' they observe;
and of Paris, 'He is represented as a fop, showing off to his wife
and, one might almost say, owning weapons merely for show.
And again he is not even in the courtyard but among the
maids.'[21] Again we find the same skill at using objects—the
spear of Hector, the armour of Paris—to underline the significance of events; the technique is in fact here capable of making
two contrasting points by means of what is at bottom the same
thing—the weapons of the warrior. We shall be returning to
this. We now leave this scene in Book 6, but not before observing that its function is carried through to the end. The
scholiast comments: 'We can see the two characters contrasted
with each other: while Hector gives precedence to assisting his
countrymen rather than to pleasure, Paris is sitting beside
Helen.'[22]

The scene from Book 6 has been handled at some length. We
have seen that in a scene which certainly was in antiquity
recognized as symbolic (a reassuring check that we are not im-
porting anachronistic subtleties), Homer made regular and
effective use of the significant power of situations and of objects. We see him doing this in a scene which exists in order to
bring out the nature of Troy and of the Trojan war;[23] this

---

[20] H. Schrade, *Götter und Menschen Homers*, 244.

[21] ΣbT in 6.319, πρὸς ὑπογραμμὸν καὶ προτροπὴν Ἀλεξάνδρου θρασὺς
φαίνεται Ἕκτωρ διὰ τοῦ δόρατος προμηνύων τὴν ἄφιξιν. ΣbT in 6.321,
τὸν καλλωπιστὴν δηλοῖ καὶ ἐναβρυνόμενον τῇ γυναικὶ καὶ μόνον οὐχὶ
πομπῆς χάριν κεκτημένον τὴν σκευήν· ἄλλως τε οὐδὲ ἐν τῇ αὐλῇ ἐστιν ἀλλὰ
ἐν μέσαις ταῖς ἐρίθοις.

[22] ΣbT in 6.390 ... καὶ ἔστιν ἰδεῖν ἀντικείμενα τὰ πρόσωπα, Ἕκτορος
μὲν προτιμήσαντος τῶν ἡδέων τὴν βοήθειαν τῶν πολιτῶν, Ἀλεξάνδρου δὲ
τῇ Ἑλένῃ παρακαθημένου.

[23] By contrast, P. Vivante in *CQ* 25 (1975), 11: 'The ὁμιλία does not subserve
the action . . .'

Paris, glamorous and frivolous, is the man to have chosen pleasure in the Judgement of the three goddesses, and so to have brought on Troy the destructive anger of Hera and Athena.[24] Indirect means are thus used to make points of great importance to the poem, and the audience, it is assumed, will understand. Methodically, we can now advance to apply this sort of interpretation to other passages.

In the second book, Agamemnon is deceived by a lying dream sent by Zeus. He summons the Achaean army *en masse*, and attempts to excite their martial ardour by an ill-advised stratagem: he will counsel despair and flight, while the other commanders are to urge them on. The effect aimed at is presumably that of making the army reject with indignation the idea of returning in disgrace from an enemy so much fewer in numbers, a point laboured by Agamemnon in his discouraging speech (2.122–30); but in fact the troops are overwhelmed with joy at the thought of going home and rush in chaotic tumult for the ships. Agamemnon, who has failed to predict this outcome, is unable to do anything to stop it. Now, when Agamemnon appeared to make his speech he is described in these terms:

Up rose mighty Agamemnon holding the sceptre which Hephaestus had toiled to make. Hephaestus gave it to the Lord Zeus, son of Cronos; Zeus gave it to Hermes the Messenger, Argus-slayer; and the Lord Hermes gave it to Pelops, driver of horses, who in turn gave it to Atreus, shepherd of the people. Atreus at death left it to wealthy Thyestes, and he left it to Agamemnon to bear, to rule over many islands and all Argos. Leaning on that sceptre he spoke to the Argives . . .

We have already heard that as soon as Agamemnon had woken from his deceptive dream, he dressed and picked up 'his ancestral sceptre, an everlasting possession' (2.46). This sceptre, then, is heavily emphasized; what is the point? As in arming-scenes (see below, p. 36ff.), we expect something singled out in advance for mention to have a role to play. First, it is reasonable to suppose that the origin of the sceptre is significant. It comes from Zeus, and when Zeus gives the sceptre to a king, he gives him honour and privilege: Nestor told Achilles not to struggle with Agamemnon, 'for he has incomparably greater honour, a sceptred king to whom Zeus gives glory' (1.278). The idea was an ancient one. In the great empires of the Near East, rulers

[24] 5.24–67, 18.358, 20.313–17.

claimed to have been given their sceptre by the supreme god.[25] Now, at this moment of the *Iliad* we know that Zeus, on whom Agamemnon relies (1.174, 'I have others who will honour me, and above all Zeus the Counsellor'), is planning to humiliate and deceive him. The god who gave him the sceptre which marks his power is also the god who has just sent him the lying dream. There is therefore a grim irony in the emphasis on Zeus as the source of his position;[26] he leans on the symbol of kingship which has already been undermined.

Again, when his plan has failed, the Achaeans are racing for the ships, and it seems that Troy will not fall after all, Agamemnon looks on helplessly; inspired by Athena, Odysseus acts. 'He came up to Agamemnon son of Atreus and took from him his ancestral sceptre, an everlasting possession'; with the sceptre he hits those of low rank who are urging flight, with it he thrashes the insubordinate Thersites, and holding it he makes the speech which restores morale and is greeted with cheers by the army. The significance is clear: this is how to be a king,[27] and Agamemnon's failure in the role is symbolized in the treatment of that inherently significant object, the royal sceptre. The point is confirmed for us in Book 9 and Book 14. Thoroughly disheartened by defeat, Agamemnon twice proposes—without hidden intention—that the Achaeans should sail home. On each occasion he is rebuked, and the situation is

[25] Thus Assur-Nâsir-Pal of Assyria: 'When I had seated myself upon the royal throne in might, and when Assur had placed in my hand the sceptre which rules the peoples ...' (Luckenbill, *Ancient Records of Assyria and Babylonia*, I (1926), 141); at Babylon, *ANET*², 332.243, 'Marduk ... who turns over the pure sceptre to the king who reveres him ...'; cf. Dirlmeier in *Philol.* 90 (1935), 75. 'Le sceptre n'est pas seulement le signe, mais le siège d'une force religieuse': L. Gernet, 'Droit et prédroit en Grèce ancienne', *Anthropologie de la Grèce antique*, 205, with reference to L. Deubner, *ARW* 30 (1933), 83 ff. See also F. J. M. de Waele, *The Magic Staff or Rod* (Nijmegen, 1927), and A. Alföldi in *AJA* 63 (1959), 15 ff., L. A. Stella, *Tradizione micenea e poesia dell' Iliade* (1978), 54 ff.

[26] F. Jacoby, *SB Berlin*, 1932.589 = *Kleine Schriften*, 1.74, speaks of 'certainly conscious contrast' between the stately introduction of Agamemnon here, and the mortifying role he is to play.

[27] 2.186, 199, 265, 279, K. Reinhardt, *Die Ilias und ihr Dichter*, 113. G. Gschnitzer, on the other hand (*Studien zum antiken Epos*, ed. Görgemanns, 8–12), thinks the 'reactionary' poet of Book 2 is concerned to show Agamemnon as a long-established ruler, and Odysseus as acting *sub auspiciis regis*; but if we are to read poems to extract political messages, we must allow for the nature of poetic logic. Codino, *Introduzione*, 86, thinks that in Odysseus' hands 'the sceptre becomes a mere single club.'

restored, by firm speeches, one by Diomede, the other by Odysseus. In Book 9 Diomede tells the king that Zeus has given him the sceptre to be honoured above all others, but has not given him courage; in Book 14 Odysseus says that 'no sceptred king with so many subjects' should have brought himself to make such a speech. We see how both speakers find it natural to speak of the sceptre, and to contrast Agamemnon's possession of it with his inadequacy as a king. Again, as with the armour of Paris and Hector, the point illuminated here by the poet is an absolutely central one to the *Iliad*. The troubles and disasters of Agamemnon arise from his position; he is supreme (has the sceptre), but he is not the greatest hero. That situation is unstable and leads to his quarrel with Achilles. Homer uses the sceptre to underline it.[28]

Another function of a sceptre—not the unique inherited one of Agamemnon—is to represent the authority of the community.[29] Heralds hold them, so do ambassadors and speakers who 'have the floor' at public assemblies. This enables the poet to make another kind of striking and symbolic gesture. When Achilles in the quarrel wishes to make the most powerful possible statement of his refusal to go on fighting for the Achaeans, he says, 'I will speak out and swear a great oath to it: I swear by this sceptre, which will never grow leaves and twigs, since it has been cut in the hills . . . now among the sons of the Achaeans judges bear it in their hands, they who defend the ordinances established by Zeus; that will be a mighty oath: there will be a time when the sons of the Achaeans, all of them, will feel the absence of Achilles . . .' (1.233 f.) When he has finished this passionate oath, in which six lines describe the history of the sceptre before Achilles reveals what it is that he is about to swear by it—a powerful device of emphasis—he flings the sceptre to the ground. By doing so he gives vivid form to his rejection of his whole position among the Achaeans. The sceptre is to be held by those who administer justice: he is suffering injustice. It is the symbol of the community and its

---

[28] Adam Parry pointed out that even the way the two men are named, in *Iliad* 1.7—Ἀτρείδης τε ἄναξ ἀνδρῶν καὶ δῖος Ἀχιλλεύς—brings out the same point: Agamemnon is 'lord of men', defined by his position; Achilles is 'god-like', defined by his nature: *HSCP* 76 (1972), 2.

[29] G. Finsler, *Homer*², 1,209: *Iliad* 1.28, 3.218, 7.277, 18.505, 23.567. L. Gernet *Anthropologie de la Grèce antique*, 239–41.

sanctities: he rejects the community and withdraws from it to his own ships. All that is clearly intended by Achilles in the choice of such a gesture, made possible by the existence of an object charged with symbolic force.

The *Odyssey* provides an example of a scene parallel yet characteristically different. Young Telemachus, aroused by Athena, takes action at last against the Suitors and summons an assembly on Ithaca, the first for twenty years. He sits in his father's seat, and the elders make way for him (ii.14)—a line heavy with meaning; the prince gives visible sign that he is claiming the position of his father the King. He makes his speech, calling on the Suitors to get out of his house, and on the community to condemn them. At the end 'he flung the sceptre to the ground, bursting into tears; and all the people felt pity for him.' Already in antiquity this scene was contrasted with that of Achilles.[30] In the *Iliad*, the dire threat of a mighty hero, who has been assured already by Athena that he will prevail over Agamemnon; in the *Odyssey*, a very young man, trying to assert himself for the first time, in a hopeless position. The tears of Telemachus contrast with the passionate self-confidence of Achilles, and the effect in the *Odyssey* is softer, almost sentimental—but still in its own way effective; and helping to show the range of use such physical objects could serve.

I give some more examples from the *Odyssey*. When Odysseus first catches sight of his house, to which after twenty years he is returning disguised as a beggar, he takes Eumaeus' hand and says, 'Eumaeus, in truth this is the fine house of Odysseus; it can easily be recognized . . .' He goes on to dwell upon its details, concluding that 'Many men are keeping revel within, for I smell the meat and hear the music of the lyre.' The pathos of his return, where the hero must still control his heart even in sight of the home he has longed for, allowing himself only to catch at his companion's hand, is delicately expressed (xvii. 260 ff.). Very similar is the famous episode of the dog Argus. The loyal dog, thrown out to die on the dunghill because his master is away, gives a symbolic vignette of the meaning of his absence; and again the pathetic effect comes closer to sentimentality than is ever allowed in the *Iliad* (xvii.290 ff.). On a larger scale, both the Bow and Bed of Odysseus are used for this

[30] *ΣbT* in 1.245, and cf. R. von Scheliha, *Patroklos*, 184.

sort of effect. When the bow is brought out, first Penelope sits down and weeps over it, then the loyal retainers weep at the sight of the master's bow (xxi.55, 82); we recognize the same sensibility. The bed, of which Telemachus when he envisages his mother's remarriage asks whether it is 'covered with cobwebs', turns into the vital key which allows husband and wife to find each other at last. Odysseus built it, as part of his house; unmoved and unrevealed to any outsiders, it embodies the solidity and wholeness of their union (xvi.35, xxiii.177 ff.). In the *Iliad*, a contrast of a different sort is achieved when the Trojans have won their first successes. When the sun has set, with the Achaeans in full retreat, Hector addresses the assembled Trojan forces out on the battlefield, 'in a clear spot, where the ground was clear of corpses' (8.491): 'In his hand he held a spear eleven cubits long . . . Leaning on the spear he addressed the Trojans . . .' We remember that in the second book Agamemnon spoke leaning on his sceptre; in this deadly setting Hector uses not the symbol of civil order but the spear, the symbol of bare military force. 'It is effective that he speaks not holding a sceptre but the symbol of valour', the scholiast perceptively comments,[31] and his speech is not one of advice and counsel but consists of military orders, which are carried out at once, without any reply. As well as the use of a spear instead of a sceptre, the setting or the attitude of an assembly can interpret its mood and purpose. The Trojans in the eighth book meet out on the battlefield because they are beleaguering the Achaeans in their camp and watching that they do not sail away in the night; the poet of Book 10, the *Doloneia*, exaggerates this motif in harmony with his general liking for gruesome and bizarre effects,[32] and makes the Achaean chieftains get up in the middle of the night and leave their fortified camp, in order to hold a meeting of the general staff 'in a clear spot, where the ground was clear of corpses falling [*sic*],[33] the place where mighty Hector turned back from his slaughter of the Argives' (10.199). What was straightforward has become eerie, at-

---

[31] Σ̔b in 8.494, καλῶς οὐ σκῆπτρον κατέχων δημηγορεῖ ἀλλὰ τὰ τῆς ἀνδρείας σημεῖα προβαλλόμενος: Reinhardt, *Die Ilias und ihr Dichter*, 182.

[32] F. Klingner, *Hermes*, 75 (1940), 337 = *Studien zur gr. und röm. Literatur*, 7–39.

[33] τάφρον δ' ἐκδιαβάντες ὀρυκτὴν ἑδριόωντο | ἐν καθαρῷ, ὅθι δὴ νεκύων διεφαίνετο χῶρος | πιπτόντων· ὅθεν αὖτις ἀνετράπετ' ὄβριμος Ἕκτωρ| ὀλλὺς Ἀργείους.

mospheric, chosen for its own sake; why should the Achaean leaders leave their camp in order to meet in such a place? When Achilles has made his appearance and threatens to return to battle, an assembly of Trojans is held, 'and they gathered for the assembly before they thought of dinner; and the assembly was held all standing, nor did any man dare to sit down . . .' (18.245). Their position, their indifference to food, characterize their mood and state.

The motif of 'food' is constantly used by the poet to make effects of will and symbolism. These are sometimes missed by modern scholars. First, there is the use of food to embody the idea of honour. Sarpedon, in his great speech to Glaucus on the theme of *noblesse oblige*, begins by saying 'Glaucus, why are we honoured especially with seats of honour and meat and full cups of wine in Lycia? . . . That is why we must stand in the front rank of the Lycians and meet the flame of war, so that the Lycian infantrymen may say, "They are not ignoble rulers, our Lycian kings, eating the fat sheep and drinking choice wine; no, their valour is good, they fight in the front rank among the Lycians" ' (12.310–21). So too Hector insults the retreating Diomede: 'Son of Tydeus, the Achaeans honoured you with seats of honour and meat and cups full of wine, but now they will dishonour you . . .', while Agamemnon calls on Idomeneus to bestir himself, saying that he has always honoured him in war and at the feast, where his cup has always stood by him full, 'as it does for me, to drink when heart bids' (4.277–62), and on the Athenian leaders with the words, 'You are the first to hear of a banquet from me' (4.343).[34] It is worth remembering that in the old Theban epic Oedipus cursed his sons because they sent him the less honourable cut of meat, and so doomed them to death; later Greek thought, less instinctively in tune with such symbolic gestures, regarded this as a most inadequate motive,[35] and indeed I think the Homeric poets would have

---

[34] This is a very common motif in Germanic epics; for instance *Beowulf*, 2605, *Nibelungenlied*, 34, 'Etzel should never show them favour again', said Volker. 'I can see them here in crowds shaking at the knees, those who eat their prince's bread so disgracefully and now leave him in the lurch . . .' Persian grandees were paid by the Great King in food: D. M. Lewis, *Sparta and Persia* (1977), 4 ff., cf. Tac., *Germ.* 14.4, *epulae . . . pro stipendio cedunt.*

[35] *Thebais*, fr. 3 Allen; Σ in Soph. *O.C.* 1375 . . . ὁ δὲ μικροψύχως καὶ τελέως ἀγενῶς ὅμως γοῦν ἀρὰς ἔθετο κατ' αὐτῶν δόξας ὀλιγωρεῖσθαι.

been reluctant to make such a point the fulcrum for a great movement of the plot, although the idea of more honourable cuts of meat was quite familiar to them.[36] Thus we see that food is a tangible form of honour; as an ancient commentator observes, 'What he is talking about is not food but honour.'[37] Possessions, too, are inseparable from the idea of 'honour', and indeed the word 'honour' is often used to mean simply 'gifts' or 'possessions'.[38] But more interestingly the eating of food is used to embody moral values.

We often find in early literature the motif of fasting. Saul vowed that Israel would fast during a battle, with disastrous results; all Siegfried's followers fasted after his murder; and so on.[39] Especially is this common after a death. Achilles, in Book 19, refuses to eat before entering battle, and tries to prevent the rest of the Achaean army from eating. The sensible Odysseus points out, sensibly, that it is better to have a meal before going into battle, and in the end everybody eats except Achilles, who is given supernatural nourishment by Athena. Denys Page[40] waxes merry about this ('more than 180 lines have now passed since luncheon stole the limelight'), but I think we need

---

[36] e.g. 7.321, viii.476, ix.160, 550. In the Irish *Feis Tige Bricrenn* a quarrel is deliberately stirred up between three heroes over the question who should have the portion reserved for the best champion; a masculine version of the Eris-apple. See E. Knott and G. Murphy, *Early Irish Literature* (1966), 119. Text is published with English trans. as *Irish Text Society*, 2 (1899). The introduction to the volume refers to the well-known fragment of Posidonius *ap*. Athen. 154 b = 87 FGH 16, on fights to the death at dinner among the Celts over the most honourable cut of meat.

[37] ΣT in 4.343, οὐ περὶ βρωμάτων ἀλλὰ περὶ τιμῆς ὁ λόγος.

[38] For instance, 9.155 = 9.297, οἵ κέ ἑ δωτίνῃσι θεὸν ὣς τιμήσουσι: 9.602, ἀλλ' ἐπὶ δώρων | ἔρχεο· ἶσον γάρ σε θεῷ τείσουσιν Ἀχαιοί. 15.189, τριχθὰ δὲ πάντα δέδασται, ἕκαστος δ' ἔμμορε τιμῆς. Cf. M. I. Finley, *The World of Odysseus*, 140 ff. Even in a context of deep pathos the poet thinks to add to the grief of a bereaved father by saying that 'distant kinsmen divided his estate', 5.158.

[39] 1 Sam. 14:24 ff., *Nibelungenlied* § 17; cf. E. Samter, *Homer* (= *Volkskunde im altsprachlichen Unterricht*, I (1923)), 116 ff., who gives other parallels.

[40] *History and the Homeric Iliad*, 314. So too G. S. Kirk, *Songs of Homer*, 360: 'The tiresome arguments about whether Achilles will or will not take any food . . .' A more perceptive discussion: W. Schadewaldt, *Iliasstudien*, 133. Odysseus, who also does not understand Achilles, is a great one for pressing the urgent claims of the belly in the *Odyssey*, xvii.473, xviii.53. J. Trumpf, *Studien zur griechischen Lyrik* (Diss. Cologne, 1958), 8–24, makes interesting points on the significance of eating and drinking together in Greek and other Indo-European traditions.

only look to Book 24 to understand its purpose. In that book
Achilles forces Priam to eat with him before releasing to him
the body of Hector. Achilles would not eat until he had slain
Hector, and even after he reluctantly breaks his fast (23.43 ff.),
he refuses to wash the blood from his body until the corpse of
Patroclus is burned; he lies out on the beach, groaning, 'in a
clear spot, where the waves were splashing on the beach',[41] till
sleep comes on him. Even after the funeral games he cannot
sleep and wanders about the beach alone (24 *init.*). It is perfectly in line with this that he ignores the 'enormous presents'
which Agamemnon gives him as compensation in Book 19,
telling him only to produce them, or to keep them himself, if he
likes (19.147); he is still unreconciled, and avoids eating with
his opponent.

Eating together is a universal mark of union, creating a
bond.[42] Poor Lycaon vainly pleads for his life on the ground
that he has eaten, as a captive, in Achilles' house; Odysseus, in
the *Odyssey*, will not eat with Circe until she has delivered his
companions from the swine-form into which she has transformed them. Nursing his revenge and full of hatred, Achilles
will not honour this universal custom, until the last book of
resolution, where the hero who 'has destroyed pity' and who
'has a disposition as savage as a lion'[43] is finally seen in the
poignant tableau where Priam kneels to kiss his hands, and rises
to the occasion. He treats his guest with courtesy and eats with
him, then they gaze at each other and admire in each other the
nobility and beauty which each possesses.[44] This has given the
poet here a metaphor which enables Achilles to return to
humanity before he meets his death. The fasting has been
turned from a taboo or cult practice into an individual expression of Achilles' extreme grief; eating with old Priam re-
solves the passionate separateness of the hero, which it had

---

[41] 23.61. This 'unnecessary' line is interestingly discussed by W. Elliger, *Landschaft in griechischer Dichtung*, 68.

[42] If illustration were needed, a nicely explicit Egyptian inscription, recording
the bringing of a Hittite princess to marry Rameses II, *ANET*³, 258: 'they ate and
drank together, being of one heart like brothers . . . for peace and brotherhood
were between them.'

[43] 21.75 ff., x.373 ff. Lycaon, 21.75 ff.; Circe, x.373 ff.; Apollo on Achilles,
24.41-4.

[44] 24.621 ff., cf. H. J. Mette in *Glotta*, 39 (1961), 52.

seemed that nothing would be able to end.[45] Among the gods, too, the same symbolism is powerful. The angry scene in the first book, Hera nagging and Zeus threatening, is resolved as they feast together. In the last book, Thetis is summoned to Olympus to be told by Zeus that her son must give up the body of Hector. As she enters, dressed in mourning, Athena makes way for her to sit next to Zeus, and Hera puts a golden goblet in her hand, and she drinks. Here we see her old opponents, the two goddesses against whose plans she intrigued in Book 1, make gestures of reconciliation, eloquent though silent.

Mention of the golden goblet leads naturally to other golden cups which appear at significant moments. As Patroclus leaves Achilles to lead the Myrmidons, a heroic venture from which we know he will not return, Achilles goes into his hut; 'he opened the lid of a chest, handsome and ornate, which silver-footed Thetis had given him to take on his ship. She had stocked it well with tunics, cloaks to keep out the wind, and soft rugs. Within there was an ornate cup; no other man drank sparkling wine from it, nor did he pour libations to any god but Father Zeus. This he took from the chest and cleansed with sulphur, then he rinsed it in fair flowing water . . .' He makes a libation from this cup and prays to Zeus for the safe return of Patroclus from battle. This is a turning-point in the plot. Patroclus will be killed, and that will dictate the rest of the action of the *Iliad*. Its importance is marked by the gesture, in

---

[45] There is an interesting parallel in the *Song of My Cid*, the most important Spanish medieval epic. I quote from the translation by W. S. Merwin (1969), § 62, p. 71. The Cid obliges his captive, Count Ramon, to eat; for two days the Count refuses. Finally the Cid says,
'Unless you eat well, Count,/and to my full satisfaction,
You will remain here,/we shall not part from each other.'
The count said: 'I will eat,/I will eat with a will.'
With those two knights/he eats quickly.
My Cid, sitting there watching,/is well pleased,
Because the Count Don Ramon/proved so expert a trencherman.
'If it pleases you, my Cid,/we are ready to go;
Tell them to give us our beasts,/and we shall ride at once:
I have not eaten so heartily/since I have been a count;
The pleasure of that meal/will not be forgotten.'
The Count is then given presents and released, unable to believe in the Cid's generosity. This episode, charming and *naïf* as it is, shows how a motif developed by Homer into high tragedy can also be treated in a very different spirit.

which we see again what looks like a regular cult act transformed into a pure expression of emotion[46] on the part of
Achilles. The special cup, which exists only for this moment,
marks the occasion as important, and also, as with the sceptre
of Agamemnon in Book 2, has a bitterly ironical overtone, for
Zeus, the god invoked and honoured with the precious cup, has
already decided on Patroclus' death (15.65). Again the
treasured human possession is used to bring out the helplessness
of man in the perspective, shared by the audience but not by
the characters, of the will of Zeus. Nor do we fail to see the
pathos of Thetis, the careful mother, packing for her doomed
son the human comforts of warm clothes; as with the house-
keeping of Andromache, these garments are worth mentioning,
even at the highest points of an epic poem, because the poet
relies on his audience to understand that they are not mere
items on a laundry list but the vehicles of profound emotion.
From studying such unobtrusive touches we gain an insight into
the Homeric achievement of emotion and pathos by means of
an apparently objective style.[47]

Nestor, too, has a special cup, famous to us because it was at
first thought to resemble a cup found by Schliemann in a
shaft grave at Mycenae.[48] It is embossed in gold, with four
handles and two doves to each handle. We see him use it only
in the scene in Book 11 where he is visited by Patroclus and
applies all his skills to get him to induce Achilles to return to
battle, or at the least to send his friend. Again this is a crucial
scene, in which the susceptible Patroclus will be so much moved
that he will beg to be allowed to fight. The wounded Eurypylus
is in Nestor's tent, and a captive woman prepares for them a
medicinal drink. The cup of Nestor, we are told, was such that
another man could move it from the table only with difficulty;
but old Nestor lifted it without effort. The idea is unexpected,
as Nestor is old and often complains of his weakness, and Leaf
proposed to delete the lines. No doubt their purpose is to linger
a little longer on the cup and the moment of rest before the im-

---

[46] Gods feast, 1.601; Thetis drinks, 24.100; Achilles' cup, 16.221, cf. R. von
Scheliha, *Patroklos*, 260.

[47] See Ch. 4 on this question.

[48] e.g. G. S. Kirk, *Songs of Homer*, 111 n.4. The cup: 11.632, cf. T. B. L. Webster,
From Mycenae to Homer, 33, A. Heubeck, *Die homerische Frage*, 222, L. A. Stella,
Tradizione micenea e poesia dell'Iliade (1978), 39. Priam's cup, 24.234.

portant dialogue begins. Perhaps also they attempt to convey the idea of the importance of what Nestor is about to do: getting Patroclus into battle is the ἀριστεία, the heroic achievement, of Nestor in the *Iliad*, and before it he is given something analogous in function to the arming-scene which regularly precedes the great martial ἀριστεία of an ordinary hero. Finally, Priam has a treasured cup, given him by Thracians when he went on an embassy. 'It was a great treasure, but Priam did not hesitate to give it, so great was his anxiety to ransom his son.' It forms the climax of the list of rich offerings which Priam takes to Achilles to ransom the body of Hector, and it is a transparent means of showing the emotion of Priam. He parted with his most treasured possession to honour Hector.

The way in which meals are described also has symbolic rather than nutritious interest. It was remarked in antiquity that heroes are shown eating nothing but roast beef,[49] the most heroic of foods; camped by the 'Hellespont rich in fish', they never turn to fish as an item of diet. Meals are never described with real truth to actual practice of life, and the point about them is the honour done to those present and the fairness of the division—'their hearts lacked for nothing in the evenly divided feast', we read constantly. Thus it is moral aspects which interest the poet,[50] and their significance; these men were simple and heroic in their tastes, and they ate together like brothers.

Nor is it only what the heroes eat which has significance; just as much attaches to what they do not eat. Repeatedly heroes are compared to wild beasts which are ὠμοφάγοι, eaters of raw flesh; the adjective in fact is only used in Homer in comparisons of warriors. Carrion birds and dogs who eat the bodies of the

[49] A lengthy discussion of heroic diet, Athenaeus *ad init.*, cf. H. Strasburger, *SB Heidelberg*, 1972, 28. Cf. also Shakespeare, *Henry V*, Act III, Scene vii, 'Give them great meals of beef and iron and steel, they will eat like wolves and fight like devils.'—'Ay, but these English are shrewdly out of beef'.

[50] A. Roemer, *Homerische Aufsätze*, 123 n. 1; H. Fränkel, *Dichtung und Philosophie*, 31. 'Wahrscheinlichkeit im naturalistischen Sinn ist nicht homerisch', observes G. Finsler, *Homer* 1.320, and 'überhaupt ist alles Sachliche dem poetischen Bedürfnis durchaus untergeordnet', 1.326. οὐδέ τι θυμὸς ἐδεύετο δαιτὸς ἐίσης, 1.468 etc. ΣbT in 19.231, τοσοῦτον εἰς ἀρετὴν ὁ ποιητὴς ὁρᾷ, ὅτι καὶ τὴν ἀναγκαίαν τροφὴν ταύτης ἕνεκα δεῖν προσφέρεσθαί φησιν: 'the poet looks so much to martial prowess that he says even necessary food should be applied towards that goal.' Cf. also *JHS* 97 (1977), 47.

slain are ὠμησταί, eaters of raw flesh.[51] That word is also applied to Achilles by Hecuba: 'Raw flesh eater, not to be trusted, he will not spare you'—ὠμηστὴς καὶ ἄπιστοϛ ἀνὴρ ὅγε, οὔ σ' ἐλεήσει | οὐδέ τί σ' αἰδέσεται, she says to Priam, trying to dissuade him from his perilous journey to the slayer of his son. And in fact Achilles says to the dying Hector (22.346), 'Would that my passionate heart would incite me to chop up your flesh and eat it raw, to pay you out for what you have done to me'; while Hecuba in her turn longs to hold Achilles' liver in her hands and devour it in revenge for Hector's death, and Zeus asks Hera whether she would satisfy her hatred for Troy only by eating Priam and his children raw. In the *Odyssey* cannibals do make their appearance—the Laestrygons and the Cyclops; and in one early epic, the *Thebais*, the hero Tydeus, wounded by his enemy Melanippus, sated his passionate hatred by gnawing his skull, so that Athena in disgust turned away with the immortality she was bringing him.[52] Such terrible acts of cannibalism, in which we are aware of the superstitious purpose of possessing the strength and power of one's adversary for oneself, represent in the *Iliad* a temptation which is avoided, something which would be too appalling to be actually allowed to happen.

Germanic parallels suggest strongly that both this and another related practice, that of eating animal flesh raw, were genuinely ancient Indo-European ideas of the way terrible heroes behaved. Early Vikings ate raw meat: 'this barbaric practice was condemned in later times.'[53] The killer of Sigurth, according to the *Eddas*, was fed on the flesh of serpents and wolves to harden him to the terrible deed. In the *Nibelungenlied* the Burgundians, besieged in Etzel's hall and deprived of refreshment, drink the blood of their enemies with gusto. Pindar knew of a tradition that the young Achilles was brought up on the raw entrails of wild beasts.[54] The werewolves of Germanic

---

[51] 7.256, 11.479, 15.592, 16.157: 11.454, 22.67.

[52] Hecuba to Priam, 24.207; Achilles to Hector, 22.346; Hecuba on Achilles, 24.212; Zeus to Hera, 4.305; Laestrygons, x.114; Cyclops, ix.289. Tydeus, Σ Gen. in 5.126, cf. E. Bethe, *Thebanische Heldenlieder*, 76, A. Severyns, *Le Cycle épique*, 219; the scene was represented on an Attic red-figured bell-krater, cf. J. D. Beazley in *JHS* 67 (1947), 1–9.

[53] L. M. Hollander, *The Poetic Eddas*², 192 n. 13.

[54] Hollander, loc. cit., 244; *Nibelungenlied*, p. 261 (Penguin trans.); D. S. Robertson, 'The food of Achilles', *CR* 54 (1940), 177–80.

legend have the same implication, as perhaps do such incidents as Sigurth eating the heart and drinking the blood of both Regin and Fafnir; in Greek legend the stories of cannibalism are numerous.[55] But we remember also that ὠμοφαγία, the eating of raw flesh, continued to be a feature of the ecstatic cult of Dionysus, who numbered among his titles that of 'Ωμηστής.[56] The ecstasy of Dionysiac cult is excluded from the Homeric poems as scrupulously as the eating of raw flesh, but Dionysus' name is found on the Pylos tablets, and Homer knows all about him and his maenads (6.130 ff., 389; 22.460). The only ecstasy permitted by the *Iliad* is that associated with fighting, and cannibalism and the eating of raw flesh must conform and be attached exclusively to the passion of war. Again we see that the physical details of life are capable of bearing symbolic value—not only what the heroes do, but also what they do not do;[57] and the intense delight with which heroes gloat over the prospect of their enemies' corpses being the prey of carrion animals and birds, it is not too much to say, draws some of its power from the existence, just below the surface, of the desire to perform this action, at once fascinating and disgusting, themselves.[58]

I turn to some simpler instances of the use of objects for emotional impact. When Achilles pursues Hector for his life round the walls of Troy, they pass the springs of the River Scamander, two springs, one hot and one cold; 'and there by them are the broad washing places, beautiful, paved with stone, where the wives of the Trojans and their beautiful daughters used to wash their shining garments, in the old days of peace, before the coming of the sons of the Achaeans':

ἔνθα δ' ἐπ' αὐτάων πλυνοὶ εὐρέες ἐγγὺς ἔασι,
καλοὶ λαΐνεοι, ὅθι εἵματα σιγαλόεντα
πλύνεσκον Τρώων ἄλοχοι καλαί τε θύγατρες
τὸ πρὶν ἐπ' εἰρήνης, πρὶν ἐλθεῖν υἷας Ἀχαιῶν (22.153-6).

All this is fantasy, of course; Scamander rose high up on Mount Ida, the hot and cold springs have no existence, and no

---

[55] W. Burkert, *Homo Necans* (1972), esp. 119–23.
[56] E. R. Dodds on Eur. *Bacchae* 139 and his *Introduction*, 14 ff.
[57] Cf. ΣbT in 1.449. οὐ γὰρ μόνον τί εἴπῃ ἀλλὰ καὶ τί μὴ εἴπῃ ἐφρόντισεν.
[58] e.g. 11.393, 452; 21.122; 22.354.

doubt there was no tradition about the location of Trojan wash-places—why should there have been?[59] As Bassett says, this is an invention for tragic contrast. The great hero and sole defender of Troy is being hunted to death beneath its walls, and the cruelty of his fate is brought out by dwelling for a moment on the peaceful countryside as it used to be, a delightful picture of handsome women at their everyday tasks. The technique is akin to that of the presentation of Andromache amid her household work as her husband's body is dragged behind Achilles' chariot.

The *Odyssey* offers a parallel, similar yet different as usual: the weather-beaten Odysseus, having dragged himself ashore naked and half-dead, has spent the night in a bank of leaves under a thicket. He is awoken by the shrill voices of girls. They have spent a morning washing clothes and having a picnic, and they are now playing ball on the beach, like nymphs. Into this enchanting and light-hearted scene bursts the much-enduring hero, a grim figure, caked with brine, with nothing but a leafy branch to hide his nakedness. All the girls run—the wrong way, towards the sea—except the princess Nausicaa[60]: οἴη δ' Ἀλκινόου θυγάτηρ μένε, 'alone did the daughter of Alcinous stand her ground' (vi.130–40). In the *Iliad* the contrast of heroic suffering with the pleasantness of the world of women is a tragic one. Hector dies, and Andromache's happiness is over for ever. In the *Odyssey* it is piquant and touching, and the poet gives Nausicaa a 'symbolic' position as she alone does not run—she is the princess, they are only servants and friends. The battered hero, persecuted by gods, menaced by monsters, the sole survivor of his crew, appears suddenly amidst the delicate girls of Phaeacia, before Nausicaa whose father and mother take such loving care of her, and who can spend her time in elegance and pleasure. But his sufferings are at an end now, and the contrast, effective in its own way, is decorative, not tragic.

At 11.164 Agamemnon, in the course of his great outburst of killing, his triumphant ἀριστεία, is pursuing the routed Trojans: 'Hector was snatched away from the flying weapons, the dust,

---

[59] 22.153; source of Scamander, 12.21. Cf. W. Elliger, *Landschaft in gr. Dichtung*, 43, S. E. Bassett, *The Poetry of Homer*, 138. See below, p. 112.

[60] F. Cauer in *NJbb.* (1900), 599, who rightly sees in this a touch of humour. On the contrast of the princess and the servants, cf. ΣT on 24.538.

the slaughter, the blood, and the turmoil; but the son of Atreus pressed on violently, exhorting the Achaeans. The Trojans fled past the tomb of ancient Ilus, son of Dardanus, over the middle of the plain, past the fig-tree, while Agamemnon constantly pursued them, shrieking, his invincible hands spattered with blood.' Ilus, the ancestor after whom Ilium (and so the *Iliad*) was named, is a venerable name and no more, from early Trojan history. His grave should be a scene of peace, but now it is surrounded by 'weapons, dust, slaughter, blood, and turmoil', as Agamemnon massacres his descendants. Again we are reminded of the lost happiness of Troy;[61] among its sacred places its people are slaughtered. Later in the same book Paris leans on the tomb to shoot at Diomede. He slightly wounds him and exults, wishing that he had succeeded in killing him and delivering the Trojans, 'who fear you as bleating goats fear a lion' (11.383). But the wound is superficial, and Diomede answers with contempt: 'That was like the dart of a woman or a child, but when I hit a man he dies at once—his wife tears her cheeks, his children are orphans, and he rots, staining the earth with his blood, with more carrion birds round him than mourning women.' Here we see that in the presence of the historic dead, even 'leaning on his tomb', Paris can do nothing heroic,[62] and the Trojans are the weak victims of the Achaeans.

Finally, something rather different in the last book. Priam is making his dangerous journey to Achilles with the ransom for the body of his son. At the tomb of Ilus Priam stops to water his mules; it is getting dark. Suddenly Hermes appears, sent by Zeus to help the old man. Priam is struck helpless with terror.[63] Hermes is a god who guides the dead, Priam is out by night on a mission concerned with a dead man; the god appears at a tomb. The appropriateness of this is perfect and obvious, but there is no irony in it this time, except the very different sort of irony that Priam does not recognize the god yet says 'A god is

---

[61] Explicit at 18.288, 'Once all men spoke of Priam's city as rich in gold and rich in bronze, but now all the splendid treasures are lost and gone', and 24.543, You too, old man, we hear were prosperous once . . .'

[62] ΣT in 11.372 ἐπὶ δὲ τῷ μνήματι τοῦ παλαιοῦ προγόνου ἔστη, μηδὲν ἄξιον ποιῶν: 'he took his stand at the tomb of his ancient ancestor, but did nothing worthy of him.' Contrast Idas and Lynceus making their last stand against the Dioscuri at their father's tomb: Pindar, *Nemean X*; Theocritus XXII.

[63] 24.349 ff. Cf. H. Schrade, *Götter und Menschen Homers*, 217, W. F. Otto, *The Homeric Gods*, 116.

taking care of me, causing me to meet such a traveller as you.'
That sort of irony is characteristic, on the whole, of the *Odyssey*.
More like the former ones, or the washing-places of the women
of Troy, is what we find at 21.405. In the largely abortive
Battle of the Gods, Athena downs Ares with 'a black stone
which was lying in the plain, rough and huge, which men of
old time had placed to be a boundary-mark for plough-land.' It
used to be a landmark in peaceful days, the sign of quiet
possession of farm land; now an angry goddess hurls it at a
furious god of war, and she knocks him sprawling on the ground.
The poet gives us again a detail which allows the episode to become transparent, so that we see the nature of war and its
consequence—the chaotic reversal of the order and sense of life
in peace.[64]

I have been emphasizing the importance for Homeric poetry
of scenes which have an emblematic quality, which define the
actors in their essential natures and relationships, and also of
the use of objects which carry an effective charge of symbolic
significance. I now go on to argue that all this is by no means
simply a matter of literary style, but arises from the way the
Homeric poet sees the world itself. Symbolic and significant
objects and gestures are a development of those which were
originally conceived as magical and charged with supernatural
power. Sometimes it is not possible to distinguish the two at
all clearly.

First, the poems contain many examples of significant and
symbolic actions. A suppliant begging for his life or for some
great favour must assume the appropriate posture. Thus we see
Thetis crouched at the feet of Zeus, holding his knees with her
left hand and reaching her right towards his chin. Zeus at
first makes no reply to her plea, and Thetis retains her posture:
'Thus she spoke, and Zeus the Gatherer of the Clouds made no
reply. Long did he sit in silence, while Thetis clung on to his
knees as she had first touched them, and asked him a second
time . . .' By remaining unmoved in her suppliant posture, she
presses home her unwelcome request upon the reluctant god,
and obliges him to give an answer. So too Odysseus in Scheria
has been told that he must 'embrace the knees' of Queen
Arete, if he is to be granted passage home. He does so, and

then sits at the hearth among the ashes, waiting for a response; there is an embarrassed silence, and the oldest man present points out that 'It is not well or seemly that a stranger should sit on the ground, in the ashes by the hearth', and that he should be raised up and accepted among them. By his presence and posture at the hearth, the sacred spot in the house, Odysseus puts a constraint on the Phaeacians which obliges them to respond. On the other hand, when Odysseus, naked and disreputable, finds himself confronted with the princess Nausicaa, his well-known prudence leads him to reflect that she will not fancy having her knees embraced by the alarming figure he knows that he presents. He therefore decides against pursuing the normal procedure of a suppliant, although this means abandoning the rights which that procedure would confer; and instead makes her, from a safe distance, an extremely courtly and flattering speech, in the course of which he lets her know that he is really a gentleman, that she is so beautiful that she must surely be more than a mortal, and generally that he knows how to behave and to talk. After hearing it, Nausicaa accepts him, not as a suppliant, but 'since you seem to be neither low nor foolish'. She accepts him, that is, as a man, on the strength of the qualities he has shown; whereas her parents accept him as a suppliant, because of the gesture which he has performed.[65]

Another, special, mode of supplication is seen in the gesture which Hecuba makes to her son Hector: 'She wept, and letting down the bosom of her dress she held up her breast with the other hand. Shedding tears she said "My son, respect this which I show, and take pity on me, if ever I held the soothing breast to you ..."' The gesture has its own power, almost independent of words.[66] Here again objects can help. The old priest Chryses, coming to beg for the return of his daughter,

[65] See above all, J. Gould, 'Hiketeia', in *JHS* 93 (1973). Thetis and Zeus, 1.500 ff.; Arete, vi.310; Odysseus at the hearth, vii.142; speech to Nausicaa, vi.141–85, esp. 164, πολὺς δέ μοι ἕσπετο λαός; Nausicaa's reply, vi.187.

[66] An Irish parallel: *Fianagecht* (ed. K. Meyer), 73.20: ' "Tis then Juchna Armdhòr ... tore her checkered coif from her head, loosed her fair yellow hair, bared her breasts, and said, "My son", said she, "it is ruin of honour ... to betray the princely Finn ... now quickly leave the hostel".' Of the Germans, Tacitus, *Germania* 8.1: women have been known to halt the rout of their men in battle, *constantia precum et obiectu pectorum*. Professor Kirk calls this 'an unsophisticated gesture' (*Songs of Homer*, 383).

'holds in his hands the garlands of Far-darting Apollo on a golden sceptre', thus showing that he is a priest, and a priest of a powerful god; and also a suppliant. Agamemnon tells him to be gone, 'lest the sceptre and garland of the god fail to protect you' (1.28); he sees but chooses to disregard the power they represent.

The taking of an oath and the making of a truce are also actions which require formal gestures. In the third book of the *Iliad* we are given a full description of the making of a truce. Priam himself must be fetched from Troy, animals are sacrificed, wine is brought by both sides and mingled—a symbolic act;[67] the wine is poured on the ground with the prayer, 'Zeus most great and glorious, and all you other gods, for those who first offend against this sworn agreement, may their brains be poured on the earth as this wine is poured' (3.299–301). Here we have the clearest possible case of an act with symbolic power, and one which was as familiar to the Hittites as to the Greeks in actual practice.[68] When Menelaus accuses Antilochus of cheating in the chariot race, he challenges him to clear himself by means of an oath: 'Come, Antilochus, as is the custom, stand before your horses and your chariot, hold in your hands your slender whip with which you drove your team, and, touching your horses, swear by Poseidon that you did not intentionally foul my chariot.'[69] By taking such an oath in such a posture Antilochus would have made himself liable to the destructive anger of the god by whom he swore—and perhaps would have devoted his own chariot, itself a symbol of kingly power, to destruction. Evidently the actual gesture is vitally important. Such a formal act is raised to sublime heights when Zeus accepts the supplication of Thetis, and nods his head to mark his assent, shaking mighty Olympus. Symbolic gesture

---

[67] 'Le mélange, dans le même cratère, des vins apportés par les deux parties contractantes est une des modalités expressives du serment chez Homère', L. Gernet, *Anthropologie de la Grèce antique*, 209.

[68] Hittites: *ANET²*, 207. 'Fill a bitumen cup with water and pour it out toward the Sun-god and speak as follows: "Whoever does something in an unclean way and offers to the King polluted water, pour you, O gods, that man's soul out like water!" ' Ibid., 353.(5), (of perjury). Greece: Gernet, loc. cit.

[69] 23.581 ff. cf. R. Hirzel, *Der Eid*, 28, Gernet, 241. So Hera offers to swear by her marriage bed, 'by which I would not swear falsely', 15.40. The oath she swears to the Sleep god is exaggerated to a cosmic scale. She lays one hand on the wide earth, the other on the sparkling sea, 14.272.

and supernatural power merge into one (1.528–9).[70]
All the acts of hospitality have a similar symbolic aspect—
acceptance, the production of food and drink, the inquiry (only
after the guest has eaten) who he is, the bath which is dwelt on
at length because 'the traveller only counts as fully at home and
accepted, when the dust of travel has been washed away'; the
gift at parting, which marks the connection of host and guest as
an enduring one to be appealed to in time to come and re-
ciprocated, as a matter of right, when opportunity offers.[71] The
giving of a gift and the receiving of a gift established a relation-
tion of ξενίη, friendship, which could be effective generations
later. Thus Diomede hails Glaucus as a hereditary friend, and
at once he appeals to the evidence of gifts:

So did he speak, and the dauntless Diomede was glad. He thrust his spear
into the fertile earth [itself a symbolic gesture, meaning 'we shall not fight
each other'] and with kindly words he addressed the shepherd of the
people: 'Indeed you are my inherited friend of long standing. Oeneus once
entertained handsome Bellerophon in his house, keeping him there for
twenty days, and they gave each other splendid gifts. Oeneus gave a belt
bright with crimson dye, while Bellerophon gave a golden cup with two
handles; and it was at home in my house when I left.'

The continued existence in Diomede's house of the gift presented on that occasion shows the life which the relationship
is capable of having still. It is another related fact, obvious to
any reader of the poems, that possessions are inseparable from
honour; to be robbed of a prize is to be dishonoured, to have
great possessions is to have what a king must have in order to
be a king.

We need to understand this world of stylized and universally
intelligible gestures in order to do justice to the powerful scene
in *Iliad* 18. In his passionate mourning for Patroclus, Achilles
lies on the ground; his mother, accompanied by her sisters, the
Nereids, comes to him, and 'with shrill lamentation she held

---

[70] Cf. formulae of Ugaritic religion: *ANET³*, 135 (vii), 31 'Mountains quake at
the voice of Baal', etc., and for instance, Psalm 144:7 'Tremble, thou earth, at the
presence of the LORD, at the presence of the GOD of Jacob.'

[71] Washing, 'Die Epen reden nachdrücklich von diesem Akt wegen seiner über
das Praktische hinausreichenden Bedeutung: der Wanderer gilt erst dann als recht
eigentlich angekommen und aufgenommen, wenn der Staub der Fremde abgespült
ist', H. Fränkel, *Wege und Formen*, 98. Gifts, cf. M. I. Finley, *The World of Odysseus*,
73 ff.

the head of her son.' This is the gesture with which the chief mourner holds the dead at a funeral, as we see later in the *Iliad*, as well as from Geometric vase-paintings. The *Iliad* will not narrate Achilles' death, but just as the poem contrives to show us the fall of Troy without narrating it, so Achilles, still alive, is held and mourned as though he were already dead; the weeping Nereids fulfil the function of the mourning women at a normal funeral, just as after his actual death they came up from the sea and lamented for him, making the blood of the Achaeans run cold. With Hector, who also is bemoaned while still alive, the poet makes the point explicit: 'His women-folk lamented for Hector in his house while he still lived, for they thought he would not return from the battle', but in Book 18 he uses the language of gesture to the same purpose.

We shall have more to say about the treatment and significance of arming for battle. Simpler and more like the incidents we have been dealing with is that when Athena changes her dress when about to enter the fighting: 'Athena, daughter of aegis-bearing Zeus, laid down on her father's threshold her embroidered *peplos*, which she had worked with her own hands; she put on the tunic of Zeus, the Gatherer of the Clouds, and armed herself with her weapons for war.'[72] The *peplos* was a distinctively feminine upper garment, and the goddess, patron of the arts and crafts, has embroidered hers herself, like a good mortal woman. She takes it off and replaces it with the masculine dress of the warrior, because she is about to exercise the other side of her nature, incompatible with women's dress and all that it implied. Another sort of use is made of this idea in the *Odyssey*. When Odysseus, disguised as an old beggar, is put up to fight with Irus, he 'girt up his rags about his middle, showing thighs fine and big, and his broad shoulders appeared, his chest and powerful arms . . .' The true nature of the hero shows through, with Athena's help; imperfectly disguised by rags and

---

[72] ἵνα δὲ μηκέτι πόλεμος εἶναι δοκῇ καταπήγνυσι τὸ ξίφος ὁ Διομήδης, ΣAbT in 6.213. Bellerophon's cup, 6.212; Thetis, 18.71; holding the head of the dead, 23.136, 24.724. Nereids at Achilles' funeral, xxiv.47; Hector, 6.500; Athena's dress, 8.384. See generally the chapter *Rechtssymbolik* in C. Sittl, *Die Gebärden der Griechen und Römer* (1890), 129 ff., and G. Neumann, *Gesten und Gebärden in der gr. Kunst* (1965), e.g. p. 3: 'Diese konzentrierten Gebärden bekunden eine tiefe Schicksalsverhaftung . . . als Abbreviaturen menschlicher Grundsituationen und Grundverfassungen . . .'

age is the mighty Odysseus, and for a moment his nature reveals itself.[73] It does so, in another way, when he speaks to the wicked servants and the Suitors in his house in a high tone, suitable to the king but not to the beggar he is supposed to be (xviii.313 ff., finishing with the heavily ironic 'I am a long-enduring man', πολυτλήμων δὲ μάλ' εἰμί, xviii.366 ff.). Finally, the Bow in his hands and the moment of vengeance arrived, Odysseus 'stripped off his rags' (xxii.1)—the old identity is cast aside, and the hero reveals himself as what he is. The gesture is thrilling, and its symbolism makes it right and inevitable. The poet of the *Odyssey* also finds a device here for showing how absolute is the change of fortune that Odysseus must undergo. Unable for ten years to get back home to Ithaca, shipwrecked by an angry god, alone in the world, Odysseus must strip off the 'clean and scented garments' which the goddess Calypso gave him, and be washed up, as naked physically as he is stripped of his rank and his position, in an unknown country where his own wits and prowess will set him upon the upward path that at last will lead him to his kingdom.[74]

As with the nod of Zeus, we can see again how closely symbolic action and supernatural power go together, when we consider two passages in which a signal is held up in battle. In Book 8 the Trojans are driving the Achaeans before them. Hector with the aid of Zeus has hemmed them in by the ships, and things look disastrous, when Agamemnon makes his way to the ship of Odysseus, which lay in the middle of the line, with a great crimson cloak in his hand; he shouts piercingly to the Achaeans to fight back. Here the effect is purely naturalistic. Agamemnon attracts their attention, by his conspicuous ensign as well as by his shouted appeal. At the beginning of Book 11, Zeus sends Eris, the Strife-goddess, to the ships of the Achaeans, 'holding in her hands the portent (τέρας) of war. She took her stand by the deep black ship of Odysseus . . .' The same five lines which describe the position of Odysseus' ship in Book 8, half-way between that of Ajax son of Telamon and that of Achilles, are repeated here exactly; then we read, 'There did the goddess stand and utter her loud and terrible cry; she put

---

[73] Odysseus and Irus, xviii.67.
[74] Calypso's clothes, v.264, 321, 372; cf. R. Harder, *Kleine Schriften* (1960), 153.

great strength into each man of the Achaeans, to fight without respite. And they felt that war was more delightful than going home to their own country in their hollow ships.' The intervention of the goddess is more awesome. The emphasis is on her great cry—we are not told what she said, if anything, whereas Agamemnon's speech is given in full; and we are left to guess what the 'portent of war' might be. But the repeated lines show how closely the scene is made to resemble a purely human one.[75] And while Agamemnon's long speech seems fully human, we observe that it has a supernatural consequence: Zeus sends an encouraging omen, an eagle clutching a fawn, and the result of the speech and the omen—of action by god and man—is that the Achaeans 'leapt all the more against the Trojans and remembered their fighting spirit' (8.252).

We thus find ourselves at a natural point of transition to another regular feature of Homeric poetry; the use of weapons and other objects which themselves contain will, action, and power. The gods possess things which are filled with power. The κεστὸς ἱμάς,[76] the 'pierced strap' which Aphrodite wears on her bosom and which she lends to Hera for the seduction of Zeus, 'contains all her enchantments: in it are love and desire and seductive words of courtship, which steal away the wits even of the wise.' The wearer becomes irresistible, all the agents contained in it being set loose against the victim. When Zeus catches sight of Hera, 'as he saw her, at once his heart was filled with desire.'

The aegis of Zeus has the same nature. We are given a full description of it when Athena puts it on: 'About her shoulders she cast the tasseled aegis, terrifying, encircled all about with panic; in it are contained strife and valour and rout which chills the blood, and in it is the head of the Gorgon, a terrifying monster, grim and terrible, the portent of aegis-bearing Zeus.' Again we see that the powers are not simply depicted on the

[75] Agamemnon's shout, 8.221; Eris, 11.3. One solid result of Milman Parry's work should be that we no longer have to argue, when identical lines occur in two passages, that one must be directly influenced by the other, as is done not only in the old-fashioned analysis of Von der Mühll (*Kritisches Hypomnema zur Ilias*, 190) but also by Schadewaldt (*Iliasstudien*, 32) and Reinhardt (*Dichter der Ilias*, 178).

[76] Campbell Bonner, 'The κεστὸς ἱμάς and the Saltire of Aphrodite', *AJP* 70 (1949), 1 ff. makes an interesting case for this being in origin the X-shaped ornament worn by the goddess Ishtar/Astarte/Aphrodite, from the third millennium BC onwards.

aegis, but inherent in it; but the Gorgon's head, no doubt, is to be imagined as actually represented, as it is on the shield of Agamemnon. The poet thinks of the aegis as visibly bearing a Gorgoneion, a representation of the severed head of the Gorgon, whose purpose when we see it represented on shields was originally to terrify the enemy,[77] and also as actually containing the power to terrify and cause panic and rout. When the aegis is used, this is how its effect is described:

As long as Phoebus Apollo held the aegis still in his hands, so long did the missiles of both sides strike, and the people fall; but when he brandished it in the faces of the Achaean horsemen, and in addition himself uttered a great shout, then he bewitched their spirit in their breasts, and they forgot their martial prowess. As when a herd of cattle or a great flock of sheep is harassed by two beasts of prey in the dark night, which come on them suddenly while the herdsman is absent, even so were the Achaeans spiritless and thrown into panic; for Apollo cast panic into them, and gave victory to Hector and the Trojans.

In the same way, when Athena finally holds up the aegis against the Suitors, 'their minds were terrified, and they fled down the hall like a herd of cattle which the flitting gadfly attacks and throws into confusion, in the spring time, when the days are long.' Poseidon strides at the head of the victorious Achaeans 'holding in his strong hand a long and terrible sword, like a lightning-flash; it is forbidden for mortals to come into contact with it, terror grips men.' Hermes has a wand which seals the eyes of men in sleep, or wakes those whom the god chooses, and in the *Odyssey* we find a regular magician's wand in the hands of Circe.[78]

The *Odyssey* contains other supernatural objects: the magic herb, moly, known only to the gods, which defends against enchantment; the lotus-plant which makes men lose the will to go home; the scarf (κρήδεμνον) of the goddess Ino which preserves from drowning. A sophisticated woman like Helen is capable of drugging one's drink, and then he who drank of it 'would not shed a tear from his eyes that day, not even if his mother and father were to die, not even if they slew his brother

[77] The κεστὸς ἱμάς, 14.215; its effect, 14.244; the aegis, 5.738; Agamemnon's shield, 11.36, cf. Leaf on 5.739.

[78] Effect of the aegis, 15.318, xxii.298; Poseidon's sword, 14.384; Hermes' wand, 24.343, v. 47, xxiv.2; Circe's wand, x.238, 389. Cf. F. J. N. de Waele, *The Magic Staff or Rod in Graeco–Italian Antiquity* (1927), 34 ff., 132 ff.

or his own son with a sword, and he were looking on; such subtle drugs did the daughter of Zeus possess, beneficent ones, which Polydamna wife of Thon had given her, of Egypt, where the fertile earth bears drugs in greatest number, many of them good when mixed, but many of them harmful.'[79] Egypt contained many extraordinary things, and this description could suit perfectly real drugs, but we are only a step from the frankly magical potions by which Circe, another *femme fatale*, can turn men into animals. The *Iliad*, however, tends to limit this sort of thing to the context of fighting (the supernatural cosmetic aid of Hera forming part of her great exploit in the poem, itself aimed at a military end in the defeat of the Trojans).[80] The gods give weapons to favoured heroes, as they did to the kings of the ancient Near East,[81] especially Assyrians. Even so second-rate a hero as Pandarus was given his bow by Apollo,[82] and the provision of divine armour to Achilles is a great theme of the poem. But here as everywhere else we see the 'heroization' so characteristic of Greek mythology in general[83] and of Homer in particular. In the Eastern sources, some of which in my view were very probably known to the Homeric tradition, the god gives his weapon to a king, to guarantee him as a conqueror against the enemies of the god and his protégé.

[79] Moly, x.305; lotus, ix.94; Ino, v.346; Helen, iv.223. Eustathius preserves a delightful note (on 6.363): 'One could say that . . . this potion is the conversation of the heroine herself'—εἴποις ἂν ὅτι... ὁ τοιοῦτος κρατὴρ τῆς ἡρωΐδος ὁμιλία ἐστίν.

[80] Her adornment of herself, 14.169 ff., is analogous to the arming of a warrior before his great exploits; cf. H. Erbse in *A und A* 16 (1970), 93, H. Patzer, SB Frankfurt (1971), 31.

[81] Tiglath-Pileser I of Assyria, *c.* 1100 BC, claimed that 'Assur my lord had put into my hand a mighty weapon which subdues the insubmissive' (Luckenbill, *Ancient Records*, i.77, cf. ii.195); 'trusting in Assur the great lord and the terrible weapons which Assur my lord gave to me . . .' says Assur-Nâsir-Pal, ibid., i.149; 'Assur and Ishtar have given me an invincible weapon', claimed Sargon. An obelisk in the British Museum shows Tiglath-Pileser being given a bow by Assur. Cf. H. Schrade, *Der verborgene Gott*, 74 ff. Long before, Hammurabi (1728–1686 BC) claimed to have 'rooted out the enemy . . . with the mighty weapon which Zababa and Inanna entrusted to me', *ANET³*, 178.24. Ezek. 30:24, 'And I will strengthen the arms of the king of Babylon, and put my sword into his hand; but I will break Pharaoh's arms . . . and they shall know that I am the LORD, when I shall put my sword into the hand of the king of Babylon, and he shall stretch it out upon the land of Egypt.'

[82] 2.827. No contradiction with the statement at 4.106 that he made it himself, cf. Kullmann, *Das Wirken der Götter*, 58, Willcock in *BICS* 17 (1970), 3.

[83] G. S. Kirk, *Myth*, 178 ff., 205.

The conception is nationalistic: our king is invincible. Alternatively, in the Ugaritic tale of Aqhat (*ANET*³, 151–5), the god-given bow has the function of causing the goddess Anath to kill Aqhat, who subsequently is 'restored to his father, perhaps only for half—the fertile half—of the year. The familiar Adonis–Tammuz theme.'[84] In neither case is the story one of human heroism, nor can it be tragic, as is the story of Achilles, recipient of divine arms, who knows even as he receives them that he is doomed to die; and in Homer both sides pray to the same gods, and Zeus loves Hector and Troy no less than Agamemnon and the Achaeans. Originally, in the versions that lie behind our *Iliad*, the god-given armour of Achilles was impenetrable,[85] so that it had to be struck from Patroclus' body in Book 16 before he could be killed, but the *Iliad* has suppressed a notion which would seem to exempt one hero from its rule that all heroes face death. The poet prefers to say only, with pregnant irony, that it is 'not easy' for mortal men to break the work of gods (20.265).

But although god-given weapons no longer mean an unbroken chain of victories and deliverance from the common rule of mortality, the ancient idea of them as terrifying and full of power lingers on in Homer. We have seen the aegis, and the sword of Poseidon. We find mention also of the whip of Zeus subduing the losing side, and of the 'uproar', κυδοιμός, wielded by Enyo, while Ares wields a great spear.[86] Men, too, inspire terror by their mere appearance in armour, and their weapons have an inhuman life of their own. It seems hardly more than the most natural metaphor when the poet speaks of an arrow 'leaping' from the bow, or a spear 'flying' at a target, or an arrow 'shrieking' as it goes, although the ancient commentators have a very sharp eye for all such metaphors and never fail to

---

[84] H. L. Ginsberg in *ANET*³, 155.
[85] P. J. Kakridis, 'Achilles' Rüstung', *Hermes*, 89 (1961), 288–97.
[86] Διὸς μάστιγι 12.37, 13.812:
    ἡ μὲν ἔχουσα κυδοιμὸν ἀναιδέα δηιοτῆτος,
    Ἄρης δ' ἐν παλάμῃσι πελώριον ἔγχος ἐνώμα, 5.593–4.
κυδοιμός here is a weapon, *pace* Liddell and Scott: see W. Theiler in *Festschrift Tièche*, 129 = *Untersuchungen zur antiken Literatur* (1972), 15; Wilamowitz, *Ilias und Homer*, 182.1, who observes 'auch da ist das ein Attribut ihres Wesens, ein Symbol ihrer Tätigkeit ... Die Attribute, welche die Götter in der ältesten Kunst führen, werden alle einmal ähnliche Bedeutung gehabt haben.'

comment on them.[87] It is more striking when we find the same
verb used of the weapon as of the warrior who wields it. Just as
men can be said to 'rush eagerly' at the enemy, so a spear can
be said to do the same: as at 17.276 Τρῶες . . . ἱέμενοί περ, 'the
Trojans, although they rushed eagerly', and 20.399 αἰχμὴ . . .
ἱεμένη ῥῆξ' ὀστέα, 'the spear, rushing eagerly, shattered the
bones.' So too with a verb like μαιμάω, 'to be very eager'; it is
equally Homeric to say of the warrior ἦ καὶ μαιμώων ἔφεπ'
ἔγχει (15.742), 'he attacked very eagerly with his spear', or of
the spear itself, 'the point pierced through his breast very
eagerly, rushing forward', αἰχμὴ δὲ στέρνοιο διέσσυτο μαιμώωσα
| πρόσσω ἱεμένη (15.542). We read often of spears 'longing to glut
their appetite for men's flesh', 'sticking in the earth before they
could enjoy the white flesh', and 'eager to sate themselves on
men's flesh',[88] and we remember that this terrible temptation
was present to the hero himself; we find too that Ares, god of
war, is to be 'sated with blood', αἵματος ἆσαι Ἄρηα.[89] Ares can be

[87] 4.125, 15.313, 470, 16.773; 5.282, 13.408, 20.99, 22.275; 1.46; ΣΤ in 1.46
ἔκλαγξαν . . . ὀιστοί: ἐπιστρέφει πρὸς εὐσέβειαν τὸ καὶ τὰ ἄψυχα αἰσθάνεσθαι
τῆς θείας δυνάμεως; ΣΤ in 10.373 ἔξεστιν εἰπεῖν ὅτι καὶ τὰ βέλη ὡς ἔμψυχα
τῷ ποιητῇ συναγωνίζεται; ΣbΤ in 2.414 ἔμφασιν ἔχει ἡ ἀπὸ τῶν ἐμψύχων
μεταφορά, etc. Eustathius loves to observe that this procedure produces what he
calls γλυκύτης, by which he seems to mean 'naif charm' (e.g. 579.3, 699.36,
112.45). In general the ancient scholars followed Aristotle (Rhet. 1411 b 22) in
treating all this as simply a matter of style. The matter is interestingly discussed
by W. Marg, Die Antike, 18 (1942), 169. In the Anglo-Saxon poem Widsith, 70
'full often the yelling spear flew screaming against the foe.' In Irish, we read in
the Cath Maige Turedh, the Second Battle of Moytura (Rev. Celt. 12 (1891), 56 ff.)
I 162: 'At that time a sword, when unsheathed, would tell of the deeds done with
it. Now the reason why demons used to speak from weapons at that time was
because weapons were worshipped by human beings at that epoch . . .'
[88] As 21.168, spear of Achilles γαίη ἐνεστήρικτο, λιλαιομένη χροὸς ἆσαι:
11.574, 15.317, many spears πάρος χρόα λευκὸν ἐπαυρεῖν | ἐν γαίη ἵσταντο,
λιλαιόμενα χροὸς ἆσαι: 21.70 ἐγχείη . . . ἔστη ἱεμένη χροὸς ἄμεναι ἀνδρομέοιο.
Cf. W. Marg in Wüϑbb 2 (1976), 9.
[89] 5.288, 20.78, 22.266. Oriental parallels abound: of men, the ninth-century
Assyrian tablet published in Archaeologia, 79 (1929), 132 ff.; in line 44 we read
'Every one of the warriors sating himself with death, as though it were a fast-day'.
Of gods, ANET³, 320, the Moabite stone of Mesha (c 830 BC): 'I took the town and
slew all the people of the town as satiation for Chemosh and Moab.' Deut. 32:41,
'For I will sharpen my sword like lightning' [cf. the sword of Poseidon, 14.386], . . .
'I will make my weapons drunk with blood, and my sword shall devour flesh, it
shall glut itself from the blood of the wounded.' Isa. 34:5, 'My sword has been
made drunk in heaven . . . the sword of the LORD is filled with blood, it is,
glutted with fat . . .' Of Pharaoh as god, ANET³, 254 (a) 'Now as for the good
god' [sc. Seti I], 'he exults at undertaking combat; he delights at an attack on
him; his heart is satisfied at the sight of blood.'

called 'insatiable for war', ἆτος πολέμοιο (5.388, 863, 6.203); so can heroes (Achilles, 13.746; Hector, 22.218; the Trojans, 13.621, etc.). Heroes are often compared to Ares by Homer, and not least in their fighting fury.[90] Fighting is a madness, and the god of war is mad, even proverbially—ἐπιμὶξ δέ τε μαίνεται Ἄρης, 'Ares rages indiscriminately' (xi.537), is evidently a cliché. 'Shall we allow keen Ares to rage madly as he does?', asks Hera (5.717), and she calls him 'this madman who knows no law', ἄφρονα τοῦτον ... ὅς οὔ τινα οἶδε θέμιστα (5.761). He for his part calls Athena 'mad' (5.875). A warrior in his berserk rage is like Ares—Hector, we read, 'raged in madness, as when the warrior Ares or destructive fire on the hills rages' (15.604); he also gets his madness from a god: 'it is not without a god that he rages so madly', says Pandarus of Diomede (5.185). His hands may be said to be mad, as he rages in battle (16.244), and so, finally, can his weapons. 'My spear too, rages in my hands', says Diomede (8.111), and later Achilles says 'The spear of Diomede, son of Tydeus, is not raging in his hands' (16.74), when the hero is wounded and unable to take the field.

This fighting madness is no mere figure of speech. Impelled by Zeus in an outburst of irresistible fury, Hector foams at the mouth, his eyes flash, and his helmet shakes terrifyingly as he fights. The word λύσσα is often used of the raging of a hero, and that word is used of the madness of a mad dog—with which Hector is identified by Teucer. The warrior raging in his armour is terrifying: the plume nods grimly on his helmet, his shield may bear a Gorgon, the bronze clashes about him, his spear rages in his hand, his face is distorted by madness, he utters a terrifying shriek, his horses 'carry the panic of Ares'.[91]

[90] This seems to differentiate the Homeric comparison from that common in Egyptian inscriptions, in which Pharaohs like Thutmose III, Amenhotep II, and Rameses II (c. 1490–1436, 1447–1421, 1301–1234 BC) compare themselves to Montu, the god of war; these comparisons are rather stately than full of berserker rage (*ANET*³, 240, D.-C. 8, 244 b 12, ibid., 17, 253 (ii) 4, 255 (ii), etc.). But the same nuance is found, on the same inscriptions; Amenhotep II also called himself 'in face terrible like that of Bastet [the slaughtering cat-goddess], like Seth in his moment of raging' (*ANET*³, 245). Assyrian kings compare themselves to the weather-god Adad: *ANET*³, 279 (Shalmaneser), 'I slew 14,000 of their warriors with the sword, descending upon them like Adad when he makes a rain-storm pour down'; ibid., 277, (b).

[91] 15.607; 8.299. The verb κομπέω used for the clashing of armour, as at 12.151, is used of the din of wild boars uprooting trees with their tusks. Panic of Ares, 2.767.

Repeatedly we see that the nerve of his opponent collapses before such an onslaught, and he takes to flight. Every reader thinks of Hector, struck with sudden panic as Achilles rushes at him.[92] So closely are the weapons identified with the hero himself that it is the same thing to say 'you dare to await my spear' as to say 'you confront my prowess', to say 'they feared his massive spear' or 'they feared god-like Hector'; it is natural for Achilles to say that the Trojans are confident, 'for they do not see the front of my helmet shining near at hand', and for Hector to shout, 'Follow hard, that we may get the shield of Nestor ... and strip the breastplate of Diomede from his shoulders, which Hephaestus made; if we took these two, I think the Achaeans would embark on their swift ships tonight.'[93]

When a hero is shown putting on his armour, this means that he will have a notable part to play in the fighting which follows; the greater the *aristeia*, the fuller the arming-scene which precedes it. So true is this that when Patroclus is shown donning all the armour of Achilles except his great spear, the omission stands for an incompleteness in the *aristeia* to follow and marks it as doomed to end in disaster. And more than this: the armour which fills the enemy with terror fills the hero who wears it with strength and rage. As Hector puts on the arms of Achilles, stripped from Patroclus' body, 'Ares entered into him, the terrible god of war, and his limbs within were filled with prowess and strength; and he strode after the famous allies, shouting aloud.' When Achilles is brought his new arms, 'the goddess Thetis laid them down before Achilles, and they clashed loudly, all cunningly wrought. All the Myrmidons were seized with trembling, and not one of them dared to look straight at the armour, but they shrank from it; but as for Achilles, as he looked he was penetrated by greater rage, and his eyes flashed terrifyingly, like flame under his brows.' When he put it on, 'there was a grinding of his teeth, his eyes shone

---

[92] 22.130 ff. e.g. also 16.278, 'When the Trojans saw the valiant son of Menoetius, himself and his squire, glittering in their armour, the spirit of each of them was troubled; their ranks were confused, ... and every man looked about for a way to escape sheer destruction.' Aristotle regarded the last line here translated, πάπτηνεν δὲ ἕκαστος ὅπῃ φύγοι αἰπὺν ὄλεθρον, as 'the most terrible line in Homer' (fr. 129 = ΣT in 16.283). 4.419–21 is another striking example.

[93] 6.126–7; 5.790, 15.652; 10.70; 8. 191.

like fire, his heart was penetrated by intolerable pain . . .' The 'pain' (ἄχος) here is that of intense grief for Patroclus and intense longing for revenge.

At supreme moments the great warrior is raised so far above his ordinary self that fire crowns his head. Athena kindles a fire from the helmet and shield of Diomede at the beginning of his great *aristeia*; in the eighteenth book Achilles, deprived of his arms by Hector and so unable to fight, is actually enabled to intervene in the battle unarmed. A passage in a rich style shows Athena casting the aegis about his shoulders, crowning his head with a golden haze, and igniting a burning fire from the man himself. Often heroes are compared to fire, as we are told of Hector that 'he rages beyond all bounds, like fire', and it clearly is of small importance whether a hero's eyes are said to shine 'like fire', or 'with fire'.[94] It is the nature of the warrior which is fiery.

At the same time as Achilles appears to the Trojans wearing the aegis and crowned with cloud and fire, he utters a great shout, and Athena shouts in answer from far away. As with so many of the things we have been looking at, we find both 'naturalistic' representations of the shout of a warrior or god— that is to say, representations which observe the limits which seem to us to be those of plausibility—and also frankly supernatural ones. There is no clear and significant line that can be drawn between the two. In the fourth book Apollo calls from Pergamus to rally the retreating Trojans; what he says is just what a Trojan leader might say at that point, and the poet does not describe any effect as produced by it. Before the Battle of the Gods, as they approach, Eris rouses herself, and Athena shrieks aloud, 'standing now by the ditch outside the stockade, and now on the echoing strand did she utter a long battle-cry; while on the other side Ares, like a black storm-cloud, called to the Trojans, now from the topmost citadel of Troy, and now

---

[94] Cf. H. Patzer, *SB Frankfurt*, 1972, 28 ff.; G. Strasburger, *Die kleinen Kämpfer der Ilias*, 116; R. S. Shannon, *The Arms of Achilles and Homeric Compositional Technique* (1975), 26 ff. Armour of Achilles, 19.12; he puts it on, 19.365; Diomede, 5.4; Achilles crowned with fire, 18.202; Hector compared to fire, 9.238; eyes shine like fire, 19.366; with fire, 12.486. Cf. H. Fränkel, *Die homerischen Gleichnisse*, 50, C. H. Whitman, *Homer and the Heroic Tradition*, 129 ff., C. Moulton, *Similes in the Homeric Poems*, 100 ff.

running on the hill Callicolone by the banks of the Simoeis.'[95] This passage is an attempt at the grandiose, which goes on to show Zeus thundering, Poseidon shaking the earth, and the god of the dead afraid that his unlovely realm will be revealed to gods and men. The shouting of the gods here exists purely for the gods, it seems; Trojans and Achaeans go on fighting regardless of it, as they are regardless of the earthquake caused by Poseidon. A speech of exhortation can have the effect of putting fresh heart ($\mu\acute{\epsilon}\nu os$, $\sigma\theta\acute{\epsilon}\nu os$) into the warriors it addresses (5.784, 11.10, 14.147), an effect described in exactly the same words whether the speaker is god or man—$\dot{\omega}s$ $\epsilon\dot{\iota}\pi\dot{\omega}\nu$ $\ddot{o}\tau\rho\upsilon\nu\epsilon$ $\mu\acute{\epsilon}\nu os$ $\kappa a\grave{\iota}$ $\theta\upsilon\mu\grave{o}\nu$ $\dot{\epsilon}\kappa\acute{a}\sigma\tau o\upsilon$, 5.792, of Hera; 15.50, of Hector; 15.514, of Ajax.

Finally we reach the clearly superhuman in the greatest of these scenes, where Achilles appears to the Trojans, glorified and set ablaze by Athena: in this terrifying guise he advances alone to the trench round the palisade and shouts aloud, while from afar Pallas Athene shouts in reply. The effect is terrific.

When they heard the brazen voice of Achilles, their spirits were all confounded; the long-maned horses turned the chariots about, foreboding disaster, and their drivers were daunted, seeing the steady fire burning fiercely over the head of Peleus' valiant son, lit by Pallas Athene. Thrice did god-like Achilles utter a great shout over the trench, and thrice were the Trojans and their famous allies thrown into confusion: then did twelve of their best warriors perish by their own chariots and weapons (18.222-31).

Near Eastern parallels abound for the terrible voice of a god in battle,[96] and Indo-European parallels for the superhuman

[95] On Athena's shout at 18.217, cf. E. K. Borthwick in *Hermes*, 97 (1969), 390 n. 1, recalling the 'tremendous shout' which Athena uttered at her birth, Pindar, *Ol.* vii. 35. Apollo shouts, 4.507; Athena and Ares, 20.48.

[96] Egypt: *ANET*[3] 253 col. i, 'Hail to thee, O Seth, Son of Nut, the Great of Strength . . . Great of Battle-cry . . .'; ibid., 249 col. ii, of Pharaoh, 'His battle-cry is like (that of) Baal in the heavens.' The God Baal, a foreigner to Egypt originally, is celebrated for his battle-cry in the Ugaritic texts, thus *ANET*[3], 135 (vii), 29, 'Baal gives forth his holy voice, Baal discharges the utterance of his lips. His holy voice convulses the earth . . . the mountains tremble.' In the Old Testament, e.g. Isa. 42:13, 'The LORD shall go forth as a mighty man, he shall stir up jealousy like a man of war; he shall cry, yea, roar; he shall prevail over his enemies'; Joel 3:16, 'The LORD shall roar from Zion, and utter his voice from Jerusalem; and the heavens and earth shall shake'; 2 Sam 22:14, Ps. 46:6, 47:3-5, Jer. 25:30. In the Akkadian story of Zu, *ANET*[3], 112.62, Marduk is enjoined: 'Let the terror of thy battle-cry cast him down, let him experience darkness . . .' ΣT in 20.48, Homer preferred his heroes to shout rather than to use the trumpet, $\tau\epsilon\rho a\sigma\tau\iota\omega\tau\acute{\epsilon}\rho as$ $o\dot{\iota}\acute{o}\mu\epsilon\nu os$ $\tau\grave{a}s$ $\tau\hat{\omega}\nu$ $\dot{a}\nu\delta\rho\hat{\omega}\nu$ $\kappa a\grave{\iota}$ $\theta\epsilon\hat{\omega}\nu$ $\mu\epsilon\gamma a\lambda o\phi\omega\nu\acute{\iota}as$, 'thinking that great shouts by men and gods were more terrific'.

rage[97] and terrifying shout of heroes. Homer carefully keeps the rage of the hero within closer limits. The hero does not cease to be a man, as Cúchulainn does; his rage carries his normal heroism to a special level and intensity. The voice is one of the alarming features of an attacking warrior, and here Achilles' appearance and voice achieve their effect with special power. The shout of the hero, not that of the goddess, is dwelt on as what terrifies the Trojans, and the twelve who die do so in a reasonably 'natural' way, impaled by the weapons of their own side in the confusion of a sudden panic. I have no doubt that behind this passage lie things more like the effect produced by the warrior scream of Cúchulainn, which makes men die simply from fear,[98] or what we read in the Icelandic *Saga of Njal* (156): before the decisive battle of Clontarf scalding blood-rain falls (a motif closely akin to the Homeric 'bloody dew' with which Zeus marks the death of his son Sarpedon), and weapons fight by themselves, and 'one man on each ship died.' Homeric weapons sympathize with the warrior who wields them in force, but the poet does not allow them to act simply by themselves. These two parallels, then, point out more unambiguously superhuman ways of handling the material, and show how precisely judged is the Homeric vision.

I turn to some other ways in which the idea of the super-

[97] In the Irish legends the 'warp' of Cúchulainn is an extreme example, which by contrast shows the restraint and 'human-ness' of Homer; for instance, *The Tain* (trans. T. Kinsella from the *Táin Bó Cuailnge* 1969, 150): 'The first warp-spasm seized Cúchulainn and made him into a monstrous thing, hideous and shapeless, unheard of . . . His body made a furious twist inside his skin, so that his feet and shins and knees switched to the rear and his heels and calves switched to the front . . . His face and features became a red bowl; he sucked one eye deep into his head . . . the other eye fell out along his cheek. His mouth weirdly distorted . . . Malignant mists and spurts of fire . . . flickered red in the vaporous clouds boiling above his head . . .' I have omitted many bizarre details from this passage (cf. also ibid., 77 and 195 and e.g. *Bricriu's Feast*, Irish Text Society, 2 (1899), § 27); the last sentence I quote gives an obvious comparison and contrast with the fire on the head of Achilles.

[98] *The Tain*, 141, 'Cúchulainn gave the warrior's scream from his throat, so that demons and devils and goblins of the glen and fiends of the air replied, so hideous was the call he uttered . . . and a hundred warriors died of fright and terror'; see also p. 238. It would be un-Homeric to make Achilles' cry 'hideous'. The poet who uses the adjective καλός, 'beautiful', 5 times in the 16 lines describing Achilles rushing on Hector and striking the fatal blow (22.312–27), prefers to say, simply and effectively, that he 'shouted'. *Beowulf*, 2550, 'Then did Beowulf, in his rage, let a cry burst forth from his breast; stout-heartedly he stormed; his voice, distinct in battle, went ringing under the grey rock. Hate was enkindled . . .'

natural pervasion of the world by power and significance is influential in the Homeric poems. Animals are occasionally spoken of in a way that shows they are conceived as not wholly different from men; the killing of an ox is βουφονεῖν, using the root *phon* which properly means the killing of a human person, and that recalls rituals in which the death of an ox was treated like that of a man. We hear of the punishment of a pig which ravaged common land: its tusks were knocked out. Inanimate objects, too, could have consciousness. The Phaeacian ships were conscious, so were the metal girls made by Hephaestus and the golden and silver dogs which guarded Alcinous' palace.[99] Often we find nature responding 'sympathetically' to the movements and emotions of gods. Thus the nod of Zeus shakes Olympus (1.530); the Oriental parallels in footnote 96 suffice to show how close this is to the actual utterances of cult. When Poseidon strides over the earth, 'the high hills and the forest shook beneath the immortal feet of Poseidon as he passed', and as he drives through the sea in his golden chariot, 'the great sea-creatures sported beneath him from their lairs on every side, and they knew him for their lord; the sea parted joyfully asunder.'[100] As Zeus embraces Hera, 'the earth beneath them sent up new growing grass, dewy lotus, crocus and hyacinth, thick and soft, which raised them high from the earth. Thereon they lay, and had above to cover them a fair golden cloud, from which fell glistening dew' (14.347—51). The union of the great gods is a true Sacred Marriage of Heaven and Earth, which makes the earth fertile and fruitful. As Poseidon leads the Achaeans into battle, the sea surges up towards their huts and ships (14.392). When Zeus grieves for his son, bloody dew falls (16.459); when he plans a destructive

---

[99] βουφονεῖν, 7.466, cf. W. Burkert, *Homo Necans* (1972), 154 ff.; συὸς ... ληιβοτείρης, xviii.29; ships, viii.556; girls, 18.376; guardian dogs, vii.91, cf. Schrade, 78.

[100] 13.18–29, cf. Judges 5.4 'LORD, when thou wentest out of Séir, when thou marchedst out of the field of Edom, the earth trembled.' J. T. Kakridis, 'Poseidons Wunderfahrt', in *WS*, Beiheft 5 (1972) = *Festschrift W. Kraus*, 188–97, tries to exclude the miraculous from this scene, arguing that the sea simply parted like the wake of a ship. The word γηθοσύνῃ seems to me to be in conflict with this reductive account. The scene in the Homeric *Hymn to Aphrodite*, 69 ff., where the animals fawn on the goddess of love as she passes, feel desire, and go off in pairs to couple in the shadowy glens, is only a fuller development of what is here given in a restrained form.

day's battle, there is thunder all night, and men turn pale with foreboding (7.478); when men anger him by violence and injustice, storms and floods destroy their harvest (16.384 ff.);[101] mist and darkness descend when Ares wishes to help the Trojans,[102] a wind blows dust in the faces of the Achaeans when Zeus plans their defeat; supernatural darkness covers the fighting over the body of Patroclus, 'for he too was dear to Zeus', and is dispersed by the god in response to a prayer. The wind the sailor needs is sent or withheld by a god; 'it does not rain or snow without divine impulsion, nor do stars appear',[103] and a god can even go so far as to make the sun set early or rise late, to suit the convenience of human protégés.[104]

As for human action and will, they too are exposed to divine interference. Gods make one warrior's spear go straight (5.290, 17.632), they turn others aside (4.130, 541, 20.98); they may break the archer's bow or the warrior's spear (15.263, 6.306).[105] Gods deceive men (Agamemnon in 2, Pandarus in 4, Hector in 22); they 'bewitch' them, θέλγειν, so that they are helpless victims (12.254, 13.434, 15.594, 21.604). They put ideas into men's minds, as when Hera 'puts it into the mind of Achilles' to summon an assembly, to find out why Apollo is angry (1.58, cf. 8.218); they fill them with emotions: desire, folly, panic, joy in battle, fighting spirit, the strength to endure, the resolution to prefer fighting on to going home, all these we find 'put into' men by gods (3.139, 19.88, 13.82, 5.513, 2.450 ff.). Gods can make the limbs light, and give a man extra speed (5.122, 22.204). Gods move among men in disguise; they may not be

[101] From this point of view the vexed passage looks less unique than some have found it. See the good discussion by Lesky, 'Homeros', RE, Suppl. xi.40, H. Lloyd-Jones, The Justice of Zeus, 6, W. Elliger, Landschaft in gr. Dichtung, 78, W. Burkert, Griechische Religion der archaischen und klassischen Epoche (1977), 375.

[102] 5.506. B. Fenik, Typical Battle Scenes in the Iliad, 53 ff. deals with this and similar passages.

[103] 12.255; 17.268, 370, 648; 1.479. S. E. Bassett, The Poetry of Homer, 168.

[104] 18.239, xxiii.243. Cf. Josh. 10:15, God makes the Sun and Moon stand still for Joshua, and Isa. 38:8, 2 Kings 20:9–11.

[105] Hammurabi prayed (ANET³, 179) 'May Zababa, the mighty warrior, the first born son of Ekur, who marches at my right hand, shatter his weapons on the field of battle! ... May Inanna ... shatter his weapons on the field of battle and conflict!' Esarhaddon of Assyria (Luckenbill, Ancient Records, ii.202) boasted, 'Ishtar ... stood at my side, broke their bows, shattered their battle line.' Jer. 49:35, 'Thus saith the LORD of hosts: Behold, I will break the bow of Elam.' Ezek. 30:24, 'I will break Pharaoh's arms.' In the Völsungasaga, 11, Odin with his spear breaks the sword of Sigmund.

identified by the men they work on at all, or they may reveal their identity at the moment of departure, or men may only later realize that it was a god (e.g. Pandarus in 4, 13.66 ff., 22.297). Heroes reckon to be able to infer divine activity behind events, as when Ajax cries, 'Even a fool could tell that Zeus himself is helping the Trojans. All their missiles strike home; whether thrown by great or small warrior, Zeus guides them all, but ours land on the ground without effect' (17.629 ff.). The poet even gives us the thoughts of a hero who is in fact being driven to face Achilles by Apollo, but who, unaware of this, takes his own decision after a lengthy monologue.[106]

Again, the future is revealed or hinted at by portents and omens. The flight of birds, a peal of thunder, a serpent devouring the young of a bird, a chance utterance, a sneeze[107]—any such event may have an ulterior significance, which is there to be detected by those with the necessary skill or insight. ' "*As* this serpent devoured the eight chicks and the mother bird, *so* shall we wage war for the same number of years, and then in the tenth we shall take the city of broad streets." That is what Calchas said, and now it is all coming true.' Such a speech reflects, in the mind of the speaker, an awareness of something like the notion later called 'sympathy', of the cosmos as a sort of living organism, in which every part is related to every other;[108] important events are foreshadowed in oracles, omens, and dreams.

Somewhere between these last two ideas comes that of fate or the gods 'calling' or 'leading' a man to his death. The greatest heroes to die in the *Iliad*, Patroclus and Hector, are the two who share the phrase 'the gods called me to death'. Their death is developed more fully than any other in the poem, and the responsibility of the gods is more clearly visible; this is the 'plan of Zeus' which involved the death of both of them, in the course of his over-all strategy for the doom of Troy, a fully Olympian conception. Not very different in the *Odyssey* is the passage about the decent Suitor Amphinomus. Odysseus warns him to get away in time, before the killing begins, 'but even so

---

[106] 21.544 ff., cf. G. Petersmann in *Grazer Beiträge*, 2 (1974), 153.

[107] 13.822. 15.376, 2.299 ff., xviii.117, xvii.541. Admittedly, the last two are characteristic of the less heroic atmosphere of the *Odyssey* rather than the *Iliad*.

[108] 2.326–30. I refer of course to Posidonius. Cf. K. Reinhardt, *Kosmos und Sympathie*.

he did not escape his doom; Athena bound him with the rest, to be slain by the hand and spear of Telemachus.' The gods 'planned the destruction' of Archelochus, and Poseidon 'bewitched the eyes of Alcathous and bound his bright limbs, so that he could not flee or avoid the spear but stood like a statue or a tree' to be slain by Idomeneus. But other expressions are more sinister, as being uncanny, less clearly Olympian, and less fully personified. The two sons of Merops of Percote defied their prophetic father's warnings not to go to Troy, κῆρες γὰρ ἆγον μέλανος θανάτοιο, 'for the evil spirits of death were leading them on.'[109] These *kēres* of death are given little description, but it emerges, almost against the poet's will, that there are thousands of them, haunting human life, and in the end no man can escape them; those who die are 'carried off' by them; they haunt the battlefield along with other demons, Strife and Turmoil, and on the Shield of Achilles 'the grim κήρ' is shown carrying one man alive, newly wounded, another unwounded, and dragging a third, dead, by the feet through the mêlée.[110] The dead Patroclus completes this grisly picture when he says that 'the hateful κήρ which received me at my birth has swallowed me up.' Fate, μοῖρα, can also 'lead men to death', or more terrifyingly 'bind' a man (4.517 ἔνθ' Ἀμαρυγκείδην Διωρέα μοῖρα πέδησεν) so that he is slain; in the end the hideous vision of the *kēr* devouring him is so appalling that the poet generally keeps it out of sight.[111] But in all these cases, whether we find the raw picture of demons or the transfigured plan of Olympian Zeus, in every case men have to realize that after all something different was going on from what they perceived with their limited vision. The real meaning of what seemed to be Hector's hopeful reliance on a loved brother to help him against Achilles was that the gods were calling him to his death. The

---

[109] Patroclus and Hector called to death, 16.693 and 22.297; plan of Zeus, 8.470, 15.53; Amphinomus, xviii.155; Archelochus, 14.464; Alcathous, 13.345; sons of Merops, 2.831 = 11.332. The word κήρ is very hard to translate. I have attempted an equivalent of L. Malten's 'Schadegeist', *RE*, *Suppl.* iv.884.4.

[110] Thousands of *kēres*, 12.326; carry men off, 2.302, xiv.207; drag the slain, 18.535 ff. These last lines are interpolated from the Hesiodic *Aspis* according to some, as F. Solmsen in *Hermes*, 83 (1965), 1 ff. = *Kleine Schriften*, 1, 16 ff.; but as Leaf says, 'they cannot be said to be alien from Epic thought.'

[111] *Kēr* has swallowed me, 23.78; fate leads to death, 5.613, 13.62; birds, 4.517, cf. iii.269, xi.292.

sons of Merops realized too late that the pattern of events was that which their father all the time foresaw; they had been doomed from the beginning. The glorification and the victories which Zeus allowed to Hector and Patroclus were really part of a different pattern—a pattern which ended with their defeat and death.

It is this set of beliefs and attitudes which make it natural for Homeric man as well as for the Homeric poet to look for significance and pattern in what happens to him. When Hector, attacking the ships, cuts through with his great sword the spear with which Ajax has been defending them, Ajax does not only suffer the loss of an effective spear: 'He recognized in his noble heart the action of the gods, and he shuddered at it: that Zeus was cutting off all their battle plans and willing the Trojans to victory. He withdrew from the flying missiles, and they cast fire into the ship . . .' Ajax 'sees' the event as symbolic, and the poet agrees: Zeus is in fact urging on the Trojans and paralysing the Achaean efforts against them. The style of this important passage—the firing of a ship is the fated turning-point of the action—is compressed and powerful,[112] and the use of the significant act is what helps to make this possible for the poet. It also is vital for so many of the important and memorable scenes in the poem—Lycaon before Achilles, Priam before Achilles, Achilles with Thetis holding his head, Hector with his child, Paris with his well-polished weapons, and so on. I turn now to a last category of its use.

The great theme of the *Iliad* is heroic life and death. What it is to be a hero is brought out by the terrible contrast between 'seeing the light of the sun' and 'having one's limbs full of movement' on the one side, and the cold, dark emptiness of death on the other. It is in keeping that whole books of the epic are dominated by death in its most tangible and least metaphorical form: the vital importance of the corpse and its treatment. From the opening of Book 1—the wrath of Achilles 'cast many brave souls of heroes into Hades, and made themselves (αὐτούς) the prey of dogs and the food of birds' (1.3–5)— to the last book devoted to the final fate of the corpse of

---

[112] Ajax' perception, 16.119, cf. 15.467; style of the passage, E. Bethe, *Homer*, 1, 31. On Lycaon, Eustath. 1224.3, γραφικῶς τὰ κατὰ τὸν Λυκάονα, etc.

Hector, the theme is never far from our minds,[113] and the fighting takes on its most ferocious and implacable aspect over the bodies of Sarpedon and Patroclus. 'It is better to die here and be buried in Troy than to allow the Trojans to drag Patroclus' body to their city and win that glory', say the Achaeans (17.416), and the poet actually says that 'as they fought like fire, you would not have said that the sun was intact, nor the moon . . .' (17.366).[114]

The threat of casting the corpse of one's opponent, or of slackers on one's own side, to carrion beasts, is common all through the poem. Like so many of the things we have observed in this chapter, the idea is one beloved of the Assyrians. 'Their corpses I forbade to be buried', boasts Esarhaddon of defeated enemies; 'I did not give his body to be buried. I made him more dead than he was before', is the hideous claim of Nâbu-bel-shumâte. Assurbanipal says, 'Their dismembered bodies I fed to the dogs, swine, wolves and eagles, to the birds of heaven and the fishes of the deep'; he went so far as to dig up the bones of the Elamite kings and boast, 'I laid restlessness upon their shades.'[115] Almost every nuance of these Assyrian atrocities is paralleled in the last books of the *Iliad*, the resemblances being so striking as to make the idea of influence upon the poet a very natural one. It is made more plausible still by 18.175 ff., the passage where Iris rouses Achilles by telling him that Hector plans to 'cut Patroclus' head from his tender neck and impale it on stakes'. This comes in the same context, that of the mutilation of the corpse, and what is envisaged by Hector is a combination of favourite Assyrian punishments, beheading and impaling, both regularly meted out to those defeated in war.[116]

---

[113] C. P. Segal, *The Theme of Mutilation of the Corpse in the Iliad* and J. M. Redfield, *Nature and Culture*, 183 ff. These works suffer, in my view, from ignoring the Eastern evidence. Also M. Faust, 'Die künstlerische Verwendung von κύων "Hund" in den homerischen Epen', *Glotta*, 48 (1970), 9–31.

[114] 'A thoroughly weak passage', in the view of Leaf. See now D. Bremer, *Licht und Dunkel*, 68.

[115] Luckenbill, *Ancient Records*, ii.210, 304, 310, 312. In the Old Testament, e.g. Deut. 28:26, 1 Sam. 17:44–6, Ps. 79:2, etc.

[116] e.g. Luckenbill, i.156, '800 of their fighting men I put to the sword and cut off their hands . . . 700 men I impaled on stakes' (Assur-Nâsir-Pal). Ibid., 168, 'I made a pillar of heads in front of his city gate, the living men I impaled on stakes'. Both punishments are commonly shown in Assyrian art. Later, Xerxes beheaded King Leonidas and impaled his head on a pole after Thermopylae (Hdt. vii.238);

What we have here is perhaps affected by reports of the Assyrian 'frightfulness', which made so deep an impression all over the Near East in the eighth and seventh centuries BC,[117] when the Assyrians destroyed, among other places, Babylon, Elam, and Egyptian Thebes, and left ruins and piles of heads to mark their passage.

But, again, like all the other things which Homer shares with the Near East, this motif too must be changed in character before it can be Homeric. As the 'terrifying weapons and glamour of Ashur', which made the Great King of Assyria conquer and destroy his enemies, turn to the *heroically* terrifying weapons of individual heroes, each of whom has his own separate destiny of achievements and eventual death in his turn, so the Assyrian reprisals against the dead, whose purpose was national propaganda, to intimidate potential enemies of the King, are turned to the expression of the final horror of the death of noble warriors, and to the last extremity of passionate heroic hatred. Brave heroes made the feast of scavenging animals: that is the ultimate expression of the horror of death in battle, the death which the hero must risk. The pursuing of revenge goes beyond death; as Achilles cries that 'even if the dead forget in Hades' halls, yet I will remember my dear companion even there' (22.389), so his persistence in abusing the 'dumb earth' that was his enemy (24.54) marks the same vehement refusal to accept even the universal leveller, death. Achilles, the greatest and most passionate of heroes, is consistently characterized in both.

At a simple level, the warriors desire to possess the armour of their enemies for its straightforward value. They also desire to possess the battlefield and the bodies of the dead because that is a visible sign of having won the day. But there are also deeper, or darker, desires. To deprive the dead of a grave is to abolish his memory,[118] to make him as if he had never been; hence the passionate concern felt in Homer for a grave to remain after

---

Herodotus describes Pausanias being tempted to mutilate the corpse of Mardonius after Plataea in revenge and as a deterrent, but nobly rejecting the action as 'fitting barbarians rather than Greeks—and even in them we look on it with resentment' (Hdt. ix.78–9).

[117] Cf. W. Burkert in *WS* 10 (1976), 5–21, Isa. 37:18, 'Of a truth, LORD, the kings of Assyria have laid waste all the nations, and their countries.'

[118] e.g. 7.84–91, 6.418, 16.676, 23.245–8, 24.798, iv.584, iii.256, i.239, xxiv.32.

one's death, to record for posterity one's existence and significance. Again, we learn from Patroclus' ghost that the unburied dead may not pass the river and enter the gates of Hades but must 'wander unceasingly', excluded from rest (23.71 ff.). The Assyrians, we have seen, deliberately inflicted this posthumous suffering on their enemies, and as the idea is known to Homer I think we must accept that it is among the motives which make the Homeric warrior desire to see his enemy unburied; like other horrors, it is pushed by the poet into the background, but is none the less potent for that. Finally there is the desire to render the dead enemy finally helpless. Later we find murderers mutilating the body of a victim by the hideous practice of μασχαλισμός, cutting off the extremities of the corpse so that the dead man shall not have the power to pursue his slayer.[119] When the Achaeans stand round Hector's corpse, every one of them gives him a wound. It is natural to think that underlying this we see the superstition at work, that so many wounds will ensure that Hector in death is really dead (as an Assyrian might put it, to make him more dead than he was before); but Homer will not bring such horrors to the surface, and the scene as we have it draws a great part of its pathos and effectiveness from the heroic contrast of the impassive corpse of Hector and the small malevolence of those who ran from him in life and can face him only when he is safely dead. 'The emotion (of triumph) is that of a low mob, and it magnifies the greatness of the dead man', is the correct comment of the scholiast.[120] As so often, events are given a character exclusively in terms of heroism; but behind the heroic the audience is aware of other powerful currents and is moved by them, without their needing to show themselves above the surface.

Finally the corpse can be used to convey the aspect of Homeric warfare which is not exhausted by the duels between heroes which generally fill up the foreground. Recent work on Iliadic fighting has tended to concentrate on these and on the individual *aristeia* of great warriors,[121] so that one can be left

[119] Cf. E. Rohde, *Psyche* (Eng. trans.), 582 ff.

[120] ΣbT in 22.371: δημώδους πλήθους τὸ πάθος, αὔξει δὲ τὴν ἀρετὴν τοῦ κειμένου.

[121] B. Fenik, *Typical Battle Scenes in the Iliad* (1968); T. Krischer, *Formale Konventionen der hom. Epik* (1971), and the literature listed there on pp. 159–60.

with the impression that the poet is interested in them exclusively.[122] Mass fighting and slaughter is harder to represent
in heroic style, but the poet uses similes[123] for this purpose, and
also he uses the bodies of the slain. Events happen 'in a clear
place where the ground showed through the corpses', warriors
go 'through the slaughter, through the corpses, among the
weapons and the dark blood'. Their chariots pass over the
bodies of the dead, 'and the axle beneath and the rail all round
were all spattered with blood, sprinkled by the drops cast up
from the horses' hooves and the wheels.' There are 'shrieks
and boasts from slayers and slain, while the earth runs with
blood'. Weapons fall from their hands and the earth runs with
blood; men fall under the wheels of pursuing chariots, which
career over them, the earth is dyed with red blood as men fall
in heaps.[124] In the first light of dawn the two sides meet as they
gather up their dead: 'There it was hard to recognize individuals, but washing off the gore with water and shedding
hot tears they lifted them on to carts. Priam forbade weeping;
in silence the Trojans piled their dead on the pyre, grieving at
heart ... in the same way on the other side the well-greaved
Achaeans piled their dead on the pyre, grieving at heart ...'
(7.423–31).[125] It is part of Homer's conception of the heroic
that wounds in battle are either slight or fatal—there are to be
no mutilated and hideously suffering warriors to blur the overriding contrast between heroic life and heroic death. The
corpse both is and is not the man.[126] It stands for him, and its
treatment enables the poet to do full justice to war and death in

---

[122] This has been thought to show how 'unrealistic' Homeric fighting is; but cf.
H. P. Varley, Ivan and Nobuku Morris, *The Samurai* (1970), 22, on the fighting of
feudal Japan: 'a typical field of battle was more likely to resemble a grouping of
separate combats than a general struggle between two armies', and also ibid., 84.

[123] Cf. H. Fränkel, *Die hom. Gleichnisse*, 21 ff.

[124] 8.491 = 10.199, 10.298, 11.534 = 20.499, 4.450 = 8.63, 15.707 ff., 16.378,
17.360.

[125] περιπαθὲς τὸ δρᾶμα, 'a scene of great pathos' is the perceptive comment of
Eustathius 688.58 on this passage, which I find highly moving. 'Such a theme
would perhaps interest the audience of a martial epic' ('ein solches Thema mochte
die Hörer kriegerischen Heldensangs interessieren'), is the best that Von der
Mühll can find to say for it.

[126] At *Iliad* 1.4 the corpses are identified as 'the heroes themselves', in contrast
to the ψυχή, the 'soul' which survives death and goes down to Hades. Cf. also
23.50 ὅσσ᾽ ἐπιεικὲς | νεκρὸν ἔχοντα νέεσθαι ὑπὸ ζόφον ἠερόεντα, 24.35
νέκυν περ ἐόντα, 24.422–3, x.10, xx.23 f.

ways which otherwise could not have been embodied in the epic. And again it was above all the Homeric talent for seeing the significant in the mere object which enables him to achieve these effects.

II

CHARACTERIZATION

Homer has the art of revealing the whole character of a man by one word
(Scholiast D on 8.85).

HITHERTO we have been dealing with devices by which
the poet confers significance on actions, scenes, and
moments in the poems. Such scenes as the interview
between Hector, Paris, and Helen in Book 3, or that between
Priam and Achilles in Book 24, are not simple records of events;
they stand for and make visible the whole relationship of the
characters to each other. They also enable the audience to see
the meaning of what happens as part of the whole pattern of
human life and the world which contains men and also gods.

The question of characterization in the Homeric poems lends
itself to being treated from the same point of view. It is one on
which much has been written, and it is all too clear how subjective most of it is, when we see how flatly scholars contradict
each other.[1] I hope that it will prove possible to establish some
general points about the existence in the poems of characteriza-

---

[1] I give only a few examples. F. Codino, *Introduzione a Omero* (1965), 137, thinks
that Agamemnon and Achilles are so little individual that they are actually inter-
changeable (cf. the justified protest of Lesky, *Gnomon*, 95 (1973), 6); whereas
Finsler, i, 327, thought that 'no more brilliant characterization had ever been
given to a person in literature' than is given to Achilles in Book 9. Alexander Pope
wrote that 'every one of his persons has something so singularly his own that no
painter could have distinguished them more by their features, than the poet has by
their manners'; J. A. Notopoulos speaks of 'the disappointment of the modern mind
in the absence of individual realism in Homer's characters' (*TAPA* 80 (1951), 29).
Bethe said the character of Achilles combined 'two fundamentally opposed
creations by two great but fundamentally opposed poets', and that it was 'an absolute psychological impossibility' that one poet should have had both conceptions in
mind (*Homer*, 1, 74 ff.); Schadewaldt found his character consistent, with two
'poles', of anger and gentleness (*Iliasstudien*, 135); Wilamowitz in 1912 snorted that
'to speak of a character of the Homeric Achilles or Odysseus at all is a piece of
stupidity, as different poets conceive the same hero differently' (*Kultur der Gegen-
wart* 1, 8, 12). And so on. A list of modern works on Homeric characters: A.
Heubeck, *Die homerische Frage* (1974), 197.

tion, and to see how it is used, rather differently in the two epics, towards the same goals.

Some people have inclined to deny the possibility of there being in the Homeric poems any consistent characterization at all. Old-fashioned analysts and modern oralists agree on this point. For the former, separate authorship of the different parts into which they resolved the poems made it hopeless to look for psychological consistency; for the latter, the rigorous constraints of the formulaic system must, it seems, prevent the singer from allowing his characters to speak or think differently from each other. Another question of principle arises: How far is it legitimate to read psychology into what happens in the poems, when this is not made explicit by the poet? The analyst Von der Mühll[2] states as an axiom that 'to depict characters, beyond the objective wording of the text, did not lie within the intentions or the powers of Homer', while the neo-analyst Kakridis[3] insists, against those who supply psychological motivations for the actions of the poet's characters, that 'in poetry only what is recorded exists: nothing else.' From the point of view of oral composition, Kirk warns that 'the depiction of the heroic character is limited both by the technique and aims of oral poetry and by the simplicity of heroic virtues and vices', and when, despite these limitations, genuine characterization is still found, he thinks it right to express this in an extraordinarily guarded fashion: 'These characters achieve a complexity which has the appearance [sic] of being consistently developed as each poem progresses. Even so we must take care not to deduce too much about the methods and the scope of operation of the main poets . . .' It almost seems as though we become so scrupulous that in the end it seems fair to question not only what is not on the surface of the poems, but even what is.[4]

---

[2] Kritisches Hypomnema zur Ilias, 286: 'Über den sachlichen Wortlaut hinaus Charaktere zu zeichnen, lag nicht in B's Absicht und Vermögen.'

[3] In Festschrift W. Schadewaldt (1970), 60: 'In der Dichtung existiert nur, was "recorded" ist, sonst nichts.'

[4] G. S. Kirk, The Songs of Homer, 265. The temptation exists especially for those who pursue the oral theory, it seems. For instance, M. W. Edwards, TAPA 97 (1966), 130, discussing the noble passage at 16.104, with its threefold repetition of the word βάλλειν, 'throw': 'It might be quoted as a fine example of inadequate technique, or as an outstanding instance of intentional breaking of the rules for special poetic effect . . .' Cf. also ibid., 153 on 23.182–3. G. S. Kirk, Homer and the Oral Tradition, 84: 'Is Homer to have ascribed to him a minute observation of

In this chapter I hope to make three points, of a fairly general character, which together will prove helpful in considering this tangled question, and which also will show the poet at work conferring depth and significance upon his creation. First, characters in the poems can be different from each other; second, they can be seen to intend things which they do not explicitly reveal as their intention; third, they can be complex, in ways which are rather different in the two poems.

The unsophisticated audience, reading the *Iliad* for the first time, has generally no doubt that the characters in the poem are clearly differentiated and recognizable. As a sixth-form boy I had no difficulty in recognizing the quarrel between Agamemnon and Achilles as a glorified version of the quarrels and contentions in any gang of young men, in which the leader and the most daring spirit were not the same person. And the two heroes were clearly contrasted with each other. The contrast is made, elegantly and suggestively, in the very first naming of the two: 1.7, 'the son of Atreus, king of men, and god-like Achilles'[5] —the one identified by his titles and rank, the other by his personal quality. It comes again when Achilles reassures Calchas the prophet: no harm will come to him, even if he points at Agamemnon, 'who now claims to be the best of the Achaeans' (1.91). As the seventh line of Book 1 looked formulaic and yet perfectly contrasted the two heroes, so line 91 employs the familiar εὔχεται εἶναι, 'claims to be', which often in Homer simply means 'is'; but it has a special bite here, as we find confirmed when we reach line 244. There Achilles ends the oath which accompanies his withdrawal from battle by saying to Agamemnon, 'And you will rend your heart within you, in vexation that you have dishonoured the best of the Achaeans', and again he ends his appeal to his mother by saying, 'Let Agamemnon, son of Atreus, the great king, see his folly in dis-

---

human, especially feminine, psychology? No definite answer can be given ...'
Against the former, see *ΣT* in 16.104–5: 'The repetition is to create tension, and the effect is above imitation in painting or sculpture.' Against the latter, Coleridge, *Literary Reminiscences*, quoted in J. W. Mackail, *Coleridge's Literary Criticism*, 139, 'The Greeks, except perhaps in Homer, seem to have had no way of making their women interesting, but by unsexing them ...' There is something which causes dismay about a sort of criticism so nervous of its own subject-matter.

[5] The point is excellently made by Adam Parry, *HSCP* 76 (1972), 2 ff.

honouring the best of the Acheans' (412). On the lips of any other hero, 'Agamemnon, who claims to be the best of the Achaeans', would have no second meaning; it is in fact used without irony by Nestor (2.82). But Achilles believes, and will very soon say, that *he* is the best man among them, and the struggle between them is over that precise point. I think the same psychology is to be seen when at line 131 Agamemnon rejects Achilles' suggestion of delayed recompense: 'Do not beguile me with craft, god-like Achilles, strong though you are, for you will not outwit me, nor convince me.' ἀγαθός περ ἐών, 'strong though you are', is a phrase which occurs four times in the *Iliad* (twice addressed to Achilles), but there is an illogicality about saying 'you will not succeed in deceiving or beguiling me, strong though you are', for strength is not what makes a man a plausible deceiver. The slight abuse of the phrase suggests that the excessive prowess of Achilles, viewed as a turbulent subordinate, is what really fuels the angry over-reaction of Agamemnon, what has always worried him. He refers to it explicitly at 178, 'if you are very strong, it is god who gave it to you', and again at 290: 'if the gods have made him a warrior, do they therefore put revilings in his mouth for him to utter?'[6]

These examples show how deftly the formulaic expression can be made to produce unique and individual effects. They could be multiplied. On a larger scale, we can see how the poet varies his treatment of a set scene in accordance with the characters involved. For instance, the scene of a warrior begging for his life comes five times in the *Iliad*, and every time the suppliant is in fact slain. The two sons of Antimachus offer rich ransom to Agamemnon if he will spare their lives, but in answer to their soft words they hear an answer far from soft: 'If you are indeed the sons of Antimachus—who once urged the Trojans to slay Menelaus when he came as envoy—now you shall pay the penalty for his disgrace.' Not only does Agamemnon kill them, he hews off the arms and head of one of them and sends his trunk rolling through the battle like a drum of stone. The incident is dramatic and ironic—the name of the rich father dooms them instead of saving them—and the ferocity of Agamemnon is in accordance with his behaviour

---

[6] I give the translation of Lang, Leaf, and Myers for the obscure line 291.

elsewhere.[7] The tender-hearted Menelaus,[8] by contrast, is more easily moved, and he is about to spare the suppliant Adrestus when Agamemnon comes running up and reminds him of his wrongs; Menelaus pushes him away, and Agamemnon kills him. The night adventure of the *Doloneia*, where the sinister and the tricky are given much greater play than in the rest of the poem,[9] appropriately contains the most deceitful of this set of scenes. Dolon, captured by Diomede and Odysseus, is told by Odysseus to 'take heart and give no thought to death'. So encouraged, he answers their questions, betraying his sleeping friends; and then Diomede kills him, observing that 'if we release you or let you go, you will fight against us another day' (10.372–453). The wily Odysseus well lives up to his reputation here, deceiving the captive without actually lying to him.

Finally we come to the examples which concern Achilles. In the old days, the hero tells us, before Patroclus was slain, he preferred to ransom or sell his captives, as he sold Lycaon, rather than to kill them (21.100 ff.); and Zeus himself confirms this (24.156). But in the darkness of his fury of revenge he is resolved to slay them all. First we see Tros, son of Alastor, attempt to embrace his knees in supplication; as he touches them, Achilles stabs him from above through the liver, so that it is thrust out of him and his lap filled with blood. The incident comes in a series of killings by Achilles, all at great speed and without a pause, and with Tros the hero does not bother to take any notice of his gesture. The greatest of these scenes is, of course, that in which poor Lycaon begs for his life. His pathetic speech ends with these lines: 'Now I am doomed to die here, for I think I shall not escape your hands since fate has brought me to you.—Yet I shall say something else to you; take it to

---

[7] W. Schadewaldt, *Iliasstudien*, 50; B. Fenik, *Typical Battle Scenes in the Iliad*, 85. Another sort of scene which can be used in the same way is that where a character is brought the news of the death of another—see G. Petersmann in *Rh. Mus.* 116 (1973), 6, who effectively compares scenes of this type. Cf. also B. C. Fenik on monologues: *Homer, Tradition and Invention* (1978), 68 ff.

[8] Antimachus' sons, 11.130 ff; Adrestus, 6.46–65. Cf. H. Spiess, *Menschenart und Heldentum in Homers Ilias* (1913), 158; J. A. Scott, *The Unity of Homer* (1921), 173; A. Parry in *HSCP* 76 (1972), 16; Σ in 4.127, 4.146; Barck in *WS* n. F.5 (1951), 5 ff. The view of C. R. Beye, *Iliad, Odyssey and Epic Tradition*, 117, that Menelaus is 'a totally second-rate person', is unintelligible to me.

[9] Cf. F. Klingner, 'Über die Dolonie', *Hermes* 75 (1940), 337–68 = *Studien zur gr. und röm. Literatur* (1964), 7–39; Reinhardt, *Der Dichter der Ilias*, 247.

heart: do not kill me, since I am not born of the same mother as Hector, who slew your comrade gentle and brave.' These last three lines struck analytical scholars as inappropriate or contradictory, and on one frivolous ground or another they liked to delete them;[10] but surely we are to hear the desperate improvization of the terrified Lycaon, as he sees his doom come upon him and tries a last appeal: 'Yet I shall say something else . . .' The reply of Achilles raises the scene to its highest form.

'Since Patroclus' death no Trojan shall escape me. Come, my friend, you too must die; why lament as you do? Patroclus died, and he was a much better man than you. Do you not see what manner of man I am, in beauty and stature? My father is noble, my mother is a goddess; and yet even over me hangs death and over-mastering fate. There will be a morning or an evening or a noon-day when my life too shall be taken by some man in battle, whether it be with a blow of the spear or with an arrow from the bow.' So he spoke, and the limbs and heart of Lycaon were unstrung. He let go his hold on the spear and squatted with his arms outspread . . .

Like all the other suppliants in battle, Lycaon is killed. The manner of his death brings out the character of his opponent. Menelaus was kind-hearted but indecisive; Agamemnon is ruthless and unreflective; Achilles kills in a passionate revenge, but not in blind ferocity. He sees his action in the perspective of human life and death as a whole, the perspective which puts slayer and slain on a level, so that it is more than a mere colloquialism that he calls Lycaon 'friend' as he kills him. This is the same contrast as we find between the brutal and unreflective way in which Agamemnon rejects the aged suppliant Chryses, and the humanity which Achilles finds it possible to share with the aged suppliant Priam ('here I sit by Troy, far from home, causing grief to you and to your children'). Achilles sees further; his dispute with Agamemnon leads him to bitter reflections on the life of heroism itself, the granting by Zeus of his prayer that the Achaeans should be forced by defeat to recall him leads to bitter disillusionment, his career of victory and slaughter makes him recognize his fundamental kinship with those whom he kills.[11]

---

[10] Tros, 20.463 ff. Lycaon, 21.36 ff., 21.94–6 del. Bayfield, Leaf, Von der Mühll,

[11] 'Here I sit by Troy', 24.541; heroism, 9.316 ff., esp. 327, 'fighting with men who are defending their wives'. 'Zeus granted my prayer, but what pleasure have I in it', 18.79; 'I too must die', 21.99 ff.; 'Priam is like my own father Peleus', 24.544 ff.

These scenes of supplication show us the poet varying a set situation, and doing so in a way that brings out the character of his heroes. But more than that: we see them as they are, not in just any circumstances of ordinary life, but as they are in the light of the great issue of life and death. Trickiness and ruthlessness are interesting traits of character, and they are developed deftly and consistently; but the really important person is Achilles, and what he sees possesses a depth and truth which transforms a mere narrative of killing into an insight into death itself. So here too, in the portrayal of character, the chief interest of the poet is in conferring importance on events and bringing out their significance. As with the scenes in which Paris and Hector are seen with their wives, and which show us not only their individual personalities but the meaning of their actions and of the poem as a whole, so these scenes of supplication and its rejection bring out, in their measured crescendo, important things about heroic life and death.[12]

The *Odyssey*, as so often, offers similarity and also difference. Odysseus is entertained and loved by two goddesses, Calypso and Circe, and he has to detach himself from each of them and also to say farewell to Nausicaa. With the glamorous Circe Odysseus happily spends a year in pleasure, 'feasting on meat inexhaustible and sweet wine'. Eventually his crew urge on him that it is time to go, and he embraces her knees in supplication, begging her to let him depart: his men are melting his heart with their lamentations, when she is not there to see. At once she answers: 'Son of Laertes, sprung from Zeus, Odysseus of the many wiles, do not remain longer in my house against your will . . .' Forthwith she plans their departure.

Very different is the loving Calypso. For seven years Odysseus has been kept prisoner on her island, without means of escape; she wishes to marry him and make him immortal, but he will have none of it. Day after day he sits gazing out to sea and

---

[12] Karl Reinhardt points out that there is a development in the killings described in the *Iliad*, and that the deaths in the first half of the poem could not be simply exchanged with those in the second half, *Der Dichter der Ilias*, 13. So too the Lycaon-scene is the climax of the set of supplications in battle, and could only stand last; an ordinary one following it would be a sore anticlimax. After it we can have only the supreme supplication, that of Priam (Book 24). These facts are perhaps not without interest for the question of artistic arrangement or mere inartistic accretion in the Homeric poems.

weeping. At last the gods intervene and send Hermes to tell Calypso that she must let him go home. She pours out her feelings to Hermes in bitterness against the gods; then she finds Odysseus and tells him that he can go, if he will, 'for I shall send you off with all my heart.' The hero is naturally astonished, and she reassures him with a smile, saying 'My mind is righteous and my heart within me is not of iron; no, it is kindly.' The pair have a last interview, recorded with great delicacy and charm. She asks if he is really so anxious to see his wife, 'for whom you yearn every day', and suggests that she, as a goddess, must be far better-looking. The tactful Odysseus at once admits that Penelope is inferior in beauty but says, 'Yet even so I wish and long every day to come home ...' Calypso never tells him why she lets him go, and Odysseus never knows; she claims the credit for her own soft heart, and in his presence only hints at her bitterness and the real reason when she says 'I shall send a favourable wind for you, so that you may reach your homeland in safety—if that is the will of the gods in heaven, who are stronger than I to devise and to carry out.'[13] We see through these words her expression of the fact that, were it not for the gods, she would not be letting him go; but for Odysseus that meaning is lost.

Lastly, there is Nausicaa. The night before she meets Odysseus, she dreamt of getting married. When he appears, at first she does not find him impressive; but when he is bathed and glorified by Athena, she says to her maids, 'I wish that such a man might be called my husband, living here, and that he might be pleased to stay here!' She goes on to give a broad hint to Odysseus: 'If you come into town with me, malicious people will talk, saying "Who is this tall and handsome stranger with Nausicaa? Where did she find him? He will be her husband next." ' And even her father seems to think the match an attractive one. But of course Odysseus is off home to his wife, and there is no place for Nausicaa. She does, however, manage to be in his way as he goes in to dinner and to have a last word with him. 'Farewell, stranger, and when you are in your homeland think sometimes of me and remember that to me first you owe the saving of your life.' Odysseus replies that if he returns

---

[13] Parting from Circe, x.460 ff.; Calypso, v; Odysseus never knows her motive, vii.263; 'the gods are stronger than I', v. 170.

home safely, 'There I shall honour you like a god all my days, for you rescued me, princess.'[14] Three scenes of parting, each of them coloured by love, and all very different.

The situation of parting with a woman in love is an emotional and difficult one, which is calculated to bring out the real nature of both parties. It was to have a great future in literature. Virgil's Dido and the *Heroides* of Ovid are among its forms. The variants on the theme in the *Odyssey* show us three very different women: the hard-boiled Circe, to whom the affair has been one of pleasure which there is no point in trying to prolong; the young Nausicaa, with whom nothing is put into words and yet everything is there, in essence rather than in actuality; and the suffering Calypso, retaining her dignity as she loses her love. Each represents a type and offers a different relationship, to which the wandering hero might have abandoned himself, forgetting his wife and home. That he resists them all brings out his unconquerable resolution, the central fact of the *Odyssey*. But we observe also two other things: these women are inscrutable, and they are complex.

Before Odysseus met Circe, Hermes gave him a marvellous herb which would defend him against her magic. When her spell failed to work, Odysseus should attack her with drawn sword, as if intending to kill her; 'and she in fear will bid you come to her bed.' This duly happens. Circe tries and fails to turn the hero into a pig, recognizes him as Odysseus, whose coming had been often foretold, and says, 'Come now, sheathe your sword, and then let us go to our bed, so that we may have union in love and sleep together, and trust each other.' This is not the behaviour of a fully human person. The immediate transition from hostile magic to the act of love—and after it Circe really is trustworthy—is dreamlike, recalling the transitions in fairy stories. The transformation of a frankly magical tale into one of complex and real humanity is clear when Circe says to the hero, not that the magic herb has protected him, but 'your mind is proof against enchantment.' Odysseus and his men never understand the formidable Circe. 'Now my heart

---

[14] 'I wish that such a man', vi.244. P. Cauer, 'Homer als Charakteristiker', *NJbb* (1900), 599 remarks on the subtlety of the transition: 'such a man . . . I wish that *he* . . .' 'People will talk': vi.275; Alcinous on the match, vii.311 ff.; farewell, viii.461.

longs to be gone, and that of my comrades, who melt my heart as they wail around me, when you are not present', he says to her, when he begs her to allow him to depart;[15] but she has not the least reluctance in the world. She tells them that they must go to the land of the dead, and the news breaks their hearts. As they make their way to the ship, she 'passes them by easily', taking the animals they need to sacrifice to the dead. They do not see her go; as Odysseus puts it, 'who could see a god against his will, passing hither or thither?'[16] From first to last she is mysterious, and they are all aware of it.

When we turn to Calypso, we find that she is inscrutable in a very different way. There is not, as there was with Circe, any doubt or mystery about her basic motive: she regards Odysseus as belonging to her, she saved him from the sea, and she intends to keep him for ever and make him immortal. She conceals her motive for letting him go, as we have seen—a neat contrast with the behaviour of Achilles in the last book of the *Iliad*. Achilles, who told Odysseus that he hated like the gates of Hell the man who thought one thing in his heart and said another, does not try to claim the credit for releasing Hector's body to Priam, saying, 'I am minded to give you Hector, and a messenger has come to me from Zeus, my own mother . . .'[17] She conceals her motive; and Hermes avoids directly threatening her, in case she is minded to disobey the order of Zeus. When she asks, 'Why have you come?' he replies, 'Zeus sent me here, much against my will. Who would choose to cross so vast an expanse of salt water, without a single city where men offer sacrifices and hecatombs to the gods? But it is impossible for another god to cross or frustrate the will of aegis-bearing Zeus.

---

[15] 'Your mind', x.329, cf. Reinhardt, *Tradition und Geist*, 82. 'Let me go', x.485–6. The treatment of these lines by G. Beck, *Philologus* 109 (1965), 18 ff., is very forced.

[16] x.569–74. The harsh criticism of D. L. Page, *The Homeric Odyssey*, 32, disregards such points.

[17] 'I hate that man . . .' 9.313; messenger from Zeus, 24.561. There is an exquisite irony in lines v.190–9. Calypso leads Odysseus to suppose that her decision comes from her own kind heart, then she leads him into the cave, and he sits down 'on the seat from which Hermes had arisen'—recalling the compulsion she had received in a detail which is significant for us but not for Odysseus. Then they dine. He eats and drinks 'what mortal men consume', she is served nectar and ambrosia. The symbolism: they belong to different worlds, to which their imminent parting will restore them.

They say there is a man with you . . .' On this passage the scholiast comments: 'While seeming to defend himself on the ground that it was unavoidable that he obey Zeus, he is really preparing her, too, to accept the facts. For disobedience to Zeus is impossible.'[18] He also is too gallant to make any allusion to Calypso's love for Odysseus, saying only that 'The wind and wave brought him here, and now Zeus orders you to send him away.'[19] It is only the unhappy goddess who talks of her love and her hopes—to Hermes, but not to the hero himself.

Their last conversation is distinguished for what is not said but hinted at.

Are you so very anxious to sail for home at once? Then farewell; but if you only knew what sufferings are in store for you before you reach your home, you would stay here, and live with me, and be immortal—however you long to see your wife, for whom you yearn every day.—But in truth I think I am not inferior to her in beauty or stature, since it is not right that mortal women should rival immortals in form and beauty.

Such a speech invites and rewards treatment as being psychologically sophisticated. The goddess is saying: 'You can go if you want to, but you would do better to stay with me; I can do so much for you! I suspect you only want to go because of that wife of yours, whom you refuse to forget: but I don't see why you prefer her to me, when I am so much better looking.' Such a speech is not easy to answer. Odysseus' reply could serve as a model for embarrassed males. He begins by granting and underlining her final point. 'Mighty goddess, be not angry with me; I know full well that prudent Penelope is inferior to you in beauty and in stature, for she is mortal, while you are immortal and for ever young.' She is a mighty goddess, he insists, separated by a great gulf from a mere mortal man; and as for his wife, of course she is far less attractive than Calypso. 'Yet still I wish and long every day to go home and see the day of my return. . .' The ancients read psychology into this speech, pointing out that Odysseus cleverly began by clearing himself on the charge of love for his wife, 'since nothing wounded Calypso as much as being slighted in comparison with her', and

---

[18] Σ in v.103: τῷ μὲν δοκεῖν ὑπὲρ ἑαυτοῦ ἀπολογεῖσθαι, ὅτι ἀναγκαῖον ἦν ἐπακοῦσαι Διί, ἔργῳ δὲ κἀκείνην παρασκευάζει δέξασθαι τὰ πράγματα. οὐ γὰρ δυνατὸν παρακούειν Διός. ἀπολογεῖται would perhaps be a better reading.
[19] Σ in v.110: δαιμονίως τὰ τοῦ ἔρωτος ἐσιώπησεν.

that he was careful to reassure Calypso that it was not for his wife's sake that he was so anxious to leave, but simply to 'go home'.[20] Avoiding any question of invidious comparison between the two ladies, making no explicit refusal of the appeal she makes to him in such delicately indirect form, he allows her to keep her dignity, as Hermes tried to do. The question of principle, whether such psychological refinements, not explicitly underlined by the poet, are really to be read into the poem, will be considered after we have glanced at the scene of parting from Nausicaa.

We have seen that Nausicaa had marriage in her mind the day she met Odysseus, that her father was also thinking about it, and that both of them had thoughts of Odysseus in the role of her husband. When events take their different course, and he is about to leave, she contrives to be where he passes and to have a last exchange with him. 'Remember me when you are far away'—'I will remember you and feel grateful to you for saving my life.' The exchange is inconclusive, on the surface, and yet the audience feels it to be satisfying and perfect. This is so because we naturally supply what is not said, what might have been; Nausicaa was ready to fall in love with Odysseus, and hopes at least to live in his memory. She has secured a last word from the glamorous stranger, and she can be confident that it will be something sweet to hear. We have in fact the equivalent, in terms of the softer ethos of the *Odyssey*, of the tragic wish of Andromache after Hector's death, that he had at least 'in dying stretched out his arms to me and spoken some memorable word, which I might remember ever after as I weep night and day' (24.743). In the *Iliad*, tragedy; in the *Odyssey*, a touching but gentle pathos.

It is time to confront the question of principle. As we have seen, some people deny that any psychology is to be read into or behind the bare words of the text. This view was heroically supported by Adolf Kirchhoff, at a passage which can serve as a test case. In the sixth book of the *Odyssey*, Nausicaa told

---

[20] Σ in v. 215: ἄριστον τὸ περὶ πρώτης ἀπολογήσασθαι τῆς περὶ τὴν Πηνελόπην φιλοστοργίας. οὐδὲν γὰρ οὕτως ἥπτετο τῆς Καλυψοῦς ὡς ἡ παρευδοκίμησις. Σ in 220: ἐπ' ἄλλα τρέπει τὸν πόθον. ἡ μὲν γὰρ ἔφη, ἱμειρόμενός περ ἰδέσθαι σὴν ἄλοχον· ὁ δὲ ὁμολογῶν τὴν ἐπιθυμίαν οὐκ ἐπὶ τὴν Πηνελόπην πεποίηται τὴν ἀπόστασιν ἀλλὰ ἐπὶ τὰ οἴκοι: so too Eustath. 1530.39.

Odysseus not to accompany her into town, as their appearance
together would cause talk, and even rumours of marriage.
Odysseus complies with these instructions and makes his own
way to her father's palace. But when her father says to him, 'I
find fault with my daughter for one thing, that she did not
bring you to our house with her maidservants', he replies 'Do
not blame your innocent[21] daughter. She did tell me to follow
with her servants, but I refused, from fear and respect, lest
your heart be angered by the sight; we men on earth are
prompt to resentment.'[22] What are we to make of this? Most
scholars, from antiquity onwards, have seen in the passage a
white lie to protect Nausicaa from her father's displeasure. Even
Kakridis, in the same article in which he asserts the axiom that
'in poetry only what is recorded exists', says of this passage,
'The epic poet trusts his audience to detect the intention of the
lie: the girl was to be protected from her father's anger', and
only Kirchhoff insisted that 'If Homer meant to make Odysseus
act chivalrously, he should have said so; this is not psychologically subtle, it is merely slapdash.'[23]

Now, there are passages in the *Odyssey* in which the poet does
explicitly tell us of a character's hidden motive. At the simplest
level there is the hypocrisy of a character like Eurymachus, who
swears to Penelope that no man will lay hands on Telemachus
while he is alive, or his blood will spurt round Eurymachus'
spear; he has not forgotten the kindness of Odysseus towards
him when he was a child. 'So he spoke to cheer her, but he himself was planning Telemachus' destruction.'[24] Odysseus is
famous for his power to conceal his feelings, and one of the
constant pleasures of the poem is observing him as he does

---

[21] This seems to be the meaning of ἀμύμονα here, despite A. Amory Parry,
Blameless Aegisthus (1973), 121 ff.

[22] vii.299–307, with Σ in 303, τεχνικῶς ἄγαν ὁ 'Οδυσσεὺς ἀπολογεῖται
ὑπὲρ τῆς κόρης. πλέον γὰρ προενόησε τοῦ τῆς παιδὸς εὐσχήμονος ἢ τοῦ ἰδίου
ξυμφέροντος, and in 305, ψεύδεται μέν, ἀλλ' ἀναγκαίως, etc.

[23] Kakridis in *Festschrift W. Schadewaldt* (1970), 53; A. Kirchhoff, *Die homerische
Odyssee*[2], 210—'nicht psychologisch fein, sondern einfach flüchtig'—the work,
needless to say, of the *Bearbeiter*; 'ihm diesen Fehler durch gezwungene Interpretation in ein Verdienst zu verwandeln, haben wir gar keine Veranlassung.' We
observe that Kirchhoff's method also led him to delete v.103–4, which makes
Hermes' speech pointless.

[24] vi.448, cf. also e.g. xiii.254, xiv.459 = xv.304, xviii.51, xviii.283, and, in the
Iliad, 10.240, where Agamemnon tries to protect his brother from going on a
dangerous mission, saying something which conceals his real purpose.

things which have a secret meaning for him, unknown to the other characters; from asking, when incognito, for the song of the Wooden Horse, 'which Odysseus brought into Troy', to serving as a beggarly hanger-on in his own home and saying, 'I too once was wealthy and had a fine house.'[25] Achilles, who himself always speaks from the heart, is aware that others do not.

More specifically, the poems contain examples of tact and delicacy, marked as such. Athena comes to Nausicaa in a dream and tells her that she should take a party of maids and friends on a day's laundry by the river: 'Your wedding day is near at hand, when you must have clean clothes to wear . . . the cream of the young men of Phaeacia are seeking your hand . . .' The real motive of the goddess is of course to get Nausicaa and her company to the isolated spot where Odysseus is in urgent need of her help, but she prefers to go about it indirectly. Nausicaa is delighted with the idea of the excursion, and asks her father for a waggon for the day. She does not mention her own marriage, but instead says that her brothers are constantly going to dances, her father needs to be well dressed, and she herself has many dirty things. 'So she spoke, for she felt shame about mentioning lusty marriage to her father; but he understood it all . . .'[26] Here we have a whole net of unspoken feelings and reticences. Athena acts indirectly, Nausicaa says something other than what she means, her father sees through the screen but makes no comment upon it.

Slightly less explicit is the following passage: the first song which the Muse inspires Demodocus to sing among the Phaeacians is the story of a great quarrel at Troy between Odysseus and Achilles. The rest of the audience is delighted with the song, but Odysseus himself, for whom it has an unsuspected and personal meaning, hides his face in his garment and weeps. 'Then the other Phaeacians did not observe that he was shedding tears, but Alcinous alone observed it, sitting beside him, and heard his deep sighs. At once he spoke out among the Phaeacian oarsmen, "Listen, leaders and counsellors of Phaeacia: we have had our fill now of the feast and the music

---

[25] viii.494, xvii.419 = xix.75. A. Roemer, *Homerische Aufsätze* (1914), 90, discusses this sort of irony.

[26] The opening scene of vi, esp. lines 66–7; cf. H. Erbse, *Beiträge zum Verständnis der Od.*, 21–3.

which goes with it. Now let us go out and turn to sport" ...'[27] If we press here the principle that only what is made explicit is to be accepted as present, then the poet has not told us that Alcinous acts as he does because he wishes to spare Odysseus, and to do it tactfully. He has not given us, expressly, any motive at all for Alcinous' action. But it is perfectly clear what is meant, and the reader who insisted on more would try our patience. The 'white lie' of Odysseus about Nausicaa belongs in the same box, and so does, for instance, a delicate touch in the first book.

Athena has come to Ithaca to rouse Telemachus into action. Odysseus is still alive, she says, on an island in the sea, 'and fierce men have him, cruel men who hold him there against his will.' Now in fact Odysseus is of course on the island of Calypso, detained by a loving nymph who wants to make him immortal. Who are these 'fierce men'? Even in the palmy days of analytic scholarship this contradiction was not seized on as evidence for a separate origin and a different version of the story, because it is so obvious that the goddess is avoiding a truth which, if revealed, would reduce poor Telemachus to despair.[28] These passages help us to understand a more vexed one in the nineteenth book. Disguised as a beggar, the hero has a confidential conversation with Penelope, and tells her that her husband will very soon be home.[29] He gives her a summary account of his adventures, which he claims to have heard from the king of Thesprotia; and this account entirely omits Calypso, taking Odysseus straight from the shipwreck to the land of the Phaeacians. Analysts failed to resist the temptation here, and 'earlier versions' and the like were freely invented. In the light of our discussion we see that the hero spares Penelope's feelings. She would not like to hear from an anonymous beggar that the talk of Thesprotia was her husband's intrigue with a goddess.

---

[27] viii.73–100. On the song, W. Marg in *Navicula Chiloniensis* (1956), 16 ff., K. Deichgräber, 'Der letzte Gesang der Ilias', *SB Mainz*, 1972, 18.

[28] i.198.

[29] xix.269 ff. On the meaning of τοῦδ᾽ αὐτοῦ λυκάβαντος, 305, see H. Erbse, *Beiträge zum Verständnis der Odyssee* (1972), 91. The passage is dealt with excellently by F. Cauer, *Grundfragen der Homerkritik*[3] (1923), 539 ff.; he too is reduced to asking sadly, 'Was it necessary to spell that out?' ('War es nötig, das auszumalen?' p. 540, n. 24). He also explains why xxiii.333 ff. do not contradict this view.

This brief survey has shown that the *Odyssey* contains passages in which the poet explicitly tells us of the psychology which we are to see underlying the words and acts of characters, and also that other passages, where this is not made explicit, come so close to them in nature that we can have no reasonable doubt that there, too, the instinctive response of the audience, to interpret the passages in the light of the psychology of human beings, is sound. We need not fear that there is an objection in principle to doing this in the Homeric poems. This does not of course mean that every possible nuance which can be read into the text by perverse ingenuity is really there, nor that we are helpless to choose between plausible and implausible interpretations. The standard must continue to be that of taste and sense, here as elsewhere in the study of literature; we cannot banish them and replace them with a rule, which will give us with objective certainty the answers to aesthetic questions.

The approach we have been following with the *Odyssey* is not so easy to apply to the *Iliad*. It is significant, however, that the most striking examples in the *Iliad* are spoken by women. Andromache, begging Hector not to risk his life on the field of battle, says that he should 'stay here on the wall, lest you make your son an orphan and your wife a widow. Make the men stand by the fig-tree, where the wall can most easily be breached . . . Three times the Achaean champions have made an assault there . . .' The passage has given birth to much discussion, some being displeased that Andromache should offer detailed tactical advice, some arguing that what she says is not true. A scholiast saw the right answer: 'This is an invention, to keep her husband from the field; and that is why Hector does not answer it' (*ΣT* in 6.434). An important part of the purpose of the visit of Hector to Troy is to show the hero confronting the seductions of the women's world, and such a point, so skilful in itself and so like the technique of many passages in the *Odyssey*, fits excellently. This sort of obliqueness and complexity, then, seemed particularly appropriate in women; but its existence shows that the poet did understand inwardness and complexity in human characters. It will not do to say, as is said for instance by Redfield, that 'Homeric man, being objective, has no innerness . . . He has no hidden depths or secret motives; he says and does what he is.'[30] It is also important that in the *Iliad* the two goddesses who hate Troy never explain why they hate it (see especially 4.30 ff. and 20.313 ff.). The reason was their chagrin at defeat in the Judgement of Paris, but that motive is concealed —and again the result is very feminine.[31]

Fortunately the *Iliad* does contain a long episode in which such feminine indirectness is both explicit and important: the seduction of Zeus by Hera. Anxious to intervene against his prohibition, she looks at Zeus as he sits on Mount Ida, 'and he was hateful to her heart.' She plans his seduction, since direct means are impossible; while he sleeps she will be able to help the Achaeans. Secretly she adorns herself, securing her door with a special key. Then she induces the goddess of love, a partisan of the Trojans, to lend the talisman which makes her irresistible. She does not, of course, say why she really wants it, but she tells a tale about the venerable deities Oceanus and Tethys, who have quarrelled and ceased to sleep together; Hera hopes to reconcile them. Aphrodite lends the charm, with the unconsciously ironical remark that 'It would not be right to deny your request, for you sleep in the arms of mighty Zeus.' Hera approaches Zeus in an innocent manner and tells him that she is off to re-establish sexual relations between Oceanus and Tethys. He proposes that they make love instead; and with a show of modest reluctance ('Dread son of Cronos, what a suggestion! If you really are desirous . . .'), the artful goddess consents. Zeus sleeps, and Poseidon is enabled to rout the Trojans . . . The whole scene[32] shows perfect mastery of the arts of indirectness and of a psychology far from transparent, and all this is incompatible with over-schematic 'historical' theories about the objectivity of Homeric characters, who have 'not yet' become capable of complexity.[33]

[30] J. M. Redfield, *Nature and Culture in the Iliad* (1975), 20; see also F. Codino, *Introduzione a Omero* (1965), 137, and the references in note 37 below.

[31] K. Reinhardt, *Das Parisurteil.*

[32] The episode is firmly part of the structure of the *Iliad*—see esp. H. Erbse in *A und A* 16 (1970), 93–112—and I share the reserve expressed by reviewers towards A. Dihle's attempt to show that it had ultimately a different origin: A. Dihle, *Homer-Probleme* (1970), 83 ff., see J. B. Hainsworth in *CR* 22 (1972), 317, M. W. Edwards in *AJP* 95 (1974), 70.

[33] So too Iris excuses herself from accepting the invitation of the Winds with a social falsehood, 23.206 and *ΣbT*; and, on feminine psychology, *ΣT* on 15.22, 18.429.

The *Iliad* is not so much concerned with mysterious and inscrutable characters, both Achilles and Agamemnon expressing their attitudes and emotions with great clarity. There are however some important passages which show us something rather similar; characteristically different, in keeping with the whole nature of the two epics. In the fourth book of the *Odyssey*, Telemachus has come to Sparta with young Pisistratus, son of Nestor. They admire Menelaus' wealth and splendour, to which he replies that he would gladly part with two-thirds of his possessions, if only the men could be alive again who died at Troy; often when he thinks of them he weeps, and then again he ceases to weep. Helen enters and identifies Telemachus as the son of Odysseus, for whom, says Menelaus, he would have liked to do so much, had not the will of some god begrudged it and robbed Odysseus of his homecoming. 'So he spoke, and in all of them he aroused the desire to weep: Argive Helen wept, daughter of Zeus, and Telemachus wept, and Menelaus, son of Atreus; nor did Nestor's son have dry eyes, for he remembered noble Antilochus, who was slain by the splendid son of the Dawn ...' So they all weep for their various losses, and Pisistratus tells them about his dead brother, until they agree that they have shed enough tears; and then they turn to dinner, and Helen slips into the wine a drug which makes them forget their sorrows. Menelaus observes that 'soon is one sated with chilly lamentation', and 'we shall give over weeping, and let us once more bethink ourselves of supper'. The passage is charming, with Menelaus mourning for his dead comrades but philosophically remarking that one soon has enough of that, Pisistratus reminding the company that he, too, has someone to mourn, and Helen using her wide experience to cheer the party up. These people weep easily, but they are soon consoled; nostalgically they look back on their own old sorrows, which do not, it seems, go very deep.

In the *Iliad* we find several scenes which have a resemblance to this one. In the nineteenth book Briseis, restored to Achilles by Agamemnon, finds Patroclus dead on her return. She laments over his body; it is the due of death that a man should be lamented by women of his kin, but Patroclus has no kinswomen at Troy, and so the poet uses Briseis and the other captive women, who echo her words with their groans.[34] Since she was not a kinswoman, he is obliged to produce a reason for her grief at Patroclus' death. He does so by making her say

'You would not have me even weep, when Achilles had slain my husband and destroyed the city of god-like Mynes; you said that you would make me Achilles' wedded wife, take me back to Phthia, and hold the wedding among the Myrmidons. So I weep passionately for your death, you who were ever gentle.' So she spoke, weeping, and the women lamented after her; Patroclus was the occasion of their grief, but each wept for her own unhappiness.[35]

Hector and Patroclus, the two heroes whose death is formally lamented by women in the *Iliad*, both possessed the quality of gentleness, and the poet supplies the motive he needs for Briseis' grief in accordance with that trait of character. The other women, captives enslaved by the disasters of war, weep for their dead master. He was gentle by nature, and they mourn his death; but as each is given the occasion to weep, she weeps for her own fate. The grief here is far deeper than that of the *Odyssey*. As Achilles tells us, he will never feel a more cruel grief than at the death of Patroclus, and, far from turning to the consolations of the feast, he refuses to taste food; while as for the women, like all slaves they must conceal their feelings and can weep for themselves only when their masters, too, have cause to weep.

Later in the same book the Achaean chieftains try to console Achilles, without avail. He utters a speech of lamentation, which ends with the thought of his father Peleus, who no doubt is either dead already or on the point of death, enfeebled by hateful old age, and constantly expecting the bitter tidings of the death of his son. 'So he spoke, weeping, and the elders groaned after him, each one of them mindful of what they had left at home.' Again the same ethos; Achilles will indeed die, and all of them have reason to think of their homes with tears.

Finally, two passages in the twenty-fourth book. Priam, mourning Hector's death, grovels in the dung of the animals in

---

[34] *ΣT* in 19.282: ἐπεὶ γὰρ ἐπ' ἀλλοδαπῆς τέθνηκε Πάτροκλος, ἔνθα μὴ πάρεισι συγγενεῖς γυναῖκες ... χορὸν αἰχμαλωτίδων πεποίηκε θρηνοῦντα, ἐξάρχοντος ἐνδόξου προσώπου.

[35] 19.295–302. I think Leaf was right to insist that Πάτροκλον πρόφασιν does not mean that their grief for Patroclus was insincere. The gentleness of Hector: 24.767 ff. 'Never could I feel a more cruel suffering', 19.321.

the courtyard. 'In the palace his daughters and the wives of his sons were making moan, remembering all those brave men who were brought low, slain at the hands of Argives.' And last of all, when Priam has appeared before Achilles and made his speech of appeal for the body of Hector, which calls on him to remember his own father, old and unhappy like Priam himself: 'So he spoke, and awoke in him a desire to weep for his father; he touched the old man's hand and gently pushed him away. And each thought of his own: Priam wept sore, crouched at the feet of Achilles, for man-slaying Hector, while Achilles wept for his father, and again at times for Patroclus; and their lamentations went up through the house . . .' In the former scene the women lament each for her own dead husband, the many brave sons of Priam who have been killed in the war. Their grief forms a counterpoint to that of Priam, for whom the death of one son, Hector, has outweighed all grief for all the others. Priam will be dragged down to Hades by his grief for Hector, he says, as Achilles says that though all forget in Hades, yet he will still remember even there his dear comrade Patroclus.[36] What in the *Odyssey* created a touching but shallow, almost enjoyable, indulgence in grief, all weeping together but each inwardly thinking of a different loss and sorrow, serves in the *Iliad* to create something more. Not only is the grief the characters feel more passionate and more lasting, but as the slave women weep, each for herself, through the funeral of their master, and still more as the great enemies Priam and Achilles meet and weep together, we see the community of suffering which links all men, even conqueror and captive, slayer and father of the slain. One of the striking pieces of 'characterization' in the poem, which raises the curtain for a moment on motives which, on the surface, might have been opaque (how could we have been sure why the Achaean chieftains or the captive women wept?) goes to serve the great aim of the poem as a whole: the presentation of symbolic scenes which show us the meaning and the universality of human doom.

---

[36] Priam's daughters, 24.166; Priam and Achilles, 24.507 ff.; 'I mourn not so much for them all as for Hector', 22.424; 'grief for Hector will kill me', 22.425; 'I shall remember Patroclus', 22.390. No Egyptian drug can obliterate the sufferings of the *Iliad*, for which there is no alleviation and the gods can only recommend endurance: 'For an enduring heart have the fates given to men', 24.49, τλητὸν γὰρ Μοῖραι θυμὸν θέσαν ἀνθρώποισιν, says Apollo.

The idea that Homeric men are simple, without depths, and with everything on the surface,[37] has often led scholars to find contradictory features in the characters depicted in the poems. For J. A. Scott, 'the character of Paris in the *Iliad* involves constant contradictions.' In Achilles, Bethe found 'two fundamentally different creations by two great but fundamentally different poets', which it is 'an absolute psychological impossibility' that one poet can have entertained, while Wilamowitz argued that in Book 9 he is 'altogether a quite different character' from what he is in Book 1. Of Agamemnon, Reinhardt thought that 'The anxious brother of Menelaus, the admirer of the wise Nestor, is a different man from the excitable and overbearing one who wrongs Achilles', the two sides being irreconcilable and deriving from separate stories. When Diomede, after fighting and wounding two gods in the fifth book, says at the beginning of the sixth that 'If you are a god, I will not fight with heavenly gods', Von der Mühll finds it 'undeniably unsatisfactory and unworthy'. Dirlmeier finds two separate conceptions in the figure of Calypso, which he refuses to try to reconcile, on the ground that we do not know that the poet wanted to create consistent characters.[38]

In fact, it surely does not need much knowledge of life and of men to find no difficulty in a character like that of Agamemnon. A good fighter, he is arrogant and brusque when confident of success, not only with Achilles in the first book but also in the rebukes he gives to the Achaean leaders in the fourth. Easily deceived and prone to misunderstand, he shows cruelty both to old Chryses and also in battle; if he were to find out that Priam was in Achilles' hut, he would exact enormous ransom before he let him go, as Achilles twice tells Priam. He shows affection for his brother Menelaus, but it is not unmixed with the fear that if Menelaus were slain, then his expedition would

[37] Cf. H. Fränkel, *Dichtung und Philosophie* (1962), 83 ff. = *Early Greek Poetry and Philosophy*; J. M. Redfield, *Nature and Culture in the Iliad*, 20; E. Auerbach, 'The Scar of Odysseus', in his *Mimesis* (1953). Against Auerbach: H. Erbse, *Beiträge zum Verständnis der Od.* (1972), 23 n. 46; R. Friedrich, *Stilwandel im hom. Epos* (1975), 55 G. S. Kirk, *Homer and the Oral Tradition* (1976), 104, A. Köhnken in *A und A* 22 (1976), 101–14.

[38] J. A. Scott, *The Unity of Homer*, 227; E. Bethe, *Homer*, 1, 74 (the sentences quoted appear in italics); Wilamowitz, *Die Ilias und Homer*, 251; Reinhardt, *Der Dichter der Ilias*, 18; Von der Mühll, *Kritisches Hypomnema zur Ilias*, 113; F. Dirlmeier, 'Die schreckliche Calypso', in *Festschrift R. Sühnel*.

be a fiasco and he himself a laughing-stock. Such a man may well, in life, be prone to despair, as Agamemnon is represented as being. In the second book the failure of his ruse with the troops leaves him helpless; the defeat in the eighth book makes him weep 'like a fountain of dark water' and propose the abandonment of the whole venture and instant flight for home; in the fourteenth book he proposes it again. We have already seen (p. 52ff.) that his relation with Achilles was uneasy and disturbed his self-esteem. That point, and the over-emphasis on his own royal position that accompanies it, is made again with great elegance and economy when he eventually has to come to terms with Achilles. While Achilles repeatedly addresses him by his titles, Agamemnon contrives to avoid addressing Achilles by name at all, and in the whole nineteenth book speaks only six lines directly to him, at the end of a long speech which begins 'My friends, Achaean heroes . . .' and is mostly devoted to an elaborate mythological story. Quite consistently with this—and with the idea that the poet has clear conceptions of his characters and works them out through the poem—at the funeral games for Patroclus the generous Achilles gives a prize to Agamemnon without a contest, saying, 'Son of Atreus, we know how far you excel all men, and how far you are the best in strength and power of your throw . . .' Agamemnon makes no answer to this chivalrous gesture. He cannot apologize with grace.

Fortunately the poet has created a speech which combines the self-confident and defeatist sides of Agamemnon in one utterance. When Menelaus is treacherously wounded, Agamemnon says,

My dear brother, the truce I made was your death . . . The Trojans have broken the truce and wounded you; they will pay for it—Zeus will avenge the breach of oaths. But I am much grieved for you, Menelaus, if you die. Then I shall go back to Argos in dishonour, for the Achaeans will at once think of going home. Then we shall leave Argive Helen for Priam and the Trojans to boast of, while your bones moulder here in Troy, your work unfinished. And some arrogant Trojan will jump on your grave and say, 'So may Agamemnon succeed in all his purposes . . .' Then may the earth open and swallow me up.

The direct juxtaposition of the two moods led to one of them being cut out and simplicity restored by many nineteenth-century scholars, but not only is it excellent and perfectly in accord with the whole characterization of Agamemnon here sketched, but also, (what perhaps will carry more weight with some), it closely resembles the change in Hector's mood from a despairing and certain prediction of the destiny of Troy and his own family at 6.465, to an optimistic prayer at 6.476.[39]

This sort of complexity is in fact characteristic of Homeric psychology. We find it in the long speech of Glaucus to Diomede. Challenged by the great hero to give his name and ancestry, he begins on a subdued note: 'Why ask my ancestry? The generations of men are as ephemeral as those of leaves' (in Greek the one word γενεή has both meanings,[40] but the English 'generation' is not, I think, capable of conveying both). Then he goes on to a resounding narrative of family pride: he is sprung from mighty Bellerophon, and he has been brought up always to strive to excel and not to shame his illustrious forebears: 'Of this ancestry and this blood am I come.' The development of feeling in the speech runs from humility to pride, and the man who declined to give his ancestry at the beginning boasts of it at the end. Only such complexity can do justice to the Homeric conception of heroism: family pride and social obligation uplift and compel the hero, who yet remains aware of inevitable death. We find a similar effect when Aeneas, confronting Achilles, first tells him all the glories of his descent, then, after concluding 'Of this ancestry and this blood am I come', at once goes on to say that 'Zeus makes the valour of a man wax or wane as he pleases, for he is the strongest of all.' It is in keeping with the same conception that Sarpedon utters

[39] Agamemnon rebukes the Achaean leaders, especially Diomede who will perform wonders in the very next book, 4.336 ff.; cruel in battle, cf. note 7 above; 'if Agamemnon knew', 24.654 and 688; weeps, 9 init., cf. 14.65 ff.; sole address to Achilles, 19.139, cf. D. Lohmann, *Die Komposition der Reden in der Ilias* (1970), 76 n. 133; Achilles awards a prize, 23.890; Menelaus wounded, 4.155 ff. References for scholars who took the butcher's knife to this splendid speech can be found, if wanted, in Ameis–Hentze, *Anhang zu Homers Ilias*, 2. Heft (1882), 15. Agamemnon's moods form a consistent character, H. Spiess, *Menschenart und Heldentum* (1913), 147, Lohmann, 44 n. 72 and 178 ('in every case Agamemnon proceeds on false presuppositions', etc.). H. Gundert speaks of 'the inner insecurity of his nature': 'Charakter und Schicksal homerischer Helden', in *NJbb* 3 (1940), 227. This seems to me to be much nearer the truth than the view of G. S. Kirk, who speaks of 'veering attitudes to Agamemnon, who is presented now as a great and admirable leader, now as a manic depressive' (*Songs of Homer*, 265).

[40] Cf. H. Fränkel, *Die homerischen Gleichnisse*, 41, W. Marg in *WüJbb* 2 (1976), 18.

the fullest and most explicit statement of *noblesse oblige*: 'We are noble and wealthy, therefore we must fight in the front rank', and then goes on to say that 'If by avoiding death today we could make ourselves immortal, then I should not fight; but we must die some day, so let us go, to win glory ourselves or to serve the glory of others.'[41] It is not unreflective or unself-conscious heroism that drives these men on. Facing death, they see both the obligation and the terror, and their speech reflects the totality of their situation and their response. Once more, in connection with its central point the *Iliad* shows its mastery of a developed psychology.

In the case of Agamemnon, we remark that the will of Zeus takes the course it does because the king has the character he has:[42] quickly provoked, high-handed with Achilles, but also quick to collapse, sending envoys to the withdrawn hero before the real turning-point of the action is reached and the Achaeans thoroughly defeated.[43] That is connected with Achilles' refusal to yield, and so with Patroclus' death and the rest of the plot.

The particular character of Patroclus, his gentleness and soft-heartedness, is also vital to the unrolling of the plot. It leads him, when sent by Achilles to find out whether the wounded man he has seen is Machaon, to linger with Nestor listening to a long speech by the old man aimed at the absent Achilles, then to sit with the wounded Eurypylus, 'amusing him with his talk and laying soothing herbs on his wound for the dark pain', until the sight and sound of the Achaean defeat become too much for him and he must run back to Achilles and beg him, in tears, to rescue them himself, or to adopt Nestor's suggestion and send Patroclus instead. All this brings to fruition the plan of Zeus.[44]

Not least is this true of Achilles. If Agamemnon were not offering compensation for his arrogant treatment, says old Phoenix, I should not urge you to throw off your anger and rescue the Argives, however great their need; and he goes on,

---

[41] Glaucus, 6.145–211; Aeneas, 20.200–42; Sarpedon, 12.310–28.

[42] This approach seems to me more rewarding than to talk of him as 'a selfish, craven, ignoble, contemptible villain' (Bassett, *Poetry of Homer*, 196).

[43] This point is made in an unpublished dissertation by Mr J. M. Lynn-George.

[44] 11.596 ff., 15.393, 11.796, 16.1–45; cf. W. Schadewaldt, *Iliasstudien*, 88. Plan of Zeus: 15.63 ff.

'Hitherto you cannot be blamed for your anger. That is how we hear the story of heroes of old, when any of them was seized by furious anger: they could be won with gifts and prevailed upon by speech.' Ajax, too, is unable to understand why Achilles persists in his resentment, when the compensation offered by Agamemnon meets the demands of the heroic code, and Achilles can only reply, 'Ajax, son of Telamon, leader of the host, all that you have said is in a way agreeable to my mind, but my heart swells with anger as I remember how arrogantly he treated me, the son of Atreus . . .'[45] It is impossible to doubt that Phoenix, at least, is devoted to Achilles and would not say to him what he did not believe, and in fact, as we see, Achilles himself has to admit that the arguments for his return are unanswerable. What prevents him is the intensity of his anger, his passionate nature.[46] It is this which prevents him from treating Agamemnon's first overbearing but vague utterance ('If they do not give me recompense for Chryseis, I will take it myself, going either to you, or to Ajax, or to Odysseus; and the man to whom I come will be angered. But of this we shall take counsel hereafter . . .'), in the same way as the poet shows us Diomede making no immediate protest when unjustly and publicly criticized by him in Book 4, and then asserting himself, firmly but calmly, in Book 9.[47] It is this which prevents him from behaving like the 'heroes of old', who could be persuaded to abandon their anger. If Achilles were like Diomede, there would be no *Iliad* at all; if he were like the ordinary angry hero, Patroclus would not be killed, and the poem would not be

---

[45] Phoenix, 9.515–26; reply to Ajax, 9.644. On Achilles' character, A. Lesky, *Gesammelte Schriften*, 75 ff., D. Lohmann, *Die Komposition der Reden*, 279 n. 118, C. Whitman, *Homer and the Heroic Tradition* (1958), ch. 9.

[46] Achilles gives the same explanation again, 16.52: 'Dire anguish comes on my heart, when he (Agamemnon) tries to dishonour his equal . . .' J. M. Redfield, *Nature and Culture in the Iliad* (1975), 106 argues that 'Achilles is the victim of his own ethic.' This seems to me to be a warning of the risks in applying too anthropological an analysis to the poem. Despite ingenious arguments that 'Achilles' refusal of the warrior's role is an affirmation of the warrior ethic', it is surely made clear by Achilles that it is not his 'ethic' which prevents his return, but on the contrary his own passionate emotion, overriding a code which for him, as for the other heroes, made his return the appropriate action. This approach also distorts the role of the gods in the poem; see below p. 145ff.

[47] Agamemnon: 1.137; Diomede: 4.401, 9.33. The Diomede scene is evidently present in order to form a contrast with the behaviour of Achilles: R. von Scheliha, *Patroklos*, 184.

tragic. The *Iliad*, to be what it is, needs just such a passionate Achilles as it contains.

He reveals his character not only by his actions but also, still more, by his utterances. He produces more similes in his speeches than the other people of the epic, and several of them are striking. He uses a very large number of words which are not used elsewhere in the poem. At times he utters shorter and more staccato speech than anybody else; at other times his speech opens up into broad rhythms and reference to distant places and great distances. 'I did not come here to fight because of the spearmen of Troy, for they have done me no wrong. Never have they driven off my cattle or horses, nor have they ravaged the harvest in deep-soiled Phthia, mother of men; for indeed there lie between us many shadowy mountains and much sounding sea . . .' So says Achilles in the first book, and the rhythm of that last line, οὔρεά τε σκιόεντα θάλασσά τε ἠχήεσσα, suddenly opens a wide and inhuman vista, the world of empty space far from the quarrels at Troy. He achieves a similar effect again, when he exults over the corpse of Iphition, son of Otryntes: 'You lie low, son of Otryntes, most formidable of men. Here is your death, though you were born by the Gygaean Lake, where your father's lands lie, by the Hyllus rich in fish and the Hermus with its whirlpools', Ὕλλῳ ἐπ' ἰχθυόεντι καὶ Ἕρμῳ δινήεντι. These great lines, with their long epithets symmetrically placed, seem to bring the action to a halt for a timeless moment of contemplation; and we realize that this is no mere poetical ornament, when we reflect that it is Achilles whose perspective on events leads him repeatedly to stress the physical distance between Troy and the home where his old father waits for him in vain, and also that it is he alone who questions and criticizes the heroic destiny of battle and death.[48]

[48] Similes in Achilles' speeches: 9.323, 16.7, 21.282, 22.262, four out of a total in the *Iliad* of fourteen (3.60, 31.196, 4.243, 6.146, 12.167, 13.101, 17.20, 20.252, 21.464, 24.41). His speech is unique for its full flood of images and similes: H. Spiess, *Menschenart und Heldentum*, 103. Unique words: I hope to publish separately a detailed account of this question. In 823 lines he utters 128 unique words; for comparison, Agamemnon utters half as many, in more than two-thirds of the number of verses, 64 in 588 lines. But these crude figures need refining. Staccato utterances, cf. ΣbT in 9.374, 'in four lines there are eight independent periods.' Distant places: 1.157, cf. 1.349 ff., 9.360, 9.381, 9.395, 16.233, 18.208, 20.390, 22.390, 23.144, 24.615, cf. A. Parry in *YCS* 20 (1966), 195, and his earlier article *The Language of Achilles*, *TAPA* 87 (1956), 1–7 = *Language and Background of Homer*,

His more passionate nature makes it impossible for him to accept compensation which would satisfy other heroes; his refusal, when offered the compensation, forces him to a degree of introspection beyond that of the others, because he is in a peculiar position. His passionate rejection and his deeper insight thus belong together. They are not simply an accumulation of characteristics in principle separate. And the focus of this, the most interesting personality in the *Iliad*, is on the central questions of the poem: the meaning and significance of heroic life and death.[49]

We have seen that in the *Odyssey* characters are remarkable for their opaqueness. The greater prominence in the poem of women, who even in the *Iliad* are more inscrutable and evasive than the male, goes with this. But so do other considerations. For instance, the inhuman and superhuman figures whom Odysseus meets on his wanderings behave in an utterly unpredictable way, not only Circe but also the queen of the Laestrygons. Odysseus' scouts met her daughter, apparently an ordinary girl drawing water at a well; they asked her the name of the king of the country, and she directed them to her father's palace. There they found the queen 'as huge as a mountain peak, and they loathed her at sight. She called her husband . . . and at once he seized one of my men and made ready his meal . . .' The appalling suddenness and unexpectedness of this event and its aftermath, the destruction of all but one of Odysseus' ships by creatures 'not like men but like giants', is fresh in the memory of the survivors when they come to the deceitful hospitality of Circe. Again we see the dreamlike and

---

ed. G. S. Kirk, 48–54. Shadowy mountains, 1.157; Hyllus, 20.392. 'Far from home', 9.359 ff., 16.233, 18.99, 23.150, 24.541. Achilles sees further into the nature of heroism than the others, and questions it, 9.310 ff., 400 ff., and especially 24.518–42. It is however not right to say that he rejects it; as against Parry see M. D. Reeve in *CQ* 23 (1973), 193–5, G. S. Kirk, *Homer and the Oral Tradition*, 51. De Quincey, in his essay on 'Homer and the Homeridae', insisted that the character of Achilles 'never could have been a gradual accumulation of successive touches. It was raised by a single flash of creative imagination . . .'

[49] So too the character of Diomede shows its complexity (not incoherence: cf. n. 34), on the same question. H. Erbse, *Rh. Mus.* 104 (1961), 188, shows convincingly that this hero, urged on by Athena even against gods, yet still sharply aware, the divine impulse withdrawn, that he is a mortal man and subject to the limits of mortality, sets in an especially clear light the position of the hero in the world, between gods and men, god-like yet vulnerable.

inexplicable logic of the events of a fairy story, all the more striking when it is juxtaposed with a more fully realized and human character like Odysseus. The psychology of Aeolus, on his floating island with his six sons married to his six daughters, who gives Odysseus the winds in a leather bag but, when he returns despairing, drives him away with insults, is also clearly not to be analysed like that of a human person. And this sort of inscrutability goes deeper and is more puzzling than mere deception, which also abounds in the adventures; even the Sirens know how to sound friendly and benevolent.[50]

Such persons shade off into the more fully human people of the poem. Over dinner in Sparta, Menelaus, reconciled with Helen and an affectionate husband, listens with apparent complacency to her story of the time when she alone, in Troy, recognized Odysseus, who had entered the city in disguise; he slew many men, 'and the other women of Troy wept aloud, but my soul rejoiced, for my heart was turned and I longed to go back home, and I lamented the madness which Aphrodite gave me, when she took me away from my own country, forsaking my marriage bed and my husband, who lacked nothing, either in mind or in beauty.' To this edifying recital by a contrite wife Menelaus replies by saying that indeed Odysseus was remarkable for intelligence and strength of will. For instance, when we were all hidden in the Trojan Horse, 'you came to the spot; doubtless a god who planned victory for the Trojans must have brought you. Deiphobus, handsome as a god, followed you. Three times you went round the horse, touching it, and calling to us each by his name, imitating the voice of the wife of each man.' Odysseus prevented any of us from replying, and put his hand forcibly over the mouth of Anticlus to keep him silent. 'So Odysseus saved all the Argives; and he held Anticlus until Pallas Athena led you away.'[51] From antiquity onwards

[50] Circe, see p. 58. Laestrygonian royal family, x.105–16; Aeolus, x.1–76; Sirens, xii.184.
[51] Helen and Menelaus, iv.259–89. There is quite a literature on these two stories and the scene as a whole. Psychological complexities of increasing subtlety are read in by F. Cauer, *NJbb* (1900), 608; A. Maniet in *Ant. Class.* 10 (1947), 37–46; R. Schmiel in *TAPA* 103 (1972), 463–72. See also J. T. Kakridis, *Homer Revisited*, 40 ff., who inclines to the view that 'Helen's inconsistent character can be explained by the special conditions of the myth' (45); that is, by supposing that 'the stories do not belong to the same stage in the development of the myth', there

readers have been perplexed to know what to make of this. Did Helen try to betray her husband and the other Achaeans to death? With what purpose and to what effect does Menelaus now tell this story? The characters make no comment upon it, and sixteen lines later Menelaus is in bed, 'and beside him lay Helen of the long robe, that divine lady.' Helen, in fact, is inscrutable. We cannot reconcile her story and that of her husband, and we have no way of analysing the situation in terms of their particular characters. Helen has a glamorous if shady past; she is quicker than her husband, whether to recognize a guest, or to interpret an omen; he gives Telemachus a foolish present which has to be changed, she gives him a suggestive one, a wedding-dress for his bride, 'a keepsake of the hands of Helen'. She has acquired in Egypt drugs to cheer people up.[52] The archetype of deceitful wives, she is also the daughter of Zeus. We cannot read her mind.

That is less surprising when we reflect that Queen Arete of the Phaeacians also remains enigmatic. Odysseus is told by Nausicaa and also by Athena to make his supplication to her; she is honoured by her husband as no other mortal woman is honoured, and her favour will mean success. Yet when he does this the result is an embarrassed silence, broken at last by an aged counsellor. Queen Arete does not speak at all for eighty lines, and when she does it is to say something quite unexpected. The temptation to add to the number of psychological explanations of her behaviour will be resisted. The point, for us, is that we find another character, and another woman, who is inscrutable, and whose character is not elucidated by the poet. Odysseus finds the goddess Athena no less opaque, as he complains bitterly to her when she has appeared to him in disguise on his first return to Ithaca.[53] Penelope herself is not less mysterious. Her behaviour towards the disguised Odysseus is so ambiguous that some have been led to suppose that really she

---

being many separate stories in circulation about Helen. This does not explain her resemblance to other characters in the *Odyssey*. It is not easy, for instance, to suppose that this explanation would apply to Arete.

[52] Guest, iv.138; omen, xv.160–78; Menelaus' present, iv.600 ff.; Helen's present, xv.125; drugs, iv.220.

[53] Nausicaa's instructions, vi.303; Athena's, vii.53. Cf. U. Hölscher, 'Das Schweigen der Arete', in *Hermes* 88 (1960), 257–65; B. Fenik, *Studies in the Odyssey*, 5 ff. Arete speaks: vii.237; Odysseus to Athena, xiii.311 ff.

recognized him all the time; and the scene in which she appears before the Suitors in all her beauty and induces them to give her gifts, while Odysseus is delighted with her conduct, has also perplexed many readers. And she gives us a last surprise by not recognizing the victorious Odysseus, after his triumph, as her husband.[54]

Deception is one of the poem's great subjects. Odysseus is famous for his tricks and guile; Penelope has more tricks than any heroine known to mythology, as the frustrated Suitors complain; Telemachus learns how to conceal his feelings and fool his enemies. Odysseus tells mighty lies in Ithaca and evidently delights in them. But not all deception is of this ultimately cheery and successful sort. Every vagrant who appeared in Ithaca while Odysseus was away told lies about him and his imminent return, breaking the heart of Penelope and Eumaeus, so that now the lonely wife cannot believe in his return even when he has come home and slain his enemies. Eumaeus' own life was blighted when cheating Phoenicians seduced his nurse and carried him away as a little child, selling him into slavery. The Suitors lie to Penelope and plan the murder of Telemachus. Agamemnon's ghost tells Odysseus how he was tricked and murdered by his wife and her lover: 'Indeed I thought I should come home most welcome to my children and my household', he says bitterly, and he urges the hero to keep his return a secret, 'for there is no more trusting in women'. Trust is the hardest thing in such a world. Athena tells Telemachus, when he lingers in Sparta, to hurry home, or his mother will marry again and carry off some of his goods for her new husband: 'You know what the heart of woman is like; she wants to increase the household of the man who marries her, and she forgets her former children and her husband once he is dead; she asks no more about him . . .' And Telemachus himself, in his lethargy of despair in the first book, answers Athena's question whether he is Odysseus' son with the cynical reply that 'My mother says I am his son, but I do not know; no man ever knew his own parentage . . .' From the Suitors' point

---

[54] Penelope before the Suitors, xviii.158–303, cf. U. Hölscher, 'Penelope vor den Freiern', in *Festschr. R. Sühnel* (1967), 27–33, H. Erbse, *Beiträge zum Verständnis der Od.*, 79 ff., U. Hölscher in *Homer: Tradition and Invention*, ed. B. Fenik (1978), 61 ff.

of view, their destruction too, was a treacherous trick.[55]

For the *Iliad* the world, though terrible, remains a place in which heroism is possible. The situations round which the poem is built are scenes which embody attitudes to the fundamental questions of acceptance of death, patriotism, heroic anger, heroic shame. The characters, too, are defined by their relation to these questions. Agamemnon mistakes his position with Zeus, thinking that he is the man whom the god delights to honour; he loses his contest with Achilles for supremacy and as a hero is not of the highest quality. Hector, brave and loyal, is deceived by the temporary help of Zeus and his own short-sightedness; he too mistakes the intentions of the god for him, and he discovers, when he cannot face Achilles and turns to run from his onset, that he had also mistaken his own prowess as a hero. Paris and Helen are characterized by their attitudes to fate and duty, he as frivolous, she as more deeply tragic. In the *Odyssey* the world is menacing, not with the sharp clarity of heroic death, but with the mysteriousness of undeclared motives, inscrutable people, liars and cheats. Disloyalty and deception, not heroic rage and strife for honour, are the causes of disaster, and Odysseus must struggle not against the clear and passionate will of Achilles, as he does in the ninth and the nineteenth books of the *Iliad*, nor with the heroes of Troy in battle, but with mutinous sailors, offensive servants, disloyal subjects, and with monsters and goddesses against whom heroic prowess is useless. The *Odyssey* is intensely interested in individuals, and it is not an accident that the people whom the hero meets, even his patron goddess and his wife, are represented almost without exception as mysterious; while Odysseus himself moves unrecognized and enigmatic among the Phaeacians, as he moves disguised about his own house. That was what interested the poet about his characters. That was what made them fit into his world.

---

[55] Odysseus, ix.19; Penelope, ii.115 ff.; lies to Penelope, xiv.361 ff.; Eumaeus, xv.403; Agamemnon, xi.430, 456; Athena on Penelope, xv.10 ff.; the scene is 'a dramatic and external representation of Telemachus' own suspicions', A. Amory Parry, *Blameless Aegisthus*, 132, cf. W. F. Otto, *The Homeric Gods*, 182. Telemachus on his ancestry, i.215; Suitors' version, xxiv.123 ff.

III

DEATH AND THE GOD-LIKE HERO

L'atrocità delle battaglie omeriche e delle morti . . . fanno all' *Iliade* tutta
la maraviglia.—Vico[1]

W ITH small exceptions, the serious poetry of Greece is
concerned with the myths; and the subject of Greek
mythology is the heroes. These are two obvious facts.
Epic dealt with the 'deeds of gods and men' (i.338),[2] and so
did the choral lyric, while even the personal lyric is full of
mythical narratives and excursions. Tragedy, too, tended to
restrict itself to the mythical period, although the *Capture of
Miletus*, by Phrynichus, and the *Persians*, by Aeschylus, show
that this was not actually a rule. The mythical period was quite
a short one, two or three generations about the time of the
Theban and Trojan wars; the rest of the past, however vivid
or striking in the memory, was felt to be different,[3] and inappropriate for serious poetic treatment. Hence no tragedies
about Pisistratus or Periander, the colonizing period, or the
Lelantine War.

There was something special about that time. Heroes, we
read, were bigger and stronger than we are—a hero of Homer
could pick up and throw a rock which 'nowadays two of the
best men in a city could barely hoist on to a waggon' (12.445)—
but that is not the important thing. In that time gods intervened
openly in human affairs, and it is their passionate concern and
personal participation which marks heroic events as possessing
significance. Aeschylus, brooding upon the morality of war and

---

[1] G. B. Vico, *Scienza Nuova*, 827.

[2] Poems on purely celestial wars did exist, the cyclic *Titanomachy* for instance;
but they are little mentioned. The 'Homeric' Hymns are heavily influenced by the
epic. 'The Greeks are a special case' in the heroes being so prominent in their
mythology: G. S. Kirk, *Myth: Its Meaning and Functions*, 179. Cf. Wilamowitz, 'Die
griechische Heldensage', *Kleine Schriften*, v. 2, 54 ff.

[3] Cf. Herodotus 1.5.3 and 3.122.2, and P. Vidal-Naquet, 'Temps des dieux et
temps des hommes', in *Rev. de l'histoire des religions*, 157 (1960), 67.

conquest, writes about King Agamemnon; Euripides, brooding upon the relation of the sexes, writes about Jason and Medea. An event like the murder of a husband by his wife, or a question like that of civil disobedience, is raised to the level at which it can be 'seen' and taken seriously, when a poet writes of Clytemnestra or Antigone. In the epic, the divine presence and concern ensure that the story of Paris and Helen is a tragedy, not a mere spicy tale,[4] and that the fall of Troy is not just one more disaster but an event of moral significance. The gods find nothing so enthralling as the spectacle of human heroism and suffering;[5] their attention marks its importance, but equally their superiority marks its smallness in another perspective. The heroes were nearer to the gods than later men. 'Born of Zeus', 'nourished by Zeus', 'honoured by Zeus'; these are standard epithets for Homeric kings and princes, and not less interesting are 'loved by Zeus' and 'god-like'.

'Like Zeus in counsel', 'the equal of Ares', 'a man equal to the gods', 'god-like', 'resembling the immortals', 'divine', 'with the appearance of a god', 'honoured by his people like a god'— no reader of Homer needs to be told that these and other such epithets are among the commonest in the poems.[6] Heroines, too, 'have beauty from the goddesses' or 'look like a goddess in face', and can be compared to Artemis or Aphrodite.[7] A hero may be compared to several gods at once, as when Agamemnon is said to be 'in eyes and head like Zeus who delights in thunder, in girdle like Ares, in chest like Poseidon' (2.478 f.). Priam says of his son Hector that 'he was a god among men, and did not seem like the son of a mortal man but of a god' (24.259). But these passages suggest complications, for Agamemnon is being led to disaster by Zeus, while Hector is dead, his body in the power of his ruthless enemy. What is it to be 'god-like'?

There is one great difference between gods and men. Gods are deathless and ageless, while men are mortal. When Apollo thrusts Diomede back into the limits of his mortality, he

---

[4] K. Reinhardt, *Das Parisurteil*.

[5] See Ch. 6.

[6] Διὶ μῆτιν ἀτάλαντος, ἶσος Ἄρηι, ἰσόθεος φώς, ἀντίθεος, ἐπιείκελος ἀθανάτοισιν, δῖος, θεοειδής, θεὸς δ' ὧς τίετο δήμῳ. Such expressions are regarded as 'relitti di una fraseologia aulica' by L. A. Stella, *Tradizione micenea e poesia dell' Iliade* (1978), 68.

[7] θεῶν ἄπο κάλλος ἔχουσα, viii.457; cf. 3.158, vi.102, 19,282.

shouts, 'Reflect, son of Tydeus, and fall back; do not try to be the equal of the gods. Never is the race of immortal gods on a level with earthbound men.' When Achilles is misled into attacking Apollo, the god says, 'Son of Peleus, why do you pursue me, when you are a mortal and I a deathless god?' (5.440, 22.8). He declines to fight with Poseidon 'for the sake of mortal men, wretched creatures, who one day flourish and another day are gone' (21.462). The heroes who are 'god-like' are subject to death, and we see them die. The epithets which belong to them as heroes contrast poignantly with their human fate. Sometimes the effect seems so light that it is not certain whether it is meant to be felt at all: as when in the boxing match the only challenger for the formidable Epeius is 'Euryalus, that man equal to a god'—who is promptly knocked out and helped off by his friends, 'with feet dragging, spitting out thick blood, with his head lolling to one side'. Similarly light is the stress in a passage like that where Briseis tells the tragic story of her life: Achilles slew her husband and destroyed 'the city of divine Mynes'. The attentive listener is aware of a certain faint resonance, in the first case of irony, in the second of pathos.

More positively striking, perhaps, are such passages as those where old Nestor indulges himself in reminiscences of his great exploit in youth: 'Would that I were young, as I was when I slew god-like Ereuthalion', and 'Ereuthalion was their champion, a man the equal of gods ... he was the biggest and strongest man I ever slew.' Ereuthalion was a Goliath-figure whom nobody but the youthful Nestor dared to face; his great stature and terrifying power are dwelt upon by his slayer, who adds 'He lay sprawling, far in both directions.' He was like a god—but I slew him. The emphasis becomes, I think, clearly deliberate when we read of Paris, when he has gaily challenged any Achaean champion and Menelaus has appeared to fight him, that 'When Paris, beautiful as a god, saw him appear, his spirit was dashed, and he slunk back into the ranks to avoid his fate ... So did he slip back into the body of the haughty Trojans, Paris as beautiful as a god, in fear of Atreus' son.' For the poet makes it very clear that the beauty of Paris is what characterizes him, and is at variance with his lack of heroism: Hector at once rebukes him as 'Evil Paris, great in beauty, woman-mad, seducer . . .' and adds that 'Your music and your gifts from Aphrodite, your hair and your beauty, would not help you when Menelaus brought you down in the dust.' This makes it clear that in the narrative Ἀλέξανδρος θεοειδής, 'Paris, beautiful as a god', was no mere 'formulaic epithet' without particular significance: δείσας Ἀτρέος υἱὸν Ἀλέξανδρος θεοειδής is one of those pregnant lines which sum up a whole character and a whole situation.

But the poet can find deeper notes of pathos and significance in this way. When 'the god-like Sarpedon' is dead, his body fought over by the two armies, 'then not even a discerning man would have recognized god-like Sarpedon, for he was covered with weapons and blood and dirt, from his head right down to his feet.' Zeus, his father, keeps his shining eyes fixed on the struggle over the body of his son, unrecognizable in blood and dirt; that is all that remains of the handsome warrior Sarpedon, who in life was like a god. The epithet helps to bring out the human pathos, and also to underline the contrast of the human, even at its greatest and most attractive, and the really divine. When Achilles has killed Hector, he starts a paean of triumph over his body: 'We have won a great victory: we have slain the god-like Hector, whom the Trojans adored like a god in Troy.' Here the epithet, and the idea of adoration by one's fellow citizens, become a triumphant taunt, in which what was largely left implicit in the boasts of Nestor is fully developed. It becomes pathetic explicitly when Hecuba laments her son: 'You were my pride night and day, and you were the defender of all the men and women of Troy, who hailed you like a god. Alive, you were their great glory; but now death and fate have caught you.'[8] The greatness of his fall and her loss emerge in this touching claim.

In the light of these passages I think it is clear that we are also to see force in the epithet 'god-like' when it is used in the context of Hector's body being dishonoured by Achilles. Thus the poet tells us that after Achilles' triumphant paean 'he

---

[8] Euryalus, ἰσόθεος φώς, 23.677; πόλιν θείοιο Μύνητος, 19.296; Ereuthalion, 4.319, 7.136, 155; Ereuthalion and Goliath, cf. Mühlestein, 'Jung Nestor Jung David', in *A und A* 17 (1972), 173 ff., E. B. Smick in *AOAT* 22 = *Essays C. H. Gordon* (1973), 177 ff.; Paris, 3.30–7; Sarpedon, 16.638–40; Hector, 22.393–4, 432–6.

wrought acts of humiliation on god-like Hector',[9] piercing his
ankles and dragging through the dust of his own country 'his
head that before was comely'.[10] The immediate juxtaposition of
'god-like Hector' and 'acts of humiliation' enables the poet to
bring out, without sentimentality, the pathos of the greatest
possible fall for a man, from god-like stature to humiliation and
helplessness. I find the same technique repeatedly in the last
book of the *Iliad*. 'Achilles in his rage was abusing god-like
Hector, and all the gods, looking on, felt pity for him.' 'He has
tied god-like Hector to his chariot, having robbed him of his
life, and is dragging him round the tomb of his friend. That is
not right or good for him; we gods may grow angry with him,
for all his strength; for he is abusing dumb earth in his rage'—
so says Apollo, and we see in the speech of the god the full
nature of man, at once capable of being 'god-like' and also
doomed to be 'dumb earth'. A last and rather different example:
when Patroclus is called by Achilles to go on the mission which
will lead to his return to battle and to his death, the poet, with
unequalled economy and power, presents him in one line: 'He
came out, the equal of Ares; and that was the beginning of his
doom.'[11] His greatness and his fragility emphasize and reflect
upon each other.

The love of the gods for men is not less capable of bearing a
range of emotional overtones. That great gods 'loved' great
kings was an age-old part of the belief of Egypt and the king-

---

[9] ἀεικέα ἔργα. Ever since antiquity, scholars have argued whether this meant
'wrong' (for Achilles to commit), or 'shameful' (for Hector to endure). The
former view is taken for instance by Finsler,[2] i, 311, and C. Segal, *The Theme of
Mutilation of the Corpse*, 13, who gives other references. The same problem arises at
23.176, κακὰ δὲ φρεσὶ μήδετο ἔργα. I have no doubt that the other view (that
for instance of Bassett, *Poetry of Homer*, 203 and Schrade, *Götter und Menschen Homers*,
199) is right. Compare 22.336 σὲ μὲν κύνες ἠδ' οἰωνοὶ | ἑλκήσουσ' ἀικῶς,
which cannot have the sense of Achilles condemning his own act; 2.264, where
Odysseus threatens Thersites with ἀεικέσσι πληγῇσι, and such lines as 7.478
παννύχιος δέ σφιν κακὰ μήδετο μητίετα Ζεύς, and 21.19 ὁ δ' ἔσθορε δαίμονι
ἶσος, | φάσγανον οἷον ἔχων, κακὰ δὲ φρεσὶ μήδετο ἔργα. In all of these the
evil is for the victim, not the doer. With the last, compare *The Battle of Maldon*,
133, of two warriors: *aegþer hyra odrum yfeles hogorde*, 'each had evil intent toward
the other.' In the *Odyssey*, viii.273, ix.316, xvii.465; iv.340.

[10] 22.395, 403. The unobtrusive but powerful device of remarking on Hector's
beauty only at the moment when it was defiled, is that of 18.122 and 19.285:
Briseis' soft neck and lovely face are mentioned only as she tears them with her
nails in mourning. Cf. Wehrli in *Gnomon* 28 (1956), 577.

[11] Gods pity Hector, 24.22-3; Apollo on Hector, 24.53-4; Patroclus, 11.604.

doms of the Levant.[12] There it was a simple and unambiguous conception. The god would be on our side and would frustrate the knavish tricks of our enemies; our king was the special favourite of mighty forces, and rebellion against him was as wicked as war against him was futile. Such an idea is to be found in Homer, as when Odysseus warns the Achaeans not to provoke their king Agamemnon: 'Great is the anger of kings nourished by Zeus: their honours come from Zeus, and Zeus the Counsellor loves them.' But the subject of the epic is not a simple and one-sided narration of 'our' king's career of conquest, like an Assyrian or Egyptian historical inscription. Zeus honours Troy, he tells us himself, more than any other city under the starry heaven,[13] and he loves Hector and his own son Sarpedon, on the Trojan side, no less than he loves Achilles and Patroclus, their slayers. And he loves Achilles, the opponent of Agamemnon, more than he loves the sceptred king himself, as Agamemnon is forced to learn.[14]

Zeus loves Hector and Sarpedon, Patroclus and Achilles; but by the end of the *Iliad* three of the four are dead, and the fourth is to be slain very soon. He loves Troy, yet Troy will fall. He loves Agamemnon, but he sends a lying dream to him to deceive and defeat him. Odysseus, indeed, loved by Zeus and Athena, will survive, but that is the exception rather than the rule in the Homeric poems, and even he reproaches his patron goddess bitterly for her failure to protect him in his sufferings. Aphrodite claims that she has 'loved exceedingly' the Helen whom she forces against her will into the shameless embrace of Paris:

'Do not provoke me, wretch, lest I be angry and forsake you, and hate you even as I have exceedingly loved you; between both sides, Trojans and Achaeans, I shall devise bitter suffering for you, and you will come to a miserable end.' So she spoke, and Helen, daughter of Zeus, was afraid. She followed in silence, shielding her face with her shining robe, and none of the Trojan women saw her; the goddess led the way.

[12] Pharaohs claimed to be 'beloved of Amon-Re', 'beloved of Montu', 'beloved of Re-Har-Akhti'; Hittite kings claimed to be 'the favourite of the Storm-god'; the Lord loved Solomon; and so on (*ANET*³, 199, 234, 253, 318; 2 Sam. 12:24). See Dirlmeier, *Philol.* 90 (1935), 73–6, who thinks the idea entered Greece from these sources, by way of the epic.

[13] Zeus loves kings, 2.196–7; loves Troy, 4.44–9.

[14] e.g. 16.433, Σαρπήδονα φίλτατον ἀνδρῶν, 6.318 Ἕκτωρ εἰσῆλθε Διὶ φίλος, 16.168 Ἀχιλλεύς... ἡγεῖτο Διὶ φίλος, 11.610 Πάτροκλε Διὶ φίλε. Agamemnon forced to learn, 9.117.

That is what it might be like to be loved by a god. Even the greatest of the sons of Zeus, Heracles himself, 'who was the dearest of men to Zeus', did not for that escape suffering and disaster. Peleus, Hera tells us, was dear above all men to the immortal gods and all the gods attended his wedding to Thetis, but now he is alone and miserable, far away from his only son, who will never come home. Amphiaraus was 'loved exceedingly by aegis-bearing Zeus and by Apollo, with all kinds of love; yet he did not reach the threshold of old age, but died at Thebes by reason of a woman's gifts'—betrayed to death by his wife for a bribe. The poet of the *Odyssey* tells us with inimitable objectivity that the singer Demodocus was blind: 'the Muse loved him exceedingly, and she gave him both good and evil; she robbed him of his sight, but she gave him sweet singing.'[15] The ancients believed that Homer was a blind man, and that belief adds to the poignancy of his representation of another singer, his counterpart in his epic.

Zeus is a father to men, and Athena sometimes looks after a favourite 'like a mother'; Zeus is said to 'care for and pity' Priam in his misery.[16] It has often been emphasized that the gods of Homer love the strong and successful, not the weak and poor,[17] but it is wrong to think that means a straightforward idealizing of successful power and force. The gods love great heroes, but that love does not protect them from defeat and death. The heroes who engross the attention of the poet of the *Iliad* are those who are doomed—Sarpedon, Patroclus, Hector, Achilles; they it is whom the gods love, and who will exchange their strength and brilliance for the cold and darkness of death. As they come nearer to that terrible transition, the shining eyes of Zeus are fixed on them all the more attentively; he loves them *because* they are doomed.[18] They in their mortal blindness cannot know, as the god allows them temporary triumph, that in his long-term plan they must die; the victories of Hector and

---

[15] Odysseus: 10.527, 11.419, 473, iii.218–23; xiii.310 ff. Aphrodite, 3.414–20. Heracles, 18.118, xi.620. Peleus, 24.61, 24.534–42. Amphiaraus, xv.244–6. Demodocus, viii.63–4.

[16] Athena, 4.130, 23.783. Zeus, 24.174.

[17] e.g. B. Snell, *Discovery of the Mind*, 33.

[18] W. Schadewaldt, *Iliasstudien*, 107. As Patroclus approaches his death, 'Never did Zeus turn away from the violent battle his shining eyes', 16.644.

Patroclus, which show Zeus' love for them, are in that perspective only a stage in their planned defeat and death.

The hero who is most often compared with the gods is Achilles. But not only is he said to be 'god-like', but also we observe in action how like the gods he is, and above all how like Zeus himself. He has sacked twenty-three cities in the Troad, he boasts, and he numbers 'Sacker of Cities' among his formulaic titles: Zeus 'has brought down the towers of many cities and will bring down many more'. His quarrel with Agamemnon over his 'honour', τιμή, is reflected in heaven when Poseidon resents the claim of Zeus to higher rank. Zeus rubs in his quelling of Hera's attempted mutiny by saying, 'In the morning, if you wish, you will see the paramount son of Cronus destroy the Argive host yet more, ox-eyed Lady Hera.' In the same words Achilles tells the envoys of Agamemnon that despite all their pleas he will go home: 'Tomorrow . . . you will see, if you wish, and if you are interested, my ships sailing at dawn on the Hellespont.' He possesses a special cup, from which no man drinks but himself, and libations are poured to no god but Zeus. He is urged to 'be like the gods', whose prepotent power does not prevent them from relenting and giving way to suppliants, but his nature is god-like in a different sense. Patroclus, who knows him better than any other man, says 'You know what he is like; he is terrible. He may well blame the innocent.' We remember what Iris says that Zeus will do, if his will is crossed: 'He will come to Olympus to cast us into confusion; he will seize in succession on the guilty and the innocent.' The poet even creates a parallel between the bringing of the mourning figure of Thetis before the gods on Olympus and the appearance of the mourning Priam before Achilles. In both scenes the incomer emerges from the darkness, dressed in mourning, and finds the other in the light, sitting at ease and drinking; the gods press a wine-cup into Thetis' hand; Achilles insists that Priam eat and drink with him.[19]

But above all it is in being irresponsible and arbitrary that

---

[19] 9.328–30; 8.372, 15.77, 21.550, 24.108 (most of these were wantonly excised or emended by Aristarchus); 2.117; Poseidon and Zeus, 15.185 ff. esp. 15.186 with 16.53, 'You shall see . . .', 8.470 and 9.359; the cup, 16.225 ff.; 'be like the gods', 9.497; the guilty and the innocent, 11.654 and 15.137 (also said of Hector, 13.775); the two scenes in Book 24: lines 93–102, 471 ff.

kings resemble gods. Achilles, we have seen, is apt to blame the innocent. The conduct to be expected of a king is viewed in the same light, and with the same apprehension, in both epics. Calchas asks in advance for a guarantee of protection before he names Agamemnon as the cause of the plague, 'for a king is too powerful when he is angry with a man of lower rank: even if he digests his wrath for a time, yet he keeps his anger in his heart thereafter, to pay him out.' In the same way we hear of Zeus: 'if the Olympian does not bring it to pass at once, he brings it out in the end, and men pay for it dearly'. Penelope describes the normal kingly behaviour, to which Odysseus was such an exception: 'This is the custom of god-like kings: one man he will hate, another he will love—but Odysseus never did violence at all to any man.'[20] The gods, in their superior power, can be arbitrary. Kings, placed on the pinnacle of mortal power, try to emulate them. Agamemnon tries to treat Achilles with mere force, as he tried with the suppliant Chryses. In both cases a greater force defeats him. Achilles is asked to be like the gods and yield; he might have replied that he emulated the gods at least as well in refusing to yield to prayer. We see in the *Iliad* Zeus accept the sacrifices but reject the prayer of the Achaeans for an early victory, reject the prayer of both sides for a negotiated peace, disregard the passionate prayer of Asius, and plan disaster for the Achaeans though they pour anxious libations to him all night long; and we see Athena reject the prayers of the women of Troy.[21] The motives which impel the gods to intervene in human affairs are personal and arbitrary,[22] all-too-human in fact. Men try to act in the same way and come to grief, for Achilles, god-like beyond any other hero and indulging his passionate and arbitrary will in rejecting prayers which he knows to be right, causes the death of Patroclus and wishes only to die himself.

While he lives, the hero is god-like and loved by the gods. In his martial rage, the high point and essence of his existence, he

[20] 1.80, 4.160–1, iv.691–3, cf. ii.230–4.

[21] 2.419 ὡς ἔφατ', οὐδ' ἄρα πώ οἱ ἐπεκραίαινε Κρονίων/ἀλλ' ὅ γε δέκτο μὲν ἱρά, πόνον δ' ἀμέγαρτον ὄφελλεν. 3.302, 12.173, 7.467 ff., 6.311.

[22] Cf. K. Reinhardt, *Das Parisurteil*, 29; H. Fränkel, *Dichtung und Philosophie*, 70; vi.188 Ζεὺς δ' αὐτὸς νέμει ὄλβον Ὀλύμπιος ἀνθρώποισιν/ἐσθλοῖς ἠδὲ κακοῖσιν, ὅπως ἐθέλῃσιν, ἑκάστῳ: 17.647, 24.527, iv.236 and O. Tsagarakis, *Major Concepts of Divine Power*, 13 f.

is like a lion, a wild boar, a storm, a river in flood, a raging forest fire, a bright star from a dark cloud; his armour blazes like the sun, his eyes flash fire, his breast is filled with irresistible fury, his limbs are light and active. The mere sight of his onset and the sound of his great battle-cry are enough to fill enemy heroes with panic. Encouraged by gods, even 'thrust on by the mighty hand of Zeus', he mows down opponents like a reaper in a cornfield, like a wind scattering the foam of the sea, like a great dolphin swallowing little fishes. Men fall and are crushed under his chariot wheels, and he drives on, his chariot rattling over them.[23] He challenges his opponent to single combat with insults and exults over his body, so that the defeated must die with the taunts of the victor[24] in his ears. He then aims to strip off his armour and abolish his identity by depriving him in death of burial, and leaving his corpse to be mauled by scavenging animals and birds.

'To be alive and to see the light of the sun' is in the Homeric poems a regular phrase, along with 'while I have breath in my lungs and my knees are active'. To die, conversely, is to 'leave the light of the sun' and to 'go into the dark', or to have one's knees or limbs 'undone'.[25] The *Iliad* is full of detailed accounts of the moment of death of the warrior. The poet dislikes any account of men being gravely wounded but not dying; a wounded man either dies quickly or recovers and fights again. The incurable Philoctetes is left far from Troy, groaning on the island of Lemnos; the Achaean chieftains wounded in Book 11 are healed and will return to battle. This works with the removal of chance as a possible cause of a hero's death (no arrow at a venture can kill a Homeric hero as Ahab or Harold were killed), and the virtual suppression of trickery and treason, and

---

[23] A lion, e.g. 11.113; wild boar, 17.282; storm, 11.746; river, 5.87; star, 11.62; sun, 19.398; eyes flash fire, 12.466, hand of Zeus, 15.695; reaper, 11.67; foam, 11.306; dolphin, 21.22; chariot wheels, 16.378.

[24] οὐ γὰρ ὁ θάνατος δεινὸν ἀλλ' ἡ περὶ τὴν τελευτὴν ὕβρις φοβερά. πῶς δὲ οὐκ οἰκτρὸν ἰδεῖν ἐχθροῦ πρόσωπον ἐπεγγελῶντος καὶ τοῖς ὠσὶ τῶν ὀνειδῶν ἀκοῦσαι; Aeschines 2.181.

[25] ζώειν καὶ ὁρᾶν φάος ἠελίοιο, e.g. 18.01; εἰς ὅ κ' αὐτμὴ | ἐν στήθεσσι μένῃ καί μοι φίλα γούνατ' ὀρώρῃ, 9.609. λείπειν φάος ἠελίοιο, 18.11; νέεσθαι ὑπὸ ζόφον ἠερόεντα, 23.51; τὸν δὲ σκότος ὄσσε κάλυψε, 4.461; λῦσε δὲ γυῖα, 4.469; ὑπὸ γούνατ' ἔλυσεν, 11.578. Cf. D. Bremer, *Licht und Dunkel*, 48. H. Lloyd-Jones in *CR* 15 (1965), 2 and in *Dionysiaca* (*Festschrift D. L. Page*), 54, discusses the etymology of Hades from α-ιδης, in which poets seem to have believed.

the fact that, in the poem, prisoners are no longer taken, all suppliants being killed.[26] The effect of all this stylization is to concentrate attention as exclusively as possible on the position of the hero, face to face with his destiny at the hands of another hero: either he must kill or be killed, dying a heroic death.

When a hero dies, dark night covers him, he is seized by hateful darkness; he is robbed of his sweet life, his soul rushes forth from the wound; it goes down to Hades bewailing its fate, leaving behind its youth and strength. The doom of death covers his eyes and nostrils, his armour rings upon him, he breathes out his life in the dust, hateful fate swallows him up, he gluts the god of war with his blood.[27] Stabbed in the back, he lies in the dust, stretching out his hands to his friends; wounded in the bladder, he crouches breathing his last, and lies stretched out on the earth like a worm. With a spear driven through his eye he collapses, arms spread wide, and his killer cuts off and brandishes his head; he lies on his back in the dust, breathing his last, while all his guts pour from his wound to the earth; he dies bellowing with pain, clutching the bloody earth, or biting the cold bronze which has severed his tongue, or wounded between the navel and the genitals, 'where the wound is most painful for poor mortal men', writhing like a roped bull about the spear.[28] His eyes are knocked out and fall bloody before his feet in the dust; stabbed in the act of begging for his life, his liver slides out and his lap is filled with his blood; the spear is thrust into his mouth, splitting his white bones, and filling his eye sockets with blood which spouts at his mouth and nose; hit in the head, his blood and brains rush from the wound.[29] Wounded in the arm and helpless, he awaits his slayer, seeing death before him; his prayer for life rejected, he crouches with arms spread out waiting for the death-stroke.[30] After death his corpse may be driven over by chariots, his hands and head may be lopped off, all his enemies may surround his corpse and stab it at their leisure, his body may be thrown into the river and gnawed by fishes, or lie unrecognizable in the

[26] H. Fränkel, *Dichtung und Philosophie*, 40, cf. W. H. Friedrich, *Verwundung und Tod in der Ilias*, and G. Strasburger, *Die kleinen Kämpfer der Ilias*.

[27] 5.659, 16.602, 10.459, 14.518, 16.855, 16.502, 5.42, 4.522, 5.289.

[28] 13.548, 13.652, 14.493, 4.524, 13.393, 5.74, 13.570.

[29] 13.617, 20.470, 16.346, 17.297.

[30] 20.481, 21.115.

mêlée.[31] His soul goes down to a dark and comfortless world, to a shadowy and senseless existence, for ever banished from the light and warmth and activity of this life.

That is what the hero faces every time he goes into battle. It is clear in Homer that the soldier would, in general, prefer not to fight.[32] Not only do the Achaeans rush for the ships and home, the moment they see a chance, but the rank and file need constant and elaborate appeals and commands to keep them in the field, and even heroes have at times to reason themselves into a fighting mood, and at others to be rebuked by their superiors or their comrades. Women attempt to hold them back from the battlefield, as we see in Book 6, where Hecuba, Helen, and Andromache in turn try to detain Hector in the safe and comfortable women's realm;[33] but the true hero, like Hector, must reject the temptation and go. We are not dealing with berserkers in the pages of Homer, whatever Mycenaean warriors may have been like in reality. |Self-respect, respect for public opinion, the conscious determination to be a good man—these motives drive the hero to risk his life;[34] and the crowning paradox of the hero, the idea of inevitable death itself. 'If we were to be ageless and immortal once we had survived this war', says Sarpedon to Glaucus, 'then I should not fight in the fore-front myself, nor should I be sending you into the battle where men win glory. But in fact countless dooms of death surround us, and no mortal man can escape or avoid them: so let us go, either to yield victory to another or to win it ourselves.'[35] If the hero were really god-

---

[31] 11.534, 11.146, 22.371, 21.120, 16.638.

[32] H. Strasburger, *HZ* 177 (1954), 232.

[33] 6.258, 354, 429; Schadewaldt, *Von Homers Welt und Werk*[4], 218. Calypso, Circe, and Nausicaa represent a series of variants on this theme in the *Odyssey*, offering the hero sanctuary from his career of suffering and adventure.

[34] Odysseus' monologue, 11.407–10; Hector to Andromache, 6.441–6.

[35] Sarpedon, 12.322–8. Heroes in very various traditions invoke this reason for their willingness to face death. For instance, Gilgamesh says to Enkidu, who attempts to dissuade him from battle with the terrible Huwawa: 'Who, my friend, can scale heaven? Only the gods live forever under the sun. As for mankind, numbered are their days . . . Should I fall, I shall have made me a name: "Gilgamesh", they will say, "against fierce Huwawa has fallen!" long after my offspring has been born in my house,' *ANET*[3], 79. Sigurd to the dragon Fafnir, who has prophesied his sufferings if he chooses heroism: 'If I knew I'd never die, I'd ride back, even though I had to forfeit all the wealth . . .', *Völsungasaga*, 18. The Burgundians refuse to save their lives by surrendering Hagen to Kriemhild: 'We

like, if he were exempt, as the gods are, from age and death, then he would not be a hero at all. It is the pressure of mortality which imposes on men the compulsion to have virtues; the gods, exempt from that pressure, are, with perfect consistency, less 'virtuous' than men. They do not need the supreme human virtue of courage, since even if they are wounded in battle they can be instantly cured; and since they make no sacrifice for each other, as Hector does for his wife and child and Odysseus for his, their marriages, too, seem lacking in the depth and truth of human marriage. We see no union on Olympus which has anything of the quality of those of Hector and of Odysseus.³⁶

Death is constantly present in the hero's thoughts. Hector knows that Troy will fall, and hopes only that he will be dead and buried first. Before his duel with Ajax he makes careful provision for the burial and memorial to be allotted to the man defeated. Achilles describes his life, fighting and ravaging the Troad, 'constantly exposing my own life in battle', and in his speech to Lycaon he says 'I too am subject to death and cruel fate: there will be a morning or an evening or a noon-day, when someone will take my life in battle, hitting me with a spear or an arrow from the bow-string.'³⁷ No hero, not even the greatest, is spared the shameful experience of fear. Hector runs from Achilles; Ajax is put to flight, 'trembling and looking at the crowd of men like a wild beast'; Achilles himself is alarmed by Agenor's spear, and later, reduced by the attack of the River Scamander to seeing a miserable death apparently unavoidable, he is told by Poseidon, 'Do not tremble too much nor be afraid.'³⁸ We have seen that in some ways the fighting described by Homer is highly stylized, and that it omits some of the characteristic horrors of war. Yet the audience remains

---

must die some time or other', said Giselher, 'and no one shall prevent us from defending ourselves like knights', *Nibelungenlied*, p. 260 of Penguin trans. *Beowulf*, 1384: 'Each of us must expect an end of living in this world; let him who may win glory before death, for that is best at last for the departed warrior.'

³⁶ Otto, *The Homeric Gods*, 242; Erbse, *A. und A.* 16 (1970), 111; cf. also Bassett, *The Poetry of Homer*, 223.

³⁷ 6.447 ff.; 7.77–91; 9.322; 21.110.

³⁸ Simone Weil, *The Iliad, or, The Poem of Force*, trans. M. McCarthy, 12; 22.136 ff.; 11.544 ff.; 20.380; 21.288. We see how different an Indo–European heroic tradition could be with the Germanic hero Volsung; before his birth, we read, he had already sworn never to yield to fear (*Völsungasaga* 5).

convinced that in fact the poet has done full justice to its
nature, that its frightfulness has not been palliated or smoothed
over. That effect is achieved, in great part, because the poet
insists on presenting death in its full significance as the end,
unsoftened by any posthumous consolation or reward; in de-
picting it dispassionately and fully in all its forms; and showing
that even heroes fear and hate it. The hero is granted by the
poet the single privilege of dying a hero's death, not a random
or undignified one, but that death haunts his thoughts in life
and gives his existence at once its limitations and its definition.

It is in accordance with this overriding interest in human life,
in its quality as intense and glorious yet transitory, and its
position poised between the eternal brightness of heaven and
the unchanging darkness of the world of the dead, that the
Homeric poems are interested in death far more than they are
in fighting. Homeric duels are short;[39] heroes do not hack
away at each other, exhausting all their strength and cunning,
as do the heroes of Germanic epic or the knights of Malory.
Recent work has emphasized the brevity and standardized
character of these encounters.[40] When a hero's time of doom
has arrived, his strength is no use to him. The armour is struck
from the shoulders of Patroclus by a god; Athena secretly gives
back to Achilles the spear with which he has missed Hector,
'and Hector, shepherd of the people, did not notice'—while as
for his doomed opponent, when his death was foreshadowed
by the Scales of Zeus, then 'Phoebus Apollo abandoned him.'[41]
In many killings the victim seems rather to wait passively for
his death than to be killed fighting.[42] The most powerful de-
scriptions of death in battle are like that of Hector, recognizing
that 'the gods have called me to my death . . . now my destiny
has caught me,' and resolving to die fighting; Patroclus, dis-
armed and exposed helpless to death; Lycaon, arms out-
stretched, seeing death before him.[43] Achilles, too, though the

---

[39] G. Strasburger, *Die kleinen Kämpfer der Ilias*, 49–50.

[40] W. H. Friedrich, *Verwundung und Tod in der Ilias;* B. Fenik, *Typical Battle-Scenes in the Iliad* (1968); T. Krischer, *Formale Konventionen der hom. Epik* (1971), 13–90.

[41] 16.791, 22.276, 22.213.

[42] W. Marg, 'Kampf und Tod in der Ilias', *Die Antike*, 18 (1941), 167 ff., *WüJbb.* 2 (1976), 10.

[43] 22.297, 16.801 ff., 21.116; cf. also 4.517 ff., 11.136 ff., 13.435, 20.481, 21.24–32.

poem does not show his death, accepts and faces it; for this is what interests the poet very much, the sight of a hero succeeding in facing his own death. It is to produce and emphasize this situation that Homeric fighting is stylized as it is, when it might for instance have been developed much more as blow-by-blow accounts for the expert, interested in the technical details of fighting. The chariot race in Book 23 is treated much more in that manner. Walter Marg called the *Iliad* 'the poem of death'.[44] I think it will be more appropriate to call it the poem of life and death: of the contrast and transition between the two. This is what the poet is concerned to emphasize, and on this he concentrates his energies and our gaze. It is part of the greatness of Achilles that he is able to contemplate and accept his own death more fully and more passionately than any other hero.

The reward of the warrior is glory. It has been argued recently that we can reconstruct with confidence some features of a very early Indo-European heroic verse lying behind Homer, and that phrases such as 'deathless glory' and 'widespread glory' are the most certain examples of expressions which can be traced back to that poetry.[45] Whether or not these speculations are correct, it seems clear enough that the great themes of epic poetry, Germanic as well as Greek, go back far into the past. Heroic anger, revenge, pride, and suffering,[46] are themes of many other stories in Greek, and of other Indo-European heroic literatures. Phoenix knows of many stories of heroic χόλος, anger and withdrawal, and is able to tell Achilles that when a hero of former time was seized, like Achilles himself, by a violent fit of anger, 'they

---

[44] *A und A* 18 (1973), 10, cf. Reinhardt, *Tradition und Geist*, 13.

[45] Conveniently, R. Schmitt, *Dichtung und Dichtersprache in indogermanischer Zeit* (1967), esp. 101 ff., idem (ed.), *Indogermanische Dichtersprache* (1967), also M. L. West, *CQ* 23 (1973). A salutary warning, that 'a mere coincidence in poetic locution between two or more Indo–European poetic languages is a necessary, but not a sufficient, condition for the inference and reconstruction of Indo–European poetic language', E. Campanile in *Indo-European Studies* 2 (1974), 247. Many of the 'parallels' alleged seem either philologically inexact or the sort of thing which can arise independently, with no proof of common origin; as, for instance, the metaphor 'shepherd of the people' occurs of rulers not only in Indo–European (Greek, Anglo–Saxon, Irish), but also in the Akkadian Gilgamesh epic and in the titles of Hammurabi of Babylon; cf. also *ANET*³, 447 (Egyptian).

[46] E. Norden, *Kleine Schriften*, 562.

were prevailed on with gifts and won over with words.' Achilles consoles himself in his enforced inaction by singing 'the glorious deeds of men'.[47] We hear of some of these tales: of Heracles, Jason, Tydeus, Oedipus, Nestor, Bellerophon, Meleager. Already for Homer's characters their stories are paradigms for their own conduct: 'You are not the man your father Tydeus was', 'Do not make the same mistake as Meleager', 'Even Heracles had to accept death'. This status of being memorable and significant after death, the status which Homer's own characters have for him, is achieved by great deeds and great sufferings. Oedipus and Niobe remained in the memory for their terrible disasters, the others for their great achievements, although some, like Bellerophon, suffered greatly too.

Hector, in confident mood, hopes to kill an Achaean champion who answers his challenge: if he does, he will allow his body to be buried by his friends and a tomb raised over it, by the shore of the sea, so that passing sailors in time to come may say, 'That is the grave of a hero of olden time, whom bright Hector slew in single combat.' That is what they will say, says Hector, 'and my glory will never die.' The shooting of Menelaus brings glory to Pandarus. Hector's last words as he nerves himself for his despairing attack on Achilles are these: 'At least let me not die unheroically and ingloriously, but achieving something great for men hereafter to hear.' Achilles chose a heroic fate, short life, and deathless fame, rather than long inglorious existence, and when Patroclus is dead he accepts his own death—'but now let me win fair fame', by slaughtering Trojans and making their wives shriek as they wipe away their tears.[48]

But in the Homeric poems glory is not a simple and straight-forward thing, won by heroic deeds and consoling the hero for his death. We are far from the unreflective heroism of the Germanic lays. Helen sees herself as a character in history, whose sin has produced suffering for everyone. She invites Hector to sit down, 'Since you above all are involved in trouble, because of me, bitch that I am, and the sin of Paris;

[47] 9.525, 189.
[48] 7.85 ff., 4.197, 22.304 (cf. iii.204), 9.410 ff., 18.121.

Zeus has imposed an evil destiny upon us, so that in later times we may be a theme of song for generations to follow.' It is surely a symbol for this that in Book 3, when she is fetched to watch the duel between Paris and Menelaus, she is discovered 'weaving at the high loom, at work upon a crimson double cloth, and in it she was weaving many ordeals of the horse-taming Trojans and the Achaeans corseleted in bronze, which they were undergoing for her sake at the hands of the god of war.' The detail, the description of what it was that Helen was weaving, is there because it is significant; when Andromache, by contrast, is discovered at her loom, we are told only that 'she was weaving in many decorations.' The point in the case of Andromache is that she was told by her husband, the last time we saw her, to attend to her housewifely work, her loom, and her servants; the faithful wife obeyed her husband, and we find her carrying out his instruction.[49] The pattern of her weaving is not important. In the case of Helen, on the other hand, it is important, because it shows her as aware of her own role in causing all the distress. What she makes in Book 3 is exactly what she says in Book 6.[50] This Helen is the same conception as we find in the *Odyssey*, when she unexpectedly produces a present of her own for the departing Telemachus, a woman's garment which she has made herself. Placing it in his hand she says, 'I too give you a present, a keepsake of the hands of Helen, for your bride to wear on the joyous day of your wedding.' (xv.125.) She is aware that the dress will have special value because of its maker, and refers to herself in the third person, as a figure in history; any bride will be flattered to wear what the legendary Helen made. And Helen is a legendary figure not for her great achievements, not even for her

---

[49] Helen to Hector, 6.355–8; her weaving, 3.125–8; Andromache's weaving, 22.441; Hector's instruction, 6.491.

[50] The same technique is to be seen in the first book of the *Odyssey*. At i.153, the singer Phemius performs for the Suitors; he sings, they occupy the hall, and in a corner Telemachus has to whisper to his guest. The important thing here is the scene: the rightful prince forced into a furtive corner in his own house. But when Athena has put new courage into Telemachus, and he strides among the Suitors like a god, then we are told what the song was: the return of the Achaeans and Athena's role in it. Odysseus is on the way home (i.325). So too at xvii.261: as Odysseus at last sees his house, he hears the music of Phemius coming from it; the usurpers are taking their pleasure, while the true king must come in secret and disguise. We need not be told the details of the song.

womanly virtue, like Penelope, but for her guilt and suffering.

The whole disaster of Achaeans and Trojans at Troy, says Alcinous, was devised by the gods, so that out of the destruction of men there should be a theme for song in later generations. The disastrous return of the Achaeans from Troy is the theme of a song, and Telemachus tells his mother that she should listen to it and realize that many others besides herself have had suffering decreed for them by Zeus. Achilles says the Achaeans will long remember his disastrous quarrel with Agamemnon, and we see in the *Odyssey* that a comparable quarrel, between Achilles and Odysseus, was the subject of an epic lay. Demodocus the singer is blind; the lyre on which Achilles accompanies himself as he sings of the 'glorious deeds of men' is one which he captured when he sacked Thebe, the city of Eetion. There, as we know from Andromache, he slew her father and her seven brothers, and left her alone in the world. Suffering produces song, and by song we understand that suffering is universal for men, comes from the gods, and must be accepted. And glory is attached particularly to the tomb of the dead, while the glorious death which Hector finally achieves is no comfort to his defenceless family and friends, upon whom the emphasis falls.[51]

Such a treatment of the idea of glory is a sophisticated one. Not only general probability, and the evidence of such simpler epics as *Beowulf*, force us to believe that behind Homer there lay a tradition in which it was seen far more simply; the fact that in the epics themselves no fewer than twenty-four persons, male and female, bear names which are compounds of κλέος, 'glory',[52] points strongly in the same direction. The parents who bestowed such names on their children meant to associate them with an unambiguously splendid thing. But the poet, who

---

[51] Helen to Telemachus, xv.125; the gods will make a song of praise for Penelope, xxiv.196–8; Alcinous, viii.577–80; ὁ δ᾽ Ἀχαιῶν νόστον ἄειδε, i.325; Telemachus to Penelope, i.353 ff., and see W. Marg, *Homer über die Dichtung*, 14; Achilles on the quarrel, 19.63; quarrel of Achilles and Odysseus, viii.73, and see W. Marg in *Navicula Chiloniensis* (1956), 16 ff.; Demodocus, viii.62 ff.; Achilles' lyre, 9.186–9; Andromache's family, 6.414 ff.; glory attaches to tombs, 7.91, iv.584, xxiv.33; death of Hector, C. M. Bowra, *Tradition and Design*, 236.

[52] They are listed in Ebeling, *Lexicon Homericum*, 816. See also the literature cited by R. Schmitt, *Dichtung und Dichtersprache in indogermanischer Zeit*, 101 n. 617, on such names in Greek and other Indo–European languages.

transforms a story of the sack of a city, a perfectly ordinary
event common in the Dark Ages,[53] into the vast and tragic
tale of Troy, and who develops the heroic theme of revenge
with the same sort of moral complexity, allows his hero to
brood upon glory, too. Achilles has been told that the price of
glory for him is a short life; he will not return from Troy, if he
chooses the heroic path. The straightforward heroic choice can
be illustrated by the great hero Cúchulainn of the Ulster cycle.
As a boy he learned that he who took up arms for the first time
on a certain day would be a mighty warrior, 'his name would
endure in Ireland . . . and stories about him would last forever.' He seized the opportunity. ' "Well", Cathbad said, "the
day has this merit: he who arms for the first time today will
achieve fame and greatness. But his life is short." "That is a
fair bargain", Cúchulainn said. "If I achieve fame I am content, though I had only one day on earth." '[54] But Achilles, who
has duly chosen the heroic path, is filled with bitterness as he
broods on Agamemnon's treatment of him. Agamemnon tries
to persuade him by the offer of enormous presents and the
promise that he will 'honour him like his only son'; the presents
are marks of honour (not merely a bribe), as we see clearly
when Phoenix says, 'If you return to battle without the presents,
you will not be so highly honoured, even if you repel the
attack.'[55]

But for Achilles the gifts have lost their symbolic value and
become mere objects, in the light of the humiliation he has
suffered at the hands of the king. If that is the way he is to be
treated, when he has been acting as a true hero, risking his life
and fighting with men defending their women-folk, then there
is no honour to be won; coward and hero are given the same
honour, man of action and man of sloth must both alike die.
And from this point of view the thought of inevitable death
ceases to be the stimulus to heroism: why should Achilles not
toddle safely home and die in bed? As for the gifts, mere
things can be no compensation for the loss of a man's life, so
that Achilles is perfectly logical to demand infinite, impossible

[53] Cf. K. Latte in *Hermes*, 92 (1964), 386 = *Kleine Schriften*, 458, G. Finsler,
Homer, i, 133.
[54] *The Tain*, trans. T. Kinsella, pp. 84–5.
[55] 9.142, 604–5, 325–7, 401.

quantities of them before he will change his mind[56]—'not even
if he gave me ten and twenty times as much, all that he has and
more, as much as makes its way to Orchomenus or to Thebes
in Egypt ... even if he gave me as much as the sand of the
sea and the dust of the earth, even so would Agamemnon not
change my purpose' (9.379 ff.). And in fact Achilles does not
return for gifts, to which in Book 19 he remains indifferent,
nor does he really regain his belief in heroism. Sitting with
Priam in the last book he still sees the war in an unheroic light.
As in Book 9 he spoke bitterly of 'fighting with men who are
defending their women-folk', and in Book 19 of 'waging war for
the sake of hateful Helen'—an intensely unheroic view of the
struggle—so here he speaks of himself yet more movingly. 'My
father Peleus was happy once and honoured by the gods, but
he had only one son after all, doomed to an untimely death;
and I am not even looking after him as he grows old, since I
have been sitting here by Troy, far from home, causing grief to
you and your children.' At the point from which Achilles speaks
now, glory is shrunk to an inconsiderable thing. Priam reminds
him of his own father, old and unhappy, and he sees himself
making pointless war, no good to either side. Priam asks for a
truce of eleven days for the funeral of Hector, and says, 'Then
on the twelfth day we will fight, if we must.'[57] For both Priam
and Achilles the war has become an endless process, unrewarding and meaningless, from which they cannot extricate
themselves.

The *Odyssey* develops similar ideas, but in a rather different
manner. In the *Iliad* Achilles expresses profound disenchant-
ment with glory as the reward of the hero, but heroic he still
remains. To the last he is a fighter, even when he has by
suffering attained a perspective like that of Zeus, who 'has
sacked many cities and will sack many more'. In the *Odyssey*,
Odysseus meets him among the dead, and congratulates him on
his felicity: honoured like a god in life, he is mighty among the

---

[56] This speech does not mean pacifism or the rejection of the heroic ideal as
such, as argued by Adam Parry, 'The Language of Achilles', *TAPA* 87 1956),
1–7 = *Language and Background of Homer*, ed. G. S. Kirk (1964), 48–54; cf. M. D.
Reeve in *CQ* 23 (1973), 193–5, G. S. Kirk, *Homer and the Oral Tradition* (1976), 51.

[57] 19.325, εἵνεκα ῥιγεδανῆς ῾Ελένης Τρωσὶν πολεμίζω. 24.534–42; 24.667,
with ΣT, ὡς ἀπειρηκὼς τῷ χρόνῳ καὶ ταῖς συμφοραῖς, 'Priam speaks as one
exhausted by time and suffering.'

dead thereafter. Achilles rejects the compliment. There is no consolation for death; he would prefer to be in the lowest position in the world, the servant of an impoverished master, than to be king of all the dead. Agamemnon himself, the sacker of Troy, of whom Odysseus says that 'his glory is now the greatest under heaven, so great a city he has sacked and destroyed many people', and to whom his son Orestes built a tomb 'so that his glory might be inextinguishable', asks bitterly, in the lower world, 'What joy have I in it, that I have endured the war to the end? Zeus planned a cruel return home for me at the hands of Aegisthus and my accursed wife.' Menelaus, happily home with Helen and his accumulated treasures, tells his guests that he would give up two-thirds of his possessions to undo the effects of the Trojan War and to have alive again all the men who perished there, far from home; often does he sit in his palace and weep for them. Nestor can say only that the tale of Troy is a tale of woe, ὀιζύς, 'all that we suffered by land and sea'; 'there all the best of us were slain: there lies war-like Ajax, there lies Achilles, and Patroclus, and my own dear son . . . Not even if you were to sit by me and question me for five years and for six years, could I tell you all the sufferings of the god-like Achaeans at Troy.'

This passive view regards heroic achievement and endurance in the light of mere suffering inflicted, and looks back on it with self-pity, not with pride. Odysseus himself, when he begins his narration of his career to the Phaeacians says 'Your heart has inclined to ask me of my grievous sufferings, so that I may mourn and lament yet more. What first then shall I tell of, what last? The Olympian gods have given me woes in plenty... I am Odysseus, Laertes' son; men know of me for my many wiles, and my fame has reached heaven.' To Agamemnon he says flatly that 'for Helen's sake many of us were slain', the least heroic description of the Trojan War as a whole. When he and his Penelope are finally united, they each tell the other their experiences: 'They took delight in the tales they told each other. The queen told of all that she endured in her house from the suitors . . . and Odysseus, sprung from Zeus, told of all the griefs he had brought upon men and of all his own travail and suffering. And she listened with delight . . .' The Phaeacians, too, are held spellbound by Odysseus' recital of his 'sufferings' and beg him to go on, receiving from him the reply that 'I should not grudge telling you even more moving sufferings of my companions.'[58]

From suffering comes song, and song gives pleasure. In the *Odyssey* it is presented with a rather more plaintive tone, in the *Iliad* the light is rather more robust, but the picture is not really different. Without his 'woes in plenty', the fame of Odysseus would not have reached heaven. Without the accursed wrath of Achilles, which made many noble heroes into food for scavenging dogs and birds, there would have been no *Iliad*. The Homeric hero is anxious for glory, and he faces the full horrors of death. But as there is no posthumous reward for the brave man in the other world, so the consolation of glory is a chilly one. Odysseus, sacker of cities, 'brought many griefs upon men' in his wanderings; as he tells us himself, at the very beginning of his recital, 'from Troy the wind took me to Ismarus: there I sacked the city and slew the men.'[59] But by the end of his wanderings he has lost all the booty he gained, his own men are all dead, and it all seems to have been as futile as the raids he tells of in his false tales. Achilles 'sits by Troy, causing grief to Priam and his sons'. These terrible events produce glory, but we are not dealing with heroes for whom that is an adequate reward. The κλέος of glory is the κλέος, the mere untrustworthy report, which we mortals hear from the past, which is contrasted with the sure knowledge possessed by the gods; and also it is the role of the singer to confer κλέος on past heroic deeds.[60] The hero dies, not so much for his own glory, not even so much for his friends, as for the glory of song, which explains to a spellbound audience the greatness and fragility of the life of man.

---

[58] xi.482–91, ix.263–6, iv.584, xxiv.95–7, iv.97 ff., iii.103–16; ix.12–20; xi.438; xxiii.301–8; xi.333–4, 381.

[59] ix.39–40, cf. the Egyptian adventure narrated at xiv.245 ff.

[60] 2.484: ἔσπετε νῦν μοι, Μοῦσαι ... ὑμεῖς γὰρ θεαί ἐστε, πάρεστέ τε, ἴστέ τε πάντα· | ἡμεῖς δὲ κλέος οἷον ἀκούομεν, οὐδέ τι ἴδμεν. i.338 ἔργ' ἀνδρῶν τε θεῶν τε, τά τε κλείουσιν ἀοιδοί.

IV

DEATH, PATHOS, AND OBJECTIVITY

The importance of these adagio themes of Mozart lies, not in the perfection of their formal finish and in their sensual beauty, but in the deep feeling from which they spring ... which, while very far from concealing the inward glow of passion, yet lends it expression without even a trace of unhealthy ferment or pretentious subjectivity.[1]

THE *Iliad*, we have been arguing, is concerned above all with the contrast and significance of heroic life and death. This concern leads to the long series of killings which can, for a modern reader, be a disconcerting aspect of the poem. Thousands of lines narrate, with clinical detail and detachment, the slaying in battle of one hero after another. Those who are slain are mostly of little significance individually, and they exist, in many cases, only for the moment in which they are seen to die. Nothing is more characteristic of the poem;[2] when we turn to the *Nibelungenlied*, or the *Song of Roland*, or the *Poem of the Cid*, we find nothing like this illumination of minor warriors who exist in order to be killed. In those epics what we have is, rather, a vast number of insignificant dead, without separate description or identity, whose simpler function is to make up a total for the great heroes to slay.

The narrative manner of Homer is, generally speaking, objective.[3] He does not indulge himself in such subjective and emotional outbursts as, for instance, this of Virgil, when he is deeply moved by his own narration of the heroic and poignant death of Nisus and Euryalus, a pair of warriors who are in love and whose disaster is strongly coloured by their passion:

[1] H. Abert, *Mozart*, II, 228.

[2] I have published a rather longer and more technical version of this chapter, with a full argument for the importance of the ancient scholia for this as for other aesthetic questions: 'Homeric Pathos and Objectivity', *CQ* 26 (1976), 161–85.

[3] 'There is no subjectivity in Homer', said Coleridge (*Table Talk* for 12 May 1830); H. Fränkel speaks of 'a more general characteristic of the Homeric style: the restrained objectivity and aristocratic withdrawnness' (*Dichtung und Philosophie*, 41). I hope it will emerge from this chapter that this and similar judgements, in one way true, are in other ways misleading.

'Fortunate pair! If my songs have any power, no day shall ever oust you from the memory of ages ...'⁴ Now, a long list of accounts of the slaying of warriors unimportant in themselves, given in an unemotional style, promises to be intolerable. How is the poet to confer significance on the slain, and to make their deaths, and the long repetition of such scenes, have some emotional meaning for the audience? In this chapter I aim to show that the dispassionate manner in which these slayings are recorded, and above all the short obituaries which many of them are given, are important and striking because they do in fact convey emotion, and because in doing so they give status and significance to their subjects. It is because they do this that they remain in the memory of the reader, and that they form one of the most telling and representative aspects of the *Iliad*.

Here again, as in the treatment of characterization but on a larger scale, it will prove possible to meet the criticism that we are reading into the poem things that really are not there at all, and misrepresenting a smooth and objective surface by the arbitrary intrusion of subjective emotion, by the order in which we proceed. I begin with passages which appear to have no emotional content, and aim to show that it is impossible to separate them from others in which such content is undeniably present. It is heartening to find that the ancient commentators, whose work is so little regarded in most recent writing on Homer, very often found in these passages the same qualities of emotion and pathos as we shall find there. While that of course does not prove that we are right, it is some reassurance that

---

⁴ Virgil, *Aeneid* ix.446: homosexual love is entirely absent from the *Iliad* and the *Odyssey*, despite attempts to detect it; most recently, M. W. Clarke in *Hermes* 106 (1978), 381–95. The passage which 'contains the only *explicit* [*sic*] implication that Achilles and Patroclus were paederastic lovers' (388), namely 24.129–30, does not really do so. The word περ, into which Clarke, like Gilbert Murray (*Rise of the Greek Epic*³, 125) reads so much, in the phrase ἀγαθὸν δὲ γυναικί περ ἐν φιλότητι | μίσγεσθαι, does not mean 'even with a woman' (as opposed to a man), but is essentially a metrical device, familiar at that point in the line; cf. K. Meister, *Die homerische Kunstsprache*, 21 and 33. Telemachus and Pisistratus sleep in one bed in Menelaus' house, but on this see J. T. Kakridis in *Gymnasium*, 78 (1971), 518 ff., who rightly observes, 'Der Gedanke, dass eine solche Sitte die jungen Leute leicht zu Unzucht verführen konnte, lag den Menschen jener Zeit fern.' The love of Achilles for Patroclus is to be compared with that of Gilgamesh for Enkidu; or, to take a parallel at one time more familiar, with the love of David for Jonathan, 'passing the love of women'. The Theban epics may well have been different, cf. Wilamowitz, *Kleine Schriften*, iv, 364.

native speakers of ancient Greek shared our perceptions; they are at least not the mere anachronisms of the twentieth century. We shall find that motifs important for the production of pathos meet us also as expressive, in other places, of other emotions, but that they play their central role in conveying the central fact of the *Iliad*, the significance of death.

In Book 11.262, Agamemnon has killed two sons of Antenor. The episode has been a highly pathetic one (see especially 11.241–7). It is summarized:

> ἔνθ' Ἀντήνορος υἷες ὑπ' Ἀτρεΐδῃ βασιλῆι
> πότμον ἀναπλήσαντες ἔδυν δόμον Ἄϊδος εἴσω.

'There the sons of Antenor, at the hands of king Agamemnon, fulfilled their doom and went down to the house of Hades.' Such a passage, free from emotive words, is easily underrated. We find an ancient commentator saying 'He describes this emotionally.' Are we convinced that the emotion is really there?

In the hope of answering this question, let us go on to a not dissimilar but clearer passage. 5.539 ff., twin sons of Diocles: their parentage; growing up, they sailed to Troy; there Aeneas slew them, as men slay a pair of lions:

> τοίω τὼ χείρεσσιν ὑπ' Αἰνείαο δαμέντε
> καππεσέτην, ἐλάτῃσιν ἐοικότες ὑψηλῇσι.

'Even so were the two defeated at Aeneas' hands and fell, like tall pine-trees.' Again, no word of explicit pathos; but the scholiast observes: 'expressed emotionally, through the tall pine-trees, because of their youth and beauty'. The simile has, implicitly, brought out the pathos a little more (once fallen, they lie low), as did the treatment of their childhood and growing up.

At 11.99, Agamemnon kills Bianor and Oileus:

> καὶ τοὺς μὲν λίπεν αὖθι ἄναξ ἀνδρῶν Ἀγαμέμνων
> στήθεσι παμφαίνοντας, ἐπεὶ περίδυσε χιτῶνας.

'And them did Agamemnon king of men leave there, with their breasts gleaming, when he had stripped them of their breast-plates.' The unusual phrase στήθεσι παμφαίνοντας means that their bared chests gleamed in the sun; in antiquity it was said that the words 'showed their youth'. Here then another phrase, a factual and apparently unemotional description, gives a colouring to the whole.

We come closer to explicitness with 16.775, one of the most unforgettable passages in Homer. Over the corpse of Cebriones the battle raged:

> ὁ δ' ἐν στροφάλιγγι κονίης
> κεῖτο μέγας μεγαλωστί, λελασμένος ἱπποσυνάων.

'But he lay in the whirl of dust, a mighty man mightily fallen, forgetful of his horsemanship.' 'A pathetic and emotional addition', said the ancients, and some modern scholars have found the lines too splendid to have been invented for so minor a character as Cebriones.[5] Again, no single word is explicitly emotional. But the contrast (see below, pp. 134ff.) is effective, and it would be an imperfect reader of the poem who detected no pathos here.

4.536, a leader from each side is killed:

> ὡς τώ γ' ἐν κονίῃσι παρ' ἀλλήλοισι τετάσθην,
> ἤτοι ὁ μὲν Θρηκῶν, ὁ δ' Ἐπειῶν χαλκοχιτώνων
> ἡγεμόνες· πολλοὶ δὲ περὶ κτείνοντο καὶ ἄλλοι.

'So were the two captains stretched in the dust side by side, one of the Thracians, the other of the mail-clad Epeians; and around them were many others likewise slain.' G. Strasburger[6] suggests that here the heroic death of the two leaders represents the general mêlée, which could not be well depicted in epic. There is, I think, truth in this; but the particular way in which their deaths are summed up seems also to be meant to bring out the tragic fact that both fought and died far from home. Enemies, they lie side by side in death, and the audience sees them in the perspective in which the gods see them, as equal in vulnerability, in mortality, in death.

The motif 'far from home', here implicit only, is developed

---

[5] Thus even a purely aesthetic perception becomes at once an implement of inquiry into Origins; see Wilamowitz, *Die Ilias und Homer* (1920), 142; W. H. Friedrich, *Verwundung und Tod in der Ilias* (1956), 106; *contra*, cf. A. Dihle, *Homer-Probleme* (1970), 23.

[6] G. Strasburger, *Die kleinen Kämpfer der Ilias*, Diss. Frankfurt/Main, 1954, 45; cf. W. Marg, *Die Antike*, 18 (1942), 168.

in a series of passages. First, its use as a reproach, 16.538, Glaucus to Hector:

> Ἕκτορ, νῦν δὴ πάγχυ λελασμένος εἰς ἐπικούρων
> οἳ σέθεν εἵνεκα τῆλε φίλων καὶ πατρίδος αἴης
> θυμὸν ἀποφθινύθουσι.

'Hector, now surely you have quite forgotten your allies who for your sake, far from their families and their homeland, breathe their lives away!' As a taunt, different in character, at 1.29, Agamemnon to Chryses: 'I will not give you back your daughter':

> πρίν μιν καὶ γῆρας ἔπεισιν
> ἡμετέρῳ ἐνὶ οἴκῳ, ἐν Ἄργεϊ, τηλόθι πάτρης,
> ἱστὸν ἐποιχομένην καὶ ἐμὸν λέχος ἀντιόωσαν.

'Before that shall old age come upon her, in my house, in Argos, far from her homeland, where she shall ply the loom and serve my bed'. On this the scholiast says shrewdly: 'He wounds the old man by gradually increasing his separation from him' [sc. in line 30]: the separation from home is emphasized to cause the father the greatest possible pain.[7] We do not forget here that Chryses is a highly pathetic character; what immediately follows brings this out with great subtlety:

> ὣς ἔφατ', ἔδεισεν δ' ὁ γέρων καὶ ἐπείθετο μύθῳ·
> βῆ δ' ἀκέων παρὰ θῖνα πολυφλοίσβοιο θαλάσσης.[8]

'So he spoke, and the old man was afraid and obeyed his command; and he walked in silence along the shore of the loud-roaring sea.'

Another way of using the motif to cause pain is seen at 20.389, Achilles exulting over the corpse of Iphition, son of Otryntes:

> κεῖσαι, Ὀτρυντιάδη, πάντων ἐκπαγλότατ' ἀνδρῶν.
> ἐνθάδε τοι θάνατος, γενεὴ δέ τοί ἐστ' ἐπὶ λίμνῃ
> Γυγαίῃ, ὅθι τοι τέμενος πατρώιόν ἐστιν.

'There you lie, son of Otryntes, most redoubtable of men. Here

---

[7] Well discussed by J. Th. Kakridis, *Homer Revisited* (1971), 131.
[8] ΣT in 1.33: 'Aptly he calls him "old man", not "priest", since he is humiliated and frightened, to make him more pathetic.'

is your death, but you were born on the Gygaean Lake, where your father's lands lie.' Achilles says this εὐχόμενος, 'triumphing': it is of course not simply a geographical or biographical excursus, but brings out the bitterness of death far away from home, which is worse than mere death itself.

It is easy to reverse this and convert an insult into a lament. At 11.814 Patroclus is moved to pity by seeing the Achaean leaders wounded:

> τὸν δὲ ἰδὼν ᾤκτειρε Μενοιτίου ἄλκιμος υἱός,
> καί ῥ᾽ ὀλοφυρόμενος ἔπεα πτερόεντα προσηύδα·
> ἆ δειλοί, Δαναῶν ἡγήτορες ἠδὲ μέδοντες,
> ὡς ἄρ᾽ ἐμέλλετε τῆλε φίλων καὶ πατρίδος αἴης
> ἄσειν ἐν Τροίῃ ταχέας κύνας ἀργέτι δημῷ.

'The brave son of Menoetius, seeing him, felt pity, and with a groan he said, "Ah, unhappy men, you leaders and counsellors of the Achaeans! How you are fated, far from your families and your homeland, to glut with your white fat the swift dogs of Troy!"' Here the emotion is made quite explicit, and the same motif ('far from home') is used to bring out the pathos felt by the speaker as in the superficially 'dispassionate' passages we have been considering. In the light of this one, there can be no great doubt as to the tone of the following passage.

At 17.300, Hippothous is killed by Ajax over Patroclus' body:

> ὁ δ᾽ ἄγχ᾽ αὐτοῖο πέσε πρηνὴς ἐπὶ νεκρῷ,
> τῆλ᾽ ἀπὸ Λαρίσης ἐριβώλακος,

'He fell close to him, prone upon the corpse, far from deep-soiled Larisa', for the poet goes on to add:

> —οὐδὲ τοκεῦσι
> θρέπτρα φίλοις ἀπέδωκε, μινυνθάδιος δέ οἱ αἰὼν
> ἔπλεθ᾽ ὑπ᾽ Αἴαντος μεγαθύμου δουρὶ δαμέντι.

'Nor did he repay his parents for rearing him; short was his life, falling beneath the spear of noble Ajax.' Here the poet has added two more of his most pathetic motifs: 'short life' and 'bereaved parents'. These two, in their fully expanded form, dominate the architecture of the whole poem, from the Achilles and Chryses scenes in *Iliad* 1 to the encounter of Achilles and Priam in 24. On this passage the ancient commentator observes, 'He has made the narrative sufficiently pathetic'; but it is not by means of explicitly emotional words that this effect is achieved.[9]

Two more examples. One is in direct speech, one in a narration by the poet. At 5.684, Sarpedon, wounded, begs Hector to rescue his body:

> Πριαμίδη, μὴ δή με ἕλωρ Δαναοῖσιν ἐάσῃς
> κεῖσθαι, ἀλλ' ἐπάμυνον· ἔπειτά με καὶ λίποι αἰὼν
> ἐν πόλει ὑμετέρῃ, ἐπεὶ οὐκ ἄρ' ἔμελλον ἔγωγε
> νοστήσας οἶκόνδε φίλην ἐς πατρίδα γαῖαν
> εὐφρανέειν ἄλοχόν τε φίλην καὶ νήπιον υἱόν.

'Son of Priam, do not leave me lying, a prey to the Achaeans, but rescue me; then let me die in your city, since I am not fated to go home to my homeland, to gladden my wife and my infant son.' On this moving appeal Eustathius, 594.13, makes the obvious comment: 'The speech contains much pathos, speaking as it does of his son being orphaned, and of being buried in a foreign land.' It is unreal, I think, not to accept that the same sort of pathos is present in such a passage as the second, although the former is spoken by a character, and so its pathos is overt, while the second is an aside by the poet. At 15.705 Hector sets fire to the ship of Protesilaus,

> ἣ Πρωτεσίλαον ἔνεικεν
> ἐς Τροίην, οὐδ' αὖτις ἀπήγαγε πατρίδα γαῖαν,

'Which had brought Protesilaus to Troy, but did not take him home again'. The poet need not have added the little expansion upon the doom of Protesilaus, the first hero to be killed at Troy, which had been developed in a highly emotional way at 2.700 ff. (cf. p. 132f.); the motive for its appearance here must be pathos, and that, again, in a 'factual' style.

It is of course not possible to separate neatly the different motifs. Already passages have been mentioned which combine several. But before passing on to others, we can observe some special developments of the motif 'far away'. At 22.445 Andromache has made her usual household preparations for Hector's return, and heated water for his bath:

---

[9] Reflection on this may suggest doubts about a highly lexicographical approach to the study of ancient (or modern) poetry and ideas. It is not only, perhaps it is not chiefly, by use of the 'most important terms of value' that emotions and judgements are conveyed.

νηπίη, οὐδ' ἐνόησεν ὅ μιν μάλα τῆλε λοετρῶν
χερσὶν Ἀχιλλῆος δάμασε γλαυκῶπις Ἀθήνη.

'Fond woman, she did not know that far away from the bath
bright-eyed Athena had slain him by Achilles' hand.' Here the
poet has with great skill made use of the motif of 'far away from
home' for Hector, who was killed in his own homeland: he is
slain far from the comforts prepared for him by his loving
wife.[10] The manner of the poet here departs from the objective
style of pure narrative. The comment 'Fond woman, she did
not know . . .' presents her to us in a definite light and a more
explicitly pathetic tone. Such passages may be seen as standing
between the expressive manner of the reported speeches, and the
dispassionate manner of the narration.[11] The quality of Homer's
treatment can be felt when one compares it with a celebrated
passage in Thackeray, presumably derivative from it,[12] directly
or indirectly. At the end of Chapter 32 of *Vanity Fair*, the
heroine waits for her husband to come back from the field of
Waterloo: 'Darkness came down on the field and city: and
Amelia was praying for her George, who was lying on his face,
dead, with a bullet through his heart.' A reader of Homer may
feel, perhaps, that this effect seems by contrast rather crude;
partly because of the abrupt rhythm, and partly because it is
introduced as a surprise, unprepared.[13] Both features are
un-epic.

    Here we can compare, for similiarity and difference, two par-
ticular developments in the *Odyssey*, where so much continued
emphasis is laid upon Odysseus' remoteness.

[10] Schadewaldt, in discussing this scene, *Von Homers Welt und Werk*[4] (1965), 328,
speaks of Homer's 'great and simple art of contrasts'.
    [11] On the distinction of the two see H. Fränkel, *Dichtung und Philosophie*[2], 43.
    [12] Thackeray records (*The Letters and Private Papers of W. M. Thackeray*, ed.
G. N. Ray (1945), i, 207) that on 10 June 1832 he made 'a vow to read some
Homer every day'.
    [13] The motif of 'ignorance of friend's fate' is used again to great effect at 17.401,
where Achilles does not know of the death of Patroclus. On that passage a scholiast
makes the point (ΣT in 17.401): 'Homer regularly arouses sympathy in this way,
when those who are suffering great disasters are unaware of their misfortunes and
have more optimistic hopes, as with Andromache in Book 22'. Nothing of this in
Leaf; the analysts tended to reject the passage in Book 17, Ameis–Hentze pointing
out that 'its content is purely negative.' Not without provocation did Adolph
Roemer refer to 'the small race of the great analysts' (*das kleine Geschlecht der grossen
Analytiker*) (*Hom. Aufsätze* (1914), 66).

First, i.57:

αὐτὰρ Ὀδυσσεὺς
ἱέμενος καὶ καπνὸν ἀποθρῴσκοντα νοῆσαι
ἧς γαίης, θανέειν ἱμείρεται (cf. vii.224).

'But Odysseus, yearning to see even the smoke rising from his homeland, is praying for death.' The wish is touching because so modest: to glimpse his own country, even at the price of death. Second, xvii.312, Eumaeus speaks of the dog Argus: 'Too true, this dog belongs to a man who died far away.' This passage combines irony (it is to Odysseus himself that Eumaeus says this), with a certain sentimentality. The suffering of devoted dogs is beneath the notice of the *Iliad*. These two passages, chosen not quite at random from the lesser epic, seem to me to stand in the same relation to those from the *Iliad* as the one poem as a whole stands to the other. On the one hand, a simple pathos of heroic life and death; on the other, greater complexity and a nearer approach to sentimentality.[14]

In the *Iliad* another special development of the motif produces a striking and memorable passage at 3.243. Here Helen tells Priam that she cannot see the Dioscuri, her brothers, among the Achaean leaders; perhaps they keep out of sight because of the disgrace she has brought upon them;

ὣς φάτο, τοὺς δ᾽ ἤδη κάτεχεν φυσίζοος αἶα
ἐν Λακεδαίμονι αὖθι, φίλῃ ἐν πατρίδι γαίῃ.

'So she spoke, but them the life-giving earth held fast back in Sparta, in their own homeland.'

The lamented Adam Parry[15] has given this passage one of the best evaluations in the modern literature of the subject. I add only that from our present point of view we have here a case where again 'dead far away' is used of those who are dead in

---

[14] On the different ethos of the two poems see F. Jacoby, 'Die geistige Physiognomie der Odyssee', *Die Antike*, 9 (1933), 159–94 = *Kleine philologische Schriften* (1961), i, 107–39; W. Burkert, 'Das Lied von Ares und Aphrodite: Zum Verhältnis von Odyssee und Ilias', *Rh. Mus.* 103 (1960), 130–44; W. Marg, 'Zur Eigenart der Odyssee', *A und A* 18 (1973), 1–14. The *Tränenseligkeit* of the *Odyssey* is brought out, e.g., by G. Beck, 'Beobachtungen zur Kirke-Episode', *Philol.* 109 (1965), 1–30.
[15] *YCS* 20 (1966), 197 ff.

their own country. The combination of this with the motif of 'ignorance of friends' suffering' places Helen in an especially touching light.

Another sort of reversal is also possible. It is terrible to die and lie buried in a foreign land;[16] it is also terrible to see one's own country ravaged, and to be slain among its friendly scenes. The poem does not fail to include this motif.

In Book 22 the Trojans must watch from their wall the pursuit and death of Hector—as Zeus says, 22.172:

$$νῦν αὖτέ ἑ δῖος Ἀχιλλεὺς$$
$$ἄστυ περὶ Πριάμοιο ποσὶν ταχέεσσι διώκει,$$

'But now god-like Achilles is pursuing him with swift feet round the city of Priam', a passage whose effectiveness comes from the close juxtaposition of 'the city of Priam' with Achilles' pursuit of Priam's son.

As Hector runs, he passes the πλυνοί, 'the fair washing-places of stone, where the wives of the Trojans and their fair daughters used to wash their shining garments, in earlier days, in peace, before the sons of the Achaeans came'. It is hard to imagine this detail being preserved in an heroic tradition, except for emotional use in just this way: doubtless S. E. Bassett was right to see in it an invention for tragic contrast.[17] The juxtaposition of women at their household work (we think of the opening of *Odyssey* vi), and the Trojan hero hunted to death, is another supreme example of Homeric use of contrasts with emotional significance.[18] We shall have to say something of 'intrinsically symbolic' figures; this contrast, too, might claim to be one.

From the motif 'far from home' we have come to that of 'near to home', and it is a natural step to that of 'near to friends'. A series of Homeric warriors are slain close to friends who cannot help them. This of course is on a 'rational' level a natural result of the way in which fighting is presented in the *Iliad*, as duels amid a general mêlée, but it is turned to great effect for pathos.

---

[16] ἐχθρὰ δ' ἔχοντας ἔκρυψεν, Aesch. *Ag.* 454.

[17] 22.153, see p. 22 above.

[18] In the *Odyssey* the analogy, characteristically less tragic and more ironic, is the abuse of Odysseus 'in his own house'. In the end he will have his revenge, and it will not be flawed, like the revenge of Achilles.

First, a light and 'dispassionate' example: 4.522 = 13.548, a warrior falls:

> ὁ δ' ὕπτιος ἐν κονίῃσι
> κάππεσεν, ἄμφω χεῖρε φίλοις ἑτάροισι πετάσσας.

'He fell on his back in the dust, stretching out his hands to his companions.' The motif can be developed with similes. Thus at 13.653, Harpalion is brought down by a spear through the pelvis:

> ἑζόμενος δὲ κατ' αὖθι φίλων ἐν χερσὶν ἑταίρων
> θυμὸν ἀποπνείων, ὥς τε σκώληξ ἐπὶ γαίῃ
> κεῖτο ταθείς:

'He squatted down on the spot, in the arms of his comrades, and breathed out his life, lying stretched like a worm on the ground'; they remove the body, grieving; his father goes with them (658), 'shedding tears, and there was no compensation for his dead son'. Friends are powerless to help Harpalion, and also to avenge him. The treatment of the whole passage, especially the figure of the father, is an accumulation of devices of pathos, made explicit in the 'grief' of the comrades and the 'tears' of the father.

In the light of this, I think it would be wrong to read as really impassive the less explicit 4.512, or indeed 11.120.[19] Here Agamemnon kills two sons of Priam[20] and strips them of their armour (line 110), γιγνώσκων, 'recognizing them'; there follows a story to explain how he knew them; simile, lion killing fawns:

> ὡς ἄρα τοῖς οὔ τις δύνατο χραισμῆσαι ὄλεθρον
> Τρώων, ἀλλὰ καὶ αὐτοὶ ὑπ' Ἀργείοισι φέβοντο.

'So none of the Trojans could ward off destruction from them, but they too were put to flight by the Argives.' The detail of

---

[19] The scene is discussed by Schadewaldt, *Iliasstudien* (1938), 47 ff.

[20] Scholars have often been struck by the number of kinsmen of Priam who are killed in the course of the *Iliad*. Many have said simply that Trojans whose death at the hands of Achaean heroes is to be worth recording must be in some way significant, and the easiest way to confer significance upon the insignificant is to make them sons of Priam. G. Strasburger, *Die kleinen Kämpfer*, 24, suggests that, in contrast to the Achaeans, the Trojans are presented as forming a unity, embodied in the household of Priam. Aesthetically, I think the principal point is that Priam is *the* old man and father whom we see suffer in the poem (apart from the death of Hector, cf. also 22.4 ff., Priam on the deaths of his sons), and the accumulation of disasters upon him can be made visible and tangible in terms of pathos. We know Priam: other pathetic fathers are, by contrast, bloodless. And the *Iliad* is greatly interested in bereaved fathers.

Agamemnon 'recognizing' them[21] is adapted no doubt from the Lycaon-episode of Book 21.[22] As that is one of the most pathetic episodes in the whole poem, the intention here, too, is surely to produce pathos; and the simile, of a lion crunching up the helpless young of a deer, has the same tendency; finally, they die in the sight of their terrified and helpless companions.

So too 15.650, Hector kills Periphetes:

> φίλων δέ μιν ἐγγὺς ἑταίρων
> κτεῖν'· οἱ δ' οὐκ ἐδύναντο καὶ ἀχνύμενοί περ ἑταίρου
> χραισμεῖν· αὐτοὶ γὰρ μάλα δείδισαν Ἕκτορα δῖον.

'He slew him near his own comrades, but they, though grieved to the heart, could not rescue their comrade; they were themselves greatly afraid of god-like Hector.' Here the word ἀχνύμενοι, 'grieved', brings out the implicit pathos.

The motif can appear as a taunt, as at 16.837, Hector to the dying Patroclus,

> ἇ δείλ', οὐδέ τοι ἐσθλὸς ἐὼν χραίσμησεν Ἀχιλλεύς.

'Poor wretch, Achilles for all his valour did not save you.' It can be applied to a patron deity. Book 5.49:[23]

> ... υἱὸν δὲ Σκαμάνδριον, αἵμονα θήρης,
> Ἀτρεΐδης Μενέλαος ἕλ' ἔγχεϊ ὀξυόεντι,
> ἐσθλὸν θηρητῆρα, δίδαξε γὰρ Ἄρτεμις αὐτὴ ...
> ἀλλ' οὔ οἱ τότε γε χραῖσμ' Ἄρτεμις ἰοχέαιρα,
> οὐδὲ ἑκηβολίαι, ᾗσιν τὸ πρίν γ' ἐκέκαστο.

'Menelaus with sharp spear slew Strophius' son Scamandrius, the skilful hunter; Artemis herself had taught him. But now she availed him not, Artemis the archer, nor the marksmanship at which he used to excel ...'

---

[21] 'An extremely prosy addition', Platt: quoted with approval by Leaf.
[22] So Schadewaldt.
[23] The contrast with the epics of the *Cycle* is great. In the *Iliad* not only divine favourites like Scamandrius and Hector, but even a son of Zeus like Sarpedon can be killed; in the *Cycle*, immortality was distributed with lavish hand. Thus Artemis gave immortality to Iphigeneia, Eos and Thetis to their sons Memnon and Achilles, and Zeus to the Dioscuri; while Circe made all the survivors immortal, it seems, in the *Telegony* (Proclus). The *Odyssey* does not stoop to this, but flinches from the austerity of the Iliadic conception (*Odyssey* iv.561, Menelaus to be immortal); cf. J. Griffin, 'The Epic Cycle and the Uniqueness of Homer', in *JHS* 97 (1977), 39–53.

It can be used to deride a fool, as at 2.872, of the Trojan Amphimachus:

ὃς καὶ χρυσὸν ἔχων πόλεμόνδ᾽ ἴεν ἠΰτε κούρη,
νήπιος, οὐδέ τί οἱ τό γ᾽ ἐπήρκεσε λυγρὸν ὄλεθρον,
ἀλλ᾽ ἐδάμη ὑπὸ χερσὶ ποδώκεος Αἰακίδαο.

'He went to war wearing gold like a girl, the fool; that did not ward off grim death, but he was slain at the hands of the swift-footed Achilles.'

The inability of friends to help leads to the motif 'lack of care (after death)'.[24] Like all of those considered here, it can appear with very different emotional colourings.

First, as a warning: so at 18.270, Polydamas warns the Trojans not to spend the night out of the city and be caught by Achilles; otherwise

ἀσπασίως γὰρ ἀφίξεται Ἴλιον ἱρὴν
ὅς κε φύγῃ, πολλοὺς δὲ κύνες καὶ γῦπες ἔδονται
Τρώων.

'He will be glad to reach strong Troy, any who survives; but many of the men of Troy the dogs and birds will devour.'

More usually, it is a threat; either to slackers on one's own side, as at 2.393, Agamemnon: any Achaean who shirks battle,

οὔ οἱ ἔπειτα
ἄρκιον ἐσσεῖται φυγέειν κύνας ἠδ᾽ οἰωνούς.

'For him hereafter there shall be no hope of escaping the dogs and birds of prey.'

It can be a threat to the enemy; thus, Hector to Ajax, 13.831:

Τρώων κορέεις κύνας ἠδ᾽ οἰωνοὺς
δημῷ καὶ σάρκεσσι, πεσὼν ἐπὶ νηυσὶν Ἀχαιῶν.[25]

'You shall glut the dogs and birds of Troy with your fat and your flesh, falling by the Achaean ships.'

[24] The material is collected by C. P. Segal, 'The Theme of Mutilation of the Corpse', *Mnemosyne*, Suppl. 17 (1971).

[25] We find both in the Old Testament; thus God curses the Israelites in case of disobedience, Deut. 28:26: 'And your dead men shall be food to the birds of the sky and to the beasts of the earth; and there shall be none to scare them away.' In battle, Goliath to David, 1 Sam. 17:44: 'Come to me, and I will give thy flesh to the birds of the air, and to the beasts of the earth.'

The threat can be expanded by the contrast with the better treatment in store for one's own dead; so Achilles to Hector, 22.335: You thought you would get away with killing Patroclus, but I was there to avenge him:

σὲ μὲν κύνες ἠδ᾽ οἰωνοὶ
ἑλκήσουσ᾽ ἀϊκῶς, τὸν δὲ κτεριοῦσιν Ἀχαιοί.

'You shall be foully torn by dogs and birds; but for him the Achaeans shall hold funeral.'

The motif can appear in the expression of real pathos by a speaker, as at 11.814 (cf. p. 108).

It can be combined with ironical pathos to form a bitter taunt, as at 16.837 (cf. p. 114).

It can also be combined with real pathos into a passionate warning; so 22.86, Hecuba to Hector:

εἴ περ γάρ σε κατακτάνῃ, οὔ σ᾽ ἔτ᾽ ἔγωγε
κλαύσομαι ἐν λεχέεσσι, φίλον θάλος, ὃν τέκον αὐτή . . .
(but)
Ἀργείων παρὰ νηυσὶ κύνες ταχέες κατέδονται.

'If he slay you, then I shall not lament over you on a bier, my own dear child . . . by the ships of the Argives swift dogs will devour you.'

The bitter taunt can be further developed, as in the words of Achilles to Lycaon's corpse, as he throws it into the river, 21.122:

ἐνταυθοῖ νῦν κεῖσο μετ᾽ ἰχθύσιν, οἵ σ᾽ ὠτειλὴν
αἷμ᾽ ἀπολιχμήσονται ἀκηδέες, οὐδέ σε μήτηρ
ἐνθεμένη λεχέεσσι γοήσεται . . .

'Lie there among the fishes, which shall lick off the blood from your wound heedlessly. Your mother shall not lay you on a bier and mourn for you . . .', but fishes will feed on the shining fat of Lycaon. Here the special circumstances of the river battle have led to the introduction of the fishes instead of the more usual dogs and birds, and the poet has succeeded in making Achilles' taunt at least as horrific, and as memorable, as the normal form.

Later in the same book, the death of Asteropaeus is followed by the same motif in the 'dispassionate' style of narrative, 21.201 :

> τὸν δὲ κατ' αὐτόθι λεῖπεν, ἐπεὶ φίλον ἦτορ ἀπηύρα,
> κείμενον ἐν ψαμάθοισι, δίαινε δέ μιν μέλαν ὕδωρ.
> τὸν μὲν ἄρ' ἐγκέλυές τε καὶ ἰχθύες ἀμφεπένοντο,
> δημὸν ἐρεπτόμενοι ἐπινεφρίδιον κείροντες . . .

'He left him there, lying on the sand, having robbed him of life, with the dark water flooding him. About him eels and fishes were at work, tearing and gnawing the fat about his kidneys . . .'

P. Von der Mühll[26] attributes this scene to his poet B and finds it unsatisfactory; in a note he points out that eels do not really behave like this. But from our point of view the 'eels and fishes' form a counterpart to the 'dogs and birds', and the passage takes its place as a member, almost as an expected member, of a long series.

Another powerful passage is the passionate outburst of Priam to Hector, reminding him of all the horrors which will accompany the sack of Troy, 22.66:

> αὐτὸν δ' ἂν πύματόν με κύνες πρώτῃσι θύρῃσιν
> ὠμησταὶ ἐρύουσιν . . .
> οὓς τρέφον ἐν μεγάροισι τραπεζῆας θυραωρούς,
> οἵ κ' ἐμὸν αἷμα πιόντες ἀλύσσοντες περὶ θυμῷ
> κείσοντ' ἐν προθύροισι . . .

'And at last I shall myself be torn at the house door by ravening dogs . . . the dogs whom I have reared in my house, lap-dogs and watch-dogs, they shall drink my blood, maddened exceedingly, and lie in the gateway.' The nightmare vision of Priam is a development, like so many others, of our familiar epic motif, with the variant that the dogs this time are no longer unspecified pariahs, but Priam's own. Of course, those who dislike it can say it is 'late'; Homeric scholars seem to share with the poet himself the idea that earlier poets, like earlier men, were 'better' than later.[27]

---

[26] *Kritisches Hypomnema zur Ilias* (1952), 317: 'Noch hässlicher ist, was folgt . . · nach Otto Körner, *Die homerische Tierwelt* (1930), 80, geht dies, was die Aale betrifft, gegen die Naturgeschichte.' Cf. Kakridis, *Homer Revisited*, 96. Some of the ancients, too, thought Homer was infallible on every art and science; see, e.g., F. Buffière, *Les Mythes d'Homère et la pensée grecque* (1956), 10 ff.

[27] 'Here too B has attached an unseemly passage', Von der Mühll, 333. 'The gratuitous exaggeration of horror combines with other considerations . . . to stamp these lines too as not original', Leaf, 428, who at once adds that 'all these suspicions rest on somewhat general grounds', and that 'the additions . . . are skilfully made.'

These passages have mostly been in direct speech. A very important one which is not is 1.1–5:

> μῆνιν ἄειδε θεὰ Πηληϊάδεω Ἀχιλῆος
> οὐλομένην, ἣ μυρί᾽ Ἀχαιοῖς ἄλγε᾽ ἔθηκε,
> πολλὰς δ᾽ ἰφθίμους ψυχὰς Ἄϊδι προΐαψεν
> ἡρώων, αὐτοὺς δὲ ἑλώρια τεῦχε κύνεσσιν
> οἰωνοῖσί τε δαῖτα.[28]

'Sing, goddess, the wrath of Achilles Peleus' son, the accursed wrath that brought on the Achaeans countless woes, and sent down to Hades many mighty souls of heroes, giving them a prey to dogs and a feast for carrion birds.' What is the tone of this prologue? The question seems to have had little interest for recent workers;[29] and yet it must be important for the whole poem. The A and T scholia say that the poet 'has devised a tragic prologue for his tragedies', τραγῳδίαις τραγικὸν ἐξεῦρε προοίμιον, and the BT scholia say of line 3: κίνησιν οὐ τὴν τυχοῦσαν ἔχει τὸ προοίμιον, εἰ μέλλει διηγεῖσθαι θανάτους πολλῶν ἰφθίμων ἡρώων, which seems to mean, 'The proem has extraordinary emotional effect,[30] as it shows that the poem is to narrate the deaths of many mighty heroes.' Here it seems to me that the ancients are vindicated, and the silence of the moderns is to be condemned. The wrath is accursed: its result was that mighty heroes became food for scavenging dogs and birds.

We have looked at the way in which Homer has used this motif, and we have found that it is used in a whole range of emotional utterances. Can it be dispassionately used? In the prologue to Book 1 the poet is attracting the attention of his audience and showing them what the poem will be about and what it will be like. Its subject is a disastrous wrath, which leads to great Achaean losses and nearly to an Achaean defeat. It is not, and can never have been, a theme for those who simply 'like to be amused'—though such a taste might have enjoyed

---

[28] δαῖτα Zenodotus: πᾶσι codd. Cf. R. Pfeiffer, *History of Classical Scholarship*, I (1968), 111.

[29] It is not discussed in M. M. Willcock, *A Commentary on Homer's Iliad*, I–VI (1970), nor by B. A. van Groningen, 'The proems of the *Iliad* and *Odyssey*', *Meded. der kon. Ned. Ak. 9.8* (1946), nor W. Kullmann, 'Ein vorhomerisches Motiv im Iliasproömium', *Philol.* 99 (1955), 167–92.

[30] For such a sense of κίνησις (not in LSJ) cf. ΣbT in i.446 ... ἀλλ᾽ οὐδὲ τοσαύτην κίνησιν ἔχει τὰ ἡδέα λεγόμενα ὁπόσην τὰ λυπηρά.

the *Odyssey*. The audience must have accepted it, those who did accept it, as a tragic work. And the prologue announces it as such: an accursed, a hateful wrath, and great warriors lying unburied; *that* was the will of Zeus. It does not present the subject as 'ding-dong battles, hair-breadth 'scapes in th'imminent deadly breach, and a culminating victory over Hector, after which Troy is doomed'. The audience reacts to the mention of the unburied dead with emotion; there are things which cannot be said without that, as we shall see again. In conclusion, then: an example of emotional writing in the dispassionate style.[31]

Another instance of some interest, again easy to overlook, comes from 24.520. Here Achilles says to Priam, 'How could you bring yourself to come to the Achaean ships alone':

ἀνδρὸς ἐς ὀφθαλμοὺς ὅς τοι πολέας τε καὶ ἐσθλοὺς
υἱέας ἐξενάριξα; σιδήρειόν νύ τοι ἦτορ.

'face to face with a man who has slain many of your brave sons? Your heart is of iron.' It is not easy in English to express 'many brave sons of yours' without slipping out of the high style altogether. Most English translators resort to saying 'so many': thus Chapman ('How durst thy person thus alone/venture in his sight that hath slain so many a worthy son,/And so dear to thee?'), Rieu ('How could you dare to come by yourself to the Achaean ships into the presence of a man who has killed so many of your gallant sons?') and Lattimore ('I am one who has killed in such numbers/such brave sons of yours'). The introduction of 'so' makes the passage more evidently emotional ('I am *so* sorry!'), and the slight change helps to bring out the quality of the original: an apparently unemotional word, which succeeds in conveying emotional force. And fortunately in this place such a judgement on the tone cannot be dismissed as subjective, as the poet has at the beginning of Achilles' utterance made his purpose explicit, saying that

---

[31] In a modern literature one might for instance compare Thomas Nashe:
      Brightness falls from the air;
      Queens have died young and fair;
      Dust hath closed Helen's eye . . .
The affective juxtaposition of 'Helen's eye' and 'dust' is the same effect as 'mighty heroes . . . the prey of dogs and birds'.

Achilles stood up (516) οἰκτίρων, 'feeling pity', and began his speech, ἆ δειλὲ . . ., 'Ah, unhappy man . . .'

Another pair of passages shows us the double motif 'unburied, far from loved ones' developed in each of the two styles.

At 11.391 Diomede boasts, taunting Paris: Your arrows have no force to wound, but as for the man whom *I* hit:

> τοῦ δὲ γυναικὸς μέν τ' ἀμφίδρυφοί εἰσι παρειαί,
> παῖδες δ' ὀρφανικοί· ὁ δέ θ' αἵματι γαῖαν ἐρεύθων
> πύθεται, οἰωνοὶ δὲ περὶ πλέες ἠὲ γυναῖκες.

'his wife's cheeks are torn, and his children are fatherless; and he rots, reddening the earth with his blood, with more birds round him than mourning women.'

Here a horrific piece of gloating, it reappears in narrative at 11.159, where Agamemnon is pursuing the routed Trojans, constantly slaying, like a destructive forest fire:

> πολλοὶ δ' ἐριαύχενες ἵπποι
> κείν' ὄχεα κροτάλιζον ἀνὰ πτολέμοιο γεφύρας,
> ἡνιόχους ποθέοντες ἀμύμονας· οἱ δ' ἐπὶ γαίῃ
> κείατο, γύπεσσιν πολὺ φίλτεροι ἠὲ ἀλόχοισιν.

'Many strong-necked horses rattled empty chariots along the highways of battle, missing their noble drivers; but they lay on the earth, far more attractive to the vultures than to their own wives.' Why this allusion to the wives of the dead warriors? The figure of the widowed wife is used in a simile for the most uncontrollable grief at *Odyssey* viii.523 (Odysseus weeps, like a widow over the body of her husband, slain defending his city and his children: the simile is given a long development); in the *Iliad* it is embodied in Andromache. It is common in highly emotional contexts, and I think it is an idea which, even when expressed without elaborate pathos, cannot help but be emotive. We have already seen that some events in the Homeric poems have a symbolic force, like the fall from the head of Andromache, as she sees Hector dead, of the head-dress (22.468), 'which golden Aphrodite had given her, on the day when she was married from her father's house to Hector of the bright helmet'. One might perhaps call such a passage 'in-

trinsically symbolic',[32] like that in which Andromache says she
will burn Hector's clothes (22.510). They enable us to see
directly into the significance of what has happened; the meaning of Hector's death is brought out in Andromache's loss of
her wedding head-dress, and in the destruction of the clothes,
the embodiment of her wifely care of him, now over and useless.

The figure of the bereaved wife of the warrior is in an analogous way intrinsically emotional; it needs only to be named to
produce an emotional response. One can reflect that there are
many other statements of fact which, even in their simplest
form, cannot be uttered without such an effect; for example,
'Mrs X has been left a widow with a young child', or 'My
brother died as an undergraduate', or 'There is a dead body
outside in the road.' It was a regular effect of new plays in the
1960s to have such utterances received by the other characters
on the stage in an inappropriately calm or flippant or irrelevant
manner; that this produced a *frisson* in the audience was because of the breach of normal expectations. As far as poetry
goes, it appears to be the case that simplicity and brevity in
such expressions heighten their effect,[33] conveying a sort of
understatement, a noble restraint which allows the event to
speak for itself.[34] And also we see why the material of these
motifs so lends itself to treatment in different emotional modes;
it is because it is itself so highly charged with potential emotion.
The one way in which it is not possible to use it is in a really
dispassionate utterance.

The idea of the 'widowed wife and orphaned child' can form

---

[32] Cf. W. Schadewaldt, *Von Homers Welt und Werk*[4], 331: 'unwillkürliche Symbole'.

[33] Saint-Simon, *Mémoires*, ii, 48 (Bibl. de la Pléiade): 'Il est des vérités dont la
simplicité sans art jette un éclat qui efface tout le travail d'une éloquence qui
grossit ou qui pallie . . .'

[34] Two more examples:

> She's gone for ever.
> I know when one is dead and when one lives;
> She's dead as earth. (Shakespeare, *King Lear* v.iii).

> Half-owre, half-owre to Aberdour,
>   'Tis fifty fathoms deep;
> And there lies gude Sir Patrick Spens
>   Wi' the Scots lords at his feet.
>   (*Ballad of Sir Patrick Spens*).

a passionate plea to the warrior not to risk his life—6.431, Andromache to Hector:

> ἀλλ' ἄγε νῦν ἐλέαιρε καὶ αὐτοῦ μίμν' ἐπὶ πύργῳ,
> μὴ παῖδ' ὀρφανικὸν θήῃς χήρην τε γυναῖκα.

'But now come, pity me and remain here on the wall, lest you make your child an orphan and your wife a widow.' At 5.684 it was used for a different sort of plea, equally pathetic: 'since I can't go home to my wife and child, at least . . .'. But it can also be used to reinforce the opposite appeal:

15.495, Hector to the Trojans, 'Fight bravely; if a man is to die today, let him die—but his wife and children will be safe':

> τεθνάτω· οὔ οἱ ἀεικὲς ἀμυνομένῳ περὶ πάτρης
> τεθνάμεν· ἀλλ' ἄλοχός τε σόη καὶ παῖδες ὀπίσσω.

Conversely, the attackers are encouraged with the hope of making widows and orphans; 4.237, Agamemnon to his men:

> τῶν [sc. τῶν Τρώων] ἤτοι αὐτῶν τέρενα χρόα γῦπες ἔδονται,
> ἡμεῖς αὖτ' ἀλόχους τε φίλας καὶ νήπια τέκνα
> ἄξομεν ἐν νήεσσιν, ἐπὴν πτολίεθρον ἕλωμεν.

'The tender flesh of the Trojans vultures shall eat, and we shall bear away in our ships their dear wives and little children, when we have taken the citadel.' The laments of Andromache in Books 22 and 24 develop the material at length, from the point of view of pathos; and the bereaved wife is the subject of a gloating outburst of passionate hate from Achilles, 18.121:

> νῦν δὲ κλέος ἐσθλὸν ἀροίμην,
> καί τινα Τρωϊάδων καὶ Δαρδανίδων βαθυκόλπων
> ἀμφοτέρῃσιν χερσὶ παρειάων ἀπαλάων
> δάκρυ' ὀμορξαμένην ἀδινὸν στοναχῆσαι ἐφείην.

'But now let me win high glory, and let me make some Trojan woman and some deep-girdled daughter of Dardanus shriek aloud, as she wipes the tears with both hands from her soft cheeks.' An ancient scholar comments: 'He already has in view the sufferings which will ensue for the enemy and sates himself in his thoughts of vengeance.'[35]

---

[35] ΣbT in 18.121.

An even more frequent motif than the orphaned children of the slain warrior is that of his bereaved parents;[36] it is as if the warrior were thought of, at his death, as being younger than we seem to find him elsewhere, or than ten years of campaign at Troy would realistically have made him. The bereaved father is a dominant figure in the plot from Chryses to Priam, who appeals to Achilles in the name of another tragic father, Peleus; it seems natural to compare Achilles' grief for Patroclus (23.222) with that of a father mourning for his son.[37]

The motif of 'bereaved parents' appears in the taunt of a killer, 14.501, Peneleos over the body of Ilioneus:

εἰπέμεναί μοι, Τρῶες, ἀγανοῦ Ἰλιονῆος
πατρὶ φίλῳ καὶ μητρὶ γοήμεναι ἐν μεγάροισιν . . .

'Pray tell the dear parents of proud Ilioneus, you Trojans, to raise the lament in their house . . .'

We find it assuming two different colours on the lips of two opposing heroes. 17.24 ff., Menelaus to Euphorbus, is a taunt: I have killed your brother Hyperenor,

οὐδέ ἕ φημι πόδεσσί γε οἷσι κιόντα
εὐφρῆναι ἄλοχόν τε φίλην κεδνούς τε τοκῆας.
ὣς θην καὶ σὸν ἐγὼ λύσω μένος . . .

'I say he did not go home on his own feet to cheer his dear wife and his noble parents. So will I quench your spirit, too.'

In Euphorbus' reply, a threat arises from the pathos of loss, 17.34:

νῦν μὲν δή, Μενέλαε διοτρεφές, ἦ μάλα τείσεις
γνωτὸν ἐμόν, τὸν ἔπεφνες, ἐπευχόμενος δ' ἀγορεύεις,
χήρωσας δὲ γυναῖκα μυχῷ θαλάμοιο νέοιο,
ἄρρητον δὲ τοκεῦσι γόον καὶ πένθος ἔθηκας.

'Now truly, noble Menelaus, you shall pay for my brother, whom you have slain and make your boast of it; you have

---

[36] A very exaggerated statement of this in C. R. Beye, *The Iliad, the Odyssey, and the Epic Tradition* (1968), 94: 'Only the very old (and Andromache) seem to have any concern for children . . .'

[37] Cf. p. 141ff. below for the same fact in early epigrams. Croesus is made by Herodotus to say to Cyrus (1.87.4): 'Nobody is mad enough to choose war rather than peace; for in peace sons bury their fathers, but in war fathers bury their sons.' There is a proverbial ring to this saying.

widowed his wife in her new bridal chamber, and brought un-
utterable woe and lamentation to his parents; I shall console
them if I slay you.' We observe that the wife is in her 'new'
house: that is, she is a young bride, for the obvious reason that
her bereavement is thus more touching.

At 17.300 we had an example of 'obituary' in the dispassionate style, which followed the motif of 'death far from
home' with that of 'short life and bereaved parents'. The
combination is developed more fully and pathetically at 5.152
ff., the two sons of Phaenops slain by Diomede:

> βῆ δὲ μετὰ Ξάνθον τε Θόωνά τε, Φαίνοπος υἷε,
> ἄμφω τηλυγέτω· ὁ δὲ τείρετο γήραϊ λυγρῷ,
> υἱὸν δ' οὐ τέκετ' ἄλλον ἐπὶ κτεάτεσσι λιπέσθαι.
> ἔνθ' ὅ γε τοὺς ἐνάριζε, φίλον δ' ἐξαίνυτο θυμὸν
> ἀμφοτέρω, πατέρι δὲ γόον καὶ κήδεα λυγρὰ
> λεῖπ', ἐπεὶ οὐ ζώοντε μάχης ἒκ νοστήσαντε[38]
> δέξατο· χηρωσταὶ δὲ διὰ κτῆσιν δατέοντο.

'He went after Xanthus and Thoon, sons of Phaenops, both
last-born; their father was worn with cruel age, and he had no
other sons for his possessions after him. Then Diomede slew
them and robbed them of their lives, both of them; to their
father he left lamentation and bitter grief, for he received them
not alive returning from battle, and distant kin divided his
estate.' Eustathius comments: 'The account is emotional,'
(533.28). We observe here that the sons barely exist at all, and
that the epithets applied to them ('sons of Phaenops', 'both
last-born')[39] relate entirely to their relationship with their
father. His feelings are the real subject of interest, and every
device is used to increase their bitterness. As with Harpalion's
father,

> μετὰ δέ σφι πατὴρ κίε δάκρυα λείβων,
> ποινὴ δ' οὔτις παιδὸς ἐγίγνετο τεθνηῶτος—

---

[38] μάχης ἒκ νοστήσαντα is used four times; revealingly, always of *failure* to
return from battle. All the other three passages refer to Hector: 17.207, 22.444,
24.705.

[39] This use of τηλύγετος of more than one son is peculiar: 'perhaps twins', says
LSJ, as if the poet had in mind a real family tree, beyond what he says in this
passage, which could be reconstructed by us by conjecture. I suppose the usage
has arisen from the desire to combine two pathetic motifs: 'the only child' and
'two sons lost at one blow'. The poet is not innocent of exaggeration.

'the father went with them, weeping; but there was no compensation for his dead son', so here pathos is the explanation of the development.

If a father can be bereaved, then we wonder how he tried to take care of his son. He can be prophetic, and foresee their doom; 11.328, Diomede and Odysseus slay the two sons of Merops:

> ἔνθ' ἑλέτην . . .
> υἷε δύω Μέροπος Περκωσίου, ὃς περὶ πάντων
> ᾔδεε μαντοσύνας, οὐδὲ οὓς παῖδας ἔασκε
> στείχειν ἐς πόλεμον φθισήνορα· τὼ δέ οἱ οὔ τι
> πειθέσθην· κῆρες γὰρ ἄγον μέλανος θανάτοιο.

'Then they slew . . . the two sons of Merops of Percote, who above all men was skilled in soothsaying. He tried to prevent his sons from going to murderous war, but they disobeyed him; the fates of black death were leading them on.' Here the force of the motif is that his foresight was vain, destiny doomed his sons; again the focus of interest is upon the absent and suffering father.

Or a father may doom his son through his own reckless wrongdoing, 5.59:

> Μηριόνης δὲ Φέρεκλον ἐνήρατο, τέκτονος υἱὸν
> Ἁρμονίδεω, ὃς χερσὶν ἐπίστατο δαίδαλα πάντα
> τεύχειν . . .
> ὃς καὶ Ἀλεξάνδρῳ τεκτήνατο νῆας ἐίσας
> ἀρχεκάκους, αἳ πᾶσι κακὸν Τρώεσσι γένοντο
> οἷ τ' αὐτῷ, ἐπεὶ οὔ τι θεῶν ἐκ θέσφατα ᾔδη.

'Meriones slew Phereclus, the son of the craftsman Harmonides, who was skilled to make all manner of works of craft . . . He it was who built for Paris the trim ships, the source of woe, which were the bane of all the Trojans and of himself, for he knew not the oracles of heaven.' Again the father predominates; again the impression is of human folly and helplessness in the face of destiny.

A father may fail to be prophetic when he should be. 5.149, the two sons of Eurydamas the interpreter of dreams are slain by Diomede:

νἱέας Εὐρυδάμαντος, ὀνειροπόλοιο γέροντος·
τοῖς οὐκ ἐρχομένοις ὁ γέρων ἐκρίνατ' ὀνείρους,
ἀλλά σφεας κρατερὸς Διομήδης ἐξενάριξε.

'The sons of Eurydamas, old interpreter of dreams; for them the old man discerned no dreams when they went, but strong Diomede despoiled them.' Again, we learn nothing of these men but the pathetic ignorance of their father, who should have known their fate.

A father may be careful of his son, but of course in vain. 20.408, Achilles kills Polydorus, Priam's son:

τὸν δ' οὔ τι πατὴρ εἴασκε μάχεσθαι,
οὕνεκά οἱ μετὰ παισὶ νεώτατος ἔσκε γόνοιο,
καί οἱ φίλτατος ἔσκε, πόδεσσι δὲ πάντας ἐνίκα·
δὴ τότε νηπιέῃσι ποδῶν ἀρετὴν ἀναφαίνων
θῦνε διὰ προμάχων, ἧος φίλον ὤλεσε θυμόν.

'His father tried to keep him from fighting, because among his children he was the youngest born and best beloved; he outstripped all in swiftness of foot. Just then in youthful folly, showing off his swift running, he was racing through the front ranks until he lost his life.' The rare noun νηπιέη, 'youthful folly', replaces the commoner νήπιος ὅς, 'the fool, who ...', always said by the poet with emotion, whether pity or derision; Priam is an important character, whose function is to lose his sons and lament over them, 24.255,

ὤμοι ἐγὼ πανάποτμος, ἐπεὶ τέκον υἷας ἀρίστους
Τροίῃ ἐν εὐρείῃ, τῶν δ' οὔ τινά φημι λελεῖφθαι,

'Woe is me, altogether unhappy; I had sons, the best men in Troy, and not one of them, I say, is left.' Polydorus exists only for this effect of his death on Priam and on Hector.

Less obvious is the allusion at 17.194. Hector puts on the armour of Achilles:

ἅ οἱ θεοὶ οὐρανίωνες
πατρὶ φίλῳ ἔπορον. ὁ δ' ἄρα ᾧ παιδὶ ὄπασσε
γηράς· ἀλλ' οὐχ υἱὸς ἐν ἔντεσι πατρὸς ἐγήρα,

'which the heavenly gods had given to his father. He when he grew old gave it to his son; but the son did not grow old in his father's armour.' Of this passage, the ancient scholars say 'It is poignant and pathetic that the son should be less fortunate than the father.' Von der Mühll,[40] on the other hand, finds it 'sentimental and in poor taste', and supposes that 'the poet imitates the tragic tone of Homer.' Tastes vary, and I find this passage a touching and effective one. As for 'sentimentality', 15.705 above seems to me exactly comparable (the ship which brought Protesilaus, but did not take him home), on which Von der Mühll says 'this passage must be old.'[41]

The more sentimental manner of the *Odyssey*, which likes to look back with a nostalgic tenderness on the heroic sufferings of the past, is well exemplified by Nestor's words at iii.108, of Troy:

> ἔνθα δ' ἔπειτα κατέκταθεν ὅσσοι ἄριστοι·
> ἔνθα μὲν Αἴας κεῖται ἀρήιος, ἔνθα δ' Ἀχιλλεύς,
> ἔνθα δὲ Πάτροκλος, θεόφιν μήστωρ ἀτάλαντος,
> ἔνθα δ' ἐμὸς φίλος υἱὸς . . .

'There all the best of us then were slain; there lies warlike Ajax, there Achilles, there Patroclus, god-like in counsel, and there lies my dear son . . .' The lapidary style of the *Iliad* is softened: 'all the best of us' were killed there (compare the lament of Menelaus, *Odyssey* iv.95 ff.), and the speaker dwells lovingly on their names, ending with 'my dear son'. 'Extremely pathetic', observe the Scholia—a different pathos from that of the greater epic.

So much for the bereaved fathers in the background of the poem. The *Iliad* is composed of small units which have the same nature as the large ones, it seems, when we reflect on the unhappy fathers in the foreground of the plot. That is confirmed by the use of another motif, not capable of being sharply distinguished from the last: that of 'short life'. Sometimes the emphasis is rather on the short life of the hero than on the grief of his family; above all, with Achilles. His early doom is, of course, another subject which cannot be mentioned without emotion.

Thus at its first appearance, 1.352, Achilles, weeping and alone, gazing out over the sea, calls:

> μῆτερ, ἐπεί μ' ἔτεκές γε μινυνθάδιόν περ ἐόντα . . .

---

[40] *Kritisches Hypomnema zur Ilias*, 258.
[41] On 15.705, see above, p. 109; Von der Mühll, 236, 'Dies wird hier alt sein.'

'Mother, since you bore me, short though my life is . . .', and his mother replies weeping, 1.413:

> ὦ μοι τέκνον ἐμόν, τί νύ σ' ἔτρεφον αἰνὰ τεκοῦσα;
> αἴθ' ὄφελες παρὰ νηυσὶν ἀδάκρυτος καὶ ἀπήμων
> ἧσθαι, ἐπεί νύ τοι αἶσα μίνυνθά περ, οὔ τι μάλα δήν.
> νῦν δ' ἅμα τ' ὠκύμορος καὶ ὀϊζυρὸς περὶ πάντων
> ἔπλεο.

'Alas, my child, why did I bear you, wretched in my motherhood? Would that you might sit by the ships without tears and suffering, since your destiny is very brief; but now you are both short-lived and also unhappy beyond all men . . .' And it is important for the last book, too, that Achilles is near his death; 24.540, Peleus, too, is unlucky:

> ἕνα παῖδα τέκεν παναώριον . . .

'He begat one son, to a most untimely death.'

There is no need to expand on the destiny of Achilles, but others too are presented in the same light. At 15.610 Zeus aids Hector:

> αὐτὸς γάρ οἱ ἀπ' αἰθέρος ἦεν ἀμύντωρ
> Ζεύς, ὅς μιν πλεόνεσσι μετ' ἀνδράσι μοῦνον ἐόντα
> τίμα καὶ κύδαινε· μινυνθάδιος γὰρ ἔμελλεν
> ἔσσεσθ'· ἤδη γάρ οἱ ἐπόρνυε μόρσιμον ἦμαρ
> Παλλὰς Ἀθηναίη ὑπὸ Πηλεΐδαο βίηφιν.[42]

'For Zeus out of heaven was his helper and gave him honour and glory, one man against many, for his life was to be short; already Pallas Athena was stirring up his day of destiny at the mighty hands of Achilles.' This is a statement of fact: Zeus is helping Hector, and his death is near. But the effect is to make us see Hector as a doomed man, to see him as he appears in the perspective of Zeus. We feel the pathos of Hector's delusive triumphs, as we feel that of Achilles' early death; and Schadewaldt[43] is right to emphasize that Zeus 'loves' Hector because his death is near.

[42] Most editors have followed the Alexandrians in rejecting these lines (see Leaf ad loc.). There are real difficulties, but the *emotional* effect is, I think, in accord with the others discussed here.

[43] *Iliasstudien*, 107 ff. The reason for giving concrete honour to his corpse is his sacrifices (24.67 ff.), but the account of his death shows him lifted up and divinely favoured, to contrast most tellingly with his end.

From our present point of view it is interesting that Zeus himself expresses the very thought here cast in the narrative form. 17.200, seeing Hector put on the armour of Achilles, Zeus:

> κινήσας ῥα κάρη προτὶ ὃν μυθήσατο θυμόν·
> 'ἆ δείλ', οὐδέ τί τοι θάνατος καταθύμιός ἐστιν,
> ὃς δή τοι σχεδὸν εἶσι, σὺ δ' ἄμβροτα τεύχεα δύνεις
> ἀνδρὸς ἀριστῆος, τόν τε τρομέουσι καὶ ἄλλοι.
> τοῦ δὴ ἑταῖρον ἔπεφνες ἐνηέα τε κρατερόν τε,
> τεύχεα δ' οὐ κατὰ κόσμον ἀπὸ κρατός τε καὶ ὤμων
> εἴλευ· ἀτάρ τοι νῦν γε μέγα κράτος ἐγγυαλίξω,
> τῶν ποινὴν ὅ τοι οὔ τι μάχης ἐκ νοστήσαντι
> δέξεται Ἀνδρομάχη κλυτὰ τεύχεα Πηλεΐωνος.'

'Shaking his head he spoke to his own heart: "Ah, poor man, and you have no thought for death, which is coming close to you; you are putting on the immortal armour of a champion of whom all men else are afraid. His comrade, gentle and brave, you have slain, and stripped the armour from his head and shoulders, as you should not. Yet now I shall grant you great might, in recompense because Andromache shall never receive from you, as you come from battle, the famous armour of Achilles." ' This impressive speech (it, too, is for Von der Mühll 'sentimental and in poor taste'), combines the motifs of 'short life', 'pathetic ignorance', and 'no return home'. It represents in fact what might be called the austere pathos of heaven; in contrast, the passionate pathos of earth is exemplified by Andromache's lament over Hector's body, 24.723:[44]

> τῇσιν δ' Ἀνδρομάχη λευκώλενος ἦρχε γόοιο
> Ἕκτορος ἀνδροφόνοιο κάρη μετὰ χερσὶν ἔχουσα·
> 'ἆνερ, ἀπ' αἰῶνος νέος ὤλεο, κὰδ δέ με χήρην
> λείπεις ἐν μεγάροισι· πάϊς δ' ἔτι νήπιος αὔτως
> ὃν τέκομεν σύ τ' ἐγώ τε δυσάμμοροι...'

'Among them white-armed Andromache raised the lament,

----

[44] Well discussed by K. Deichgräber, *Der letzte Gesang der Ilias*, SB Mainz, 1972, 118 ff.

holding in her arms the head of man-slaying Hector: "My husband, you have lost your life young, leaving me a widow in your house, and our son is still a little child, born of two unhappy parents ..." '

These last three passages form an ascending scale of pathos. First, the objective manner in which the poet in his own narration conveys his sense of tragedy, then the perspective of Zeus, in which human suffering is touching but not shattering, and finally the view of the human victim whose life is destroyed.

There are other important passages in which the divine perspective is conveyed in a 'dispassionate' tone, and they are important for the poem.

At 15.361 Apollo clears the way for the triumphant Trojans into the Achaean camp, kicking down for them the wall erected so laboriously in Book 8:

> ἔρειπε δὲ τεῖχος Ἀχαιῶν
> ῥεῖα μάλ', ὡς ὅτε τις ψάμαθον πάϊς ἄγχι θαλάσσης,
> ὅς τ' ἐπεὶ οὖν ποιήσῃ ἀθύρματα νηπιέῃσιν
> ἂψ αὖτις συνέχευε ποσὶν καὶ χερσὶν ἀθύρων,
> ὥς ῥα σύ, ἤϊε Φοῖβε, πολὺν κάματον καὶ ὀϊζὺν
> σύγχεας Ἀργείων, αὐτοῖσι δὲ φύζαν ἐνῶρσας.

'He cast down the Achaean wall most easily, like a boy playing in the sand by the sea, who makes castles in the sand in his childish play and then in sport destroys them with hands and feet. Even so did you, archer Apollo, destroy the long toil and labour of the Argives, and arouse panic fear among them.' I point particularly to the phrase πολὺν κάματον καὶ ὀϊζὺν Ἀργείων: much toil and labour of the Argives, destroyed by Apollo easily, as a child destroys a sand-castle. The juxtaposition is an eloquent one, and conveys the poet's sense of the pathos of vain human effort, and also the divine scale, on which nothing achieved or endured by men can be really serious.[45]

A second similar passage is the opening of Book 13. At the end of Book 12, Hector has smashed his way into the Achaean camp, his eyes flashing fire,

---

[45] See H. Fränkel, *Dichtung und Philosophie*², 60; W. F. Otto, *The Homeric Gods* (Eng. trans.), 241 ff.

ὅμαδος δ' ἀλίαστος ἐτύχθη.
Ζεὺς δ' ἐπεὶ οὖν Τρῶάς τε καὶ Ἕκτορα νηυσὶ πέλασσε,
τοὺς μὲν ἔα παρὰ τῇσι πόνον τ' ἐχέμεν καὶ ὀϊζὺν
νωλεμέως, αὐτὸς δὲ πάλιν τρέπεν ὄσσε φαεινώ,
νόσφιν ἐφ' ἱπποπόλων Θρῃκῶν καθορώμενος αἶαν ...
ἐς Τροίην δ' οὐ πάμπαν ἔτι τρέπεν ὄσσε φαεινώ.

'A din unceasing arose. Now Zeus, when he had brought the
Trojans and Hector to the ships, left them to undergo pain and
labour there continually; and he turned away his shining
eyes,[46] gazing far off upon the land of the Thracians, breeders
of horses ... to Troy he turned no more his shining eyes.'
Here again the same contrast: the unperturbed superiority of
the gods 'who live at ease', in contrast with the suffering of
earth. Zeus 'turns away his shining eyes', and leaves the men to
their unending labour and pain. And the phrase 'to undergo
pain and labour continually' admirably exemplifies the emotive
use of factual words.[47]

The ascending scale of pathos can be found again with the
motif 'the young husband slain'. We have observed that the
Homeric warrior is characteristically seen as young, and that
the widowed wife is a natural figure of Homeric pathos. A
pathos still more intense is produced by combining the two
ideas.

First, the idea of 'bridegroom' used as a bitter taunt, 13.381.
The boastful Othryoneus had offered to drive the Achaeans
from Troy, in exchange for the hand of a daughter of Priam
free of bride-price. He is slain by Idomeneus, who exults over
his body:

ἀλλ' ἔπε', ὄφρ' ἐπὶ νηυσὶ συνώμεθα ποντοπόροισιν
ἀμφὶ γάμῳ (dragging away his corpse).

'Nay, come with me, that we may make a covenant by the sea-
going ships about your marriage ...'

[46] See below, p. 197.
[47] Those scholars who notice the passage are not much impressed by it. C.
Michel, Erläuterungen zum N der Ilias (1971), 30, is content to quote with approval
the 'recognition by earlier scholars' that it is 'an all too transparently invented
device', with no other point than to leave freedom of manoeuvre to Poseidon.
Ameis–Hentze (Anhang, 10) go so far as to say that 'the poet's lack of skill could
not betray itself more clearly than in this inept invention ...'

Next a passage whose pathos is implicit only. 13.428, the slaying of Alcathous:

> γαμβρὸς δ' ἦν Ἀγχίσαο,
> πρεσβυτάτην δ' ὤπυιε θυγατρῶν, Ἱπποδάμειαν,
> τὴν περὶ κῆρι φίλησε πατὴρ καὶ πότνια μήτηρ.

'He was son-in-law to Anchises, and had married Hipodameia, the eldest of his daughters, whom her father and her lady mother loved best.' The addition of the last line (she was the *favourite* daughter), brings out the grief which will be felt at her husband's death; just as at 5.152 ff. both sons were 'last-born', to increase the father's suffering.

A little more explicit is 13.171, the death of Imbrius:

> ναῖε δὲ Πήδαιον πρὶν ἐλθεῖν υἷας Ἀχαιῶν,
> κούρην δὲ Πριάμοιο νόθην ἔχε Μηδεσικάστην.
> αὐτὰρ ἐπεὶ Δαναῶν νέες ἤλυθον ἀμφιέλισσαι,
> ἂψ εἰς Ἴλιον ἦλθε, μετέπρεπε δὲ Τρώεσσι,
> ναῖε δὲ πὰρ Πριάμῳ· ὁ δέ μιν τίεν ἶσα τέκεσσι.

'He lived in Pedaeum before the sons of the Achaeans came, and he was married to a daughter of Priam, born out of wedlock, Medesicaste; but when the curved ships of the Danaans came, he went back to Troy and was foremost among the Trojans. He lived with Priam, who honoured him like his own sons.' Slain by Ajax, he falls like an ash tree, felled upon a mountain, which

> χαλκῷ ταμνομένη τέρενα χθονὶ φύλλα πελάσσῃ,

'smitten with the axe brings its delicate leaves to the ground'. Eustathius, quoting lost predecessors, says: 'The comparison is emotional, and the poet speaks as though he sympathized with the tree: so say older writers.'[48] The whole account of Imbrius' death is so constructed as to place the emphasis first on his family relationships (almost a son to Priam), and secondly on his fall, like a tree whose 'delicate leaves' are brought to the ground.[49]

The next stage is represented by the mention of Protesilaus in the Catalogue, 2.698 ff.; as for the men from Phylace,

[48] Eustath. 926.54.
[49] Cf. M.-L. von Franz, *Die aesthetischen Anschauungen der Iliasscholien*, 34.

τῶν αὖ Πρωτεσίλαος ἀρήιος ἡγεμόνευε
ζωὸς ἐών· τότε δ' ἤδη ἔχεν κάτα γαῖα μέλαινα.
700 τοῦ δὲ καὶ ἀμφιδρυφὴς ἄλοχος Φυλάκῃ ἐλέλειπτο
καὶ δόμος ἡμιτελής· τὸν δ' ἔκτανε Δάρδανος ἀνὴρ
νηὸς ἀποθρώσκοντα πολὺ πρώτιστον Ἀχαιῶν.
οὐδὲ μὲν οὐδ' οἳ ἄναρχοι ἔσαν, πόθεόν γε μὲν ἀρχόν ...
708 ... οὐδέ τι λαοὶ
δεύονθ' ἡγεμόνος, πόθεόν γε μὲν ἐσθλόν ἐόντα.

'Of these was war-like Protesilaus leader, while he lived; but he now was held by the black earth. His wife, her cheeks torn in mourning, was left in Phylace, and his house half-built; a Dardanian warrior slew him as he leapt from his ship, first of the Achaeans by far. Not that they were leaderless, though they sorrowed for their leader ... Yet did the host not lack a leader, only they sorrowed for the noble dead.' His house was unfinished, therefore he was newly married; he was the first to leap ashore, therefore a true hero. His wife tore her cheeks in mourning for him, and his men missed him, under the command of another. This last point is repeated. For the ancient commentators this was beautiful and pathetic; for the analysts it is a blemish ('nothing more than a stop-gap', Jachmann;[50] '708–9 look like a gloss ... filled up from previous lines so as to make two hexameters', Leaf) and suggest un-Homeric authorship. The neatness with which the passage fits in with our others is striking,[51] and some will continue to find it moving, as the ancients did. Especially noteworthy is the prevalence, in so fully amplified a passage, of implicit over explicit pathos.

The series is concluded by Iphidamas. At 11.221 ff. we are given an account of his upbringing and marriage; at 11.241 he is slain by Agamemnon:

ὣς ὁ μὲν αὖθι πεσὼν κοιμήσατο χάλκεον ὕπνον
οἰκτρός, ἀπὸ μνηστῆς ἀλόχου, ἀστοῖσιν ἀρήγων,
κουριδίης, τῆς οὔ τι χάριν ἴδε, πολλὰ δ' ἔδωκε ...

---

[50] 'By the repetition he has made the pathos more moving', Σb. Contra, G. Jachmann, Der homerische Schiffskatalog und die Ilias (1958), 118 ff. He will not allow that the passage is the work of 'a poet' at all.
[51] The phrase Δάρδανος ἀνήρ for the slayer of Protesilaus is certainly odd; heroes are not normally slain by nameless persons. Perhaps it was the peculiar bitterness of Protesilaus' fate, foretold by an oracle, to be killed by an unknown hand?

'So there he fell and slept a sleep of bronze, pitiable man, far from his wedded wife, helping his people—far from his bride, of whom he had known no joy, and much he had given to get her ...' The particular interest of this passage is the explicit epithet οἰκτρός 'pitiable';[52] the poet himself gives utterance to the pity he feels for the unlucky young husband.

As we look back over the last series, can we find a point where dispassionate objectivity gives place to the expression of sympathy and pathos? Does it not rather appear that even the first of them, the account of Alcathous' death, is so presented as to have a pathetic colouring? Perhaps this is confirmed by 23.222; Achilles at the funeral of Patroclus:

> ὡς δὲ πατὴρ οὗ παιδὸς ὀδύρεται ὀστέα καίων,
> νυμφίου, ὅς τε θανὼν δειλοὺς ἀκάχησε τοκῆας,
> ὡς Ἀχιλεὺς ἑτάροιο ὀδύρετο ὀστέα καίων.

'As a father laments when he burns the bones of his son, newly married, whose death has broken the hearts of his parents, so did Achilles lament as he burnt the bones of his comrade.' This simile, which exists to convey the emotion of passionate grief, singles out the death of the newly married son as the most heartbreaking of all deaths; to present the slaying of warriors in that light is to present it in its most pitiful aspect.

A last series completes this argument. It is a little more complex but of the same character. The motif is 'beauty brought low'. It has already played a part in some of the passages we have discussed; see 16.775, 11.391, 11.159.

First, an example in the 'dispassionate' manner. At 13.578, Helenus slays Deipyrus, whose helmet rolls in the dust:

> ἡ μὲν ἀποπλαγχθεῖσα χαμαὶ πέσε, καί τις Ἀχαιῶν
> μαρναμένων μετὰ ποσσὶ κυλινδομένην ἐκόμισσε·
> τὸν δὲ κατ' ὀφθαλμῶν ἐρεβεννὴ νὺξ ἐκάλυψεν.

'Dislodged, it fell to the earth, and one of the Achaeans picked it up as it rolled between his feet. But dark night covered the eyes of Deipyrus.' This is not far removed from grim passages where a head (13.202) or a limbless trunk (11.145) is sent rolling through the battle, and though it is perceptibly 'emotional' it is not so clear what the emotion is.

---

[52] 'He says this sympathetically', ΣT in 11.243.

This is clearer with 15.537, where Meges lops off the plume from the helmet of Dolops:

ῥῆξε δ' ἀφ' ἵππειον λόφον αὐτοῦ, πᾶς δὲ χαμᾶζε
κάππεσεν ἐν κονίῃσι νέον φοίνικι φαεινός.
ἦος ὁ τῷ πολέμιζε μένων, ἔτι δ' ἔλπετο νίκην . . .

'He broke off his horse-hair plume, and it fell in the dust, newly shining with its crimson dye. Now while he still fought on and hoped for victory . . .' (Menelaus slew him from behind). That the detail of the plume, resplendent with new colour and fallen to the earth, is indeed pathetic, is strongly suggested by the next lines; 'he still fought hopefully on', but at once was slain. The pathos is, however, coloured with irony at Dolops' expense.

More emphatic is 17.51, the death of Euphorbus:

αἵματί οἱ δεύοντο κόμαι Χαρίτεσσιν ὁμοῖαι
πλοχμοί θ', οἳ χρυσῷ τε καὶ ἀργύρῳ ἐσφήκωντο.

'Blood soaked his hair that was like the hair of the Graces, and the love-locks tightly bound with gold and silver.' As a cherished olive plant, protected and in flower, is uprooted by a storm and lies stretched on the ground: so did Euphorbus fall and lie. The simile is a developed and pathetic one, related to that which Thetis applies to her own cherished son (18.56); the flowers on the sapling recall Euphorbus' hair, and the care lavished on the plant reminds the reader of what he had been told (17.36 ff.) of Euphorbus' mourning parents. Eustathius rightly observes, 'the poet pities him as he lies on the earth',[53] for the whole account of the death is strongly pathetic in colour.

Related is the description of Achilles' horses mourning the death of Patroclus, 17.437.[54] They stood motionless, like images on a grave:

οὔδει ἐνισκίμψαντε καρήατα· δάκρυα δέ σφι
θερμὰ κατὰ βλεφάρων χαμάδις ῥέε μυρομένοισιν
ἡνιόχοιο πόθῳ· θαλερὴ δ' ἐμιαίνετο χαίτη
ζεύγλης ἐξεριποῦσα παρὰ ζυγὸν ἀμφοτέρωθεν.
μυρομένω δ' ἄρα τώ γε ἰδὼν ἐλέησε Κρονίων,
κινήσας δὲ κάρη προτὶ ὃν μυθήσατο θυμόν·
'ἆ δειλώ . . .'

---

[53] Eustath. 1904.38, οἰκτείρει χαμαὶ κείμενον.
[54] Cf. 11.159.

'... abasing their heads to the ground. Hot tears flowed from
their eyes to the earth as they mourned for the driver they
missed, and their rich manes were soiled as they drooped from
beneath the yoke-cushion on either side of the yoke. The son of
Cronos felt pity for them as he saw them mourning, and he
shook his head and said, "Alas, unlucky pair ..." ' The grief
of the immortal horses, which moves the pity of Zeus, finds expression in the soiling of their manes. We find other passages
where beauty is mentioned only when it is spoiled or defiled.
Briseis, lamenting over Patroclus' corpse, tears 'her breast and
tender neck and lovely face'.[55] The lines which follow the
motif have been quoted because they make explicit the pathos
which is to be felt in the passage as a whole.

That fine passage is excelled by the next, 16.793. Apollo
strikes Patroclus with the flat of his hand,[56] and his armour falls
from him:

> τοῦ δ' ἀπὸ μὲν κρατὸς κυνέην βάλε Φοῖβος Ἀπόλλων·
> ἡ δὲ κυλινδομένη καναχὴν ἔχε ποσσὶν ὑφ' ἵππων
> 795 αὐλῶπις τρυφάλεια, μιάνθησαν δὲ ἔθειραι
> αἵματι καὶ κονίῃσι· πάρος γε μὲν οὐ θέμις ἦεν
> ἱππόκομον πήληκα μιαίνεσθαι κονίῃσιν,
> ἀλλ' ἀνδρὸς θείοιο κάρη χαρίεν τε μέτωπον
> ῥύετ' Ἀχιλλῆος· τότε δὲ Ζεὺς Ἕκτορι δῶκεν
> 800 ᾗ κεφαλῇ φορέειν, σχεδόθεν δέ οἱ ἦεν ὄλεθρος.

'And from his head Phoebus Apollo smote his helmet, which
went rattling away with a din beneath the hooves of the horses,
the helmet with upright socket, and the crest was defiled with
blood and dust. In former time it was never suffered that the
helmet with its horsehair plume should be defiled in the dust;
no, it defended the head and comely face of a man divine, even
Achilles. But then Zeus gave it to Hector to wear on his head;
and his destruction was near at hand.' This is great poetry, and
it combines a number of our motifs. The fall of the helmet in
the dust is made almost more moving than Patroclus' death
itself. The contrast of *now* and *then*, the helmet on the head of
the splendid hero and its degradation in the dirt, is completed

[55] 19.285, cf. ΣT in 19.282-302, 'What pathetic feeling can she fail to arouse,
uttering pitiful words, shedding tears, and maiming the most beautiful parts of her
body?' See also F. Wehrli in *Gnomon*, 28 (1956), 577.

[56] Cf. 15.361 for the contrast of the effortless action of the god and the catastrophe
it produces for man.

by the statement that Hector, too, did he but know it, is also marked for death. In his human ignorance of destiny he embraces his doom.[57] This series will be completed by 22.401 below; but first two other passages call for comment, which present the motif in the developed form, 'unrecognizable in death and mutilation'. At 16.638 battle rages over the body of Sarpedon:

οὐδ' ἂν ἔτι φράδμων περ ἀνὴρ Σαρπήδονα δῖον
ἔγνω, ἐπεὶ βελέεσσι καὶ αἵματι καὶ κονίῃσιν
ἐκ κεφαλῆς εἴλυτο διαμπερὲς ἐς πόδας ἄκρους.

'And now not even a clear-sighted man could have recognized god-like Sarpedon, for with spears and blood and dust he was covered wholly, from head to foot.' We feel the horror of this description, especially of so attractive a character as Sarpedon: if we need reassurance of the correctness of our perception, it is provided by the importance given to the preservation of Hector's corpse in Book 24.

In 7.421 ff., the dead are collected and burned.[58] In the early morning both sides set about the grim task:

οἱ δ' ἤντεον ἀλλήλοισιν.
ἔνθα διαγνῶναι χαλεπῶς ἦν ἄνδρα ἕκαστον,
ἀλλ' ὕδατι νίζοντες ἄπο βρότον αἱματόεντα,
δάκρυα θερμὰ χέοντες, ἀμαξάων ἐπάειραν,
οὐδ' εἴα κλαίειν Πρίαμος μέγας· οἱ δὲ σιωπῇ
νεκροὺς πυρκαϊῆς ἐπενήνεον ἀχνύμενοι κῆρ.

'The two sides met. Then it was hard to recognize each man, but they washed off the clotted blood and, shedding hot tears, loaded them on to waggons. But great Priam had forbidden them to wail aloud, so they heaped them on the pyre in silence, grieving at heart.' This is another passage which fared better at the hands of ancient than modern criticism. Eustathius says 'The action is pathetic.'[59] The pathos is that of the lesser warriors, of those whose bodies are not rescued by heroic companions but allowed to lie all night disregarded (8.491 =

---

[57] Analysis can find no better words for the passage than 'Überdichtung', and 'ein Zusatz von B' (Von der Mühll, ad loc.).
[58] A 'late insertion', according, e.g. to Wilamowitz, Glaube der Hellenen², i, 299.
[59] Eustath. 688.65.

10.199), driven over by chariot wheels (11.537, 20.501), and eaten by scavengers (1. *init.*).

These last two examples bring out the truth of the dictum of W. Marg,[60] that the *Iliad* is a poem of death rather than of fighting. The subject of the poem is life and death, contrasted with the greatest possible sharpness. Alive, a hero; dead, a mindless ghost and a corpse not even recognizable, unless the gods will miraculously intervene.

This scale of pathos is concluded by 22.401. Hector's body is dragged behind Achilles' chariot:

τοῦ δ᾽ ἦν ἑλκομένοιο κονίσαλος, ἀμφὶ δὲ χαῖται
κυάνεαι πίτναντο, κάρη δ᾽ ἅπαν ἐν κονίῃσι
κεῖτο πάρος χαρίεν· τότε δὲ Ζεὺς δυσμενέεσσι
δῶκεν ἀεικίσσασθαι ἑῇ ἐν πατρίδι γαίῃ.

'And as he was dragged a cloud of dust arose, and his dark hair spread loose, and in the dust lay all his head that before was comely; now Zeus had given him over to his enemies to outrage him in his own homeland.' Homeric pathos can go no further than this. Zeus, who 'loved' Hector and glorified him in his triumphs, has now brought him down as far as a man can fall. The motif 'beauty brought low' is combined with that of 'suffering in one's own country'. The bitterness of the ill-treatment of Hector's head, 'which before was comely', is increased by his enemy having power to inflict it in his own fatherland, before the eyes of his own people. It is a triumph of the Homeric style and its control that all this weight of feeling can be contained in four lines; and lines which still admit, at one level, of being described as 'objective'.

This investigation has had two purposes. One has been to show how pervasive in the *Iliad* is the expression of pathos. The poem opens with the tears of Chryses and ends with a book devoted to lamentation. The tragedy of human life is brought out by the treatment of every age-group. Heroes are killed and their corpses abused; women and children are made widows and orphans, and enslaved by their conquerors; old men weep helplessly, with no other comfort than to be told that 'the gods allot suffering to every man, but they are themselves free from

[60] *A und A* 18 (1973), 10.

care.'[61] The 'obituaries' allow the poet to show us parents, wives, and children, who could not otherwise be brought on to the battlefield and seen in their suffering and pain. It is the universality of the Homeric vision which led to this highly exceptional device, which confers significance on the victims of the great heroes, who in most warlike epics count for nothing. It is no accident that in the *Odyssey*, whose intentions and whose conception of significance are so different, there are no such obituary notices. The Suitors, destroyed by Odysseus, are never presented in such a light; they are morally bad, as characters in the *Iliad* are not, and the importance of their death is not the terrible transition from light to darkness which faces all men, even heroes, but the justification of the gods and their ways. Not a poignant vignette showing us the individual man as he was in life and the emotional cost to others of his death, but a relieved cry, 'Father Zeus, after all you gods still exist on high Olympus, if the suitors have truly paid the price for their wicked violence' (xxiv.351); that is the appropriate comment on their death.

Secondly, we have tested the often proclaimed objectivity of Homer. This is vitally important, since it presents in another form the question which confronted us in connection with characterization: is it in principle wrong to read into the bare words of the text of Homer anything more than what they explicitly contain? If this were the case, then we should find ourselves prevented from saying many of the things which we most want to say, and obliged to accept that the experience of reading Homer would be unsatisfactory when compared to reading other poetry. To defend as intellectually respectable the instinctive responses of the audience; that has been among our aims. It has perhaps led to some labouring of the obvious, but I hope that in this area, too, it has been shown that the *Iliad* does undeniably contain pregnant utterances and scenes full of emotional weight, not explicitly spelt out but still present. The whole distinction between 'objective' and 'subjective' has in fact turned out to be less clear than is often suggested. Passages can be seen to produce the same emotional effect, whether expressed objectively in narrative by the poet, or subjectively in speech by one of his characters.

[61] 24.525 ff., Achilles to Priam.

It is now time to conclude with an account of the 'obituary notices' themselves, which as a striking feature of the Homeric style have often attracted attention. In the light of our discussion some treatments of them seem inadequate. Bowra says:

> The poet holds his audience by the reality and solidity of his narrative, and to maintain this he resorts to a constant, lively invention, especially of small touches which do not much affect the main story ... Their task is to enliven a tale so crowded with persons that they may easily become faint or tedious. This is especially the case in the battle scenes, where many are killed or wounded and must be given momentary attention. This is secured by some small touch of information ...[62]

The defect of this explanation is that it takes no serious account of the content and the tone of the passages. They are thus reduced to mere ornaments, empty of emotional significance, as if we could just as well have been told the deceased's size in shoes, or his favourite colour, or his taste in toothpaste. But in fact they include some of the most striking lines in the poem, and cumulatively they 'affect the main story' very much, for they are one of the devices which make us interpret it in a certain way and not in other ways.

Schadewaldt[63] says: 'When a man falls in battle, Homer lingers for a moment on his person and his fate, and so brings out the significance of the death; and this gives a warm, human ring (*einen warmen, menschlichen Klang*).' With this we come closer to the point, but 'a warm, human ring' seems less than adequate as a description of the effect of these accounts of death, and of human lives seen as interesting only in the immediate shadow of death. Kirk[64] writes that one of the two 'main devices that bring reality and life to the scenes of warfare ... used with almost unlimited richness and variety ... is the lapidary sketch of the minor victims—for it was a difficulty that most of the victims *had* to be insignificant figures, almost unknown to the rest of the poem ... Hundreds of otherwise obscure Trojan and Achaean warriors are brilliantly illuminated at the moment of their death.' Again the vital thing seems to be omitted: the way in which these deaths affect our perception of the nature of heroism and of the world in which

---

[62] C. M. Bowra, *Homer* (1972), 56.
[63] *Von Homers Welt und Werk*[4], 326.
[64] *The Songs of Homer*, 342.

the hero struggles and dies. They are 'illuminated' with a very particular light, and nothing is less in the Homeric manner than to dilate upon lifelike details for their own sake.[65] The austere Muse of the *Iliad* has no interest in them except to illustrate the actions, the thoughts, and the death of the hero.[66]

Reinhardt[67] remarks of *Iliad* 20.391 that it is 'almost reminiscent of the form of the later epigrams for the tomb'; the same comparison is perhaps implicit in Kirk's epithet 'lapidary', and a similar perception is occasionally expressed in the Scholia. For we do find in some archaic epigrams the same reticent power which has proved so striking in these Homeric passages. Thus in a sixth-century epigram from Eretria (no. 862 Peek):[68]

> Πλειστίας.
> Σπάρτα μὲν πατρίς ἐστιν, ἐν εὐρυχόροισι δὲ Ἀθάναις
> ἐθράφθε, θανάτο δὲ ἐνθάδε μοῖρ' ἔχιχε.

'Pleistias. Sparta is his fatherland, in spacious Athens he was brought up: death's lot came on him here.' This poem exploits the motif of 'far from home', and feels no need to make explicit the pathos of Pleistias' distant death. Equally reticent is No. 73 Peek, sixth century, from Corcyra:

> σᾶμα τόδε Ἀρνιάδα· χαροπὸς τόνδ' ὤλεσεν Ἄρες
> βαρνάμενον παρὰ ναυσὶν ἐπ' Ἀράθθοιο ῥhοϝαῖσι,
> πολλὸν ἀριστεύοντα κατὰ στονόεσσαν ἀϝυτάν.

'This is the grave of Arniadas; the furious war-god slew him as he fought by the ships on Arathus' streams, a great champion in the cruel battle.'

Richard Heinze pointed out that 'in the overwhelming majority of cases, where the erector of a metrical inscription of the early period is identifiable, it is a father who pays this

---

[65] e.g. ΣΤ in 1.366: μεγαλοφυῶς δὲ συντέμνει τὰ περισσὰ τῶν λόγων καὶ τῶν ἱστοριῶν.

[66] M. P. Nilsson, *Die Antike* 14 (1938), 31, points out that mythological 'digressions', too, are never included merely for their own sake (he excepts *Il.* 16. 173–92, *Od.* xv.223–56), but always are transformed by being given a psychological point.

[67] *Die Ilias und ihr Dichter* (1961), 430: 'erinnernd fast an eine Form des späteren Grabepigramms'. ΣbΤ on 6.460: 'It has the character of an epitaph which he makes with emotion for his brother's grave.'

[68] *Griechische Vers-Inschriften I: Grabepigramme*, ed. W. Peek (1955), 862.

tender honour to a dead son.'[69] That observation chimes with a striking aspect of the pathos of the *Iliad* (above, p. 123ff.); and moreover, as Heinze saw, the epitaphs must really be created to satisfy a deep emotion of loss and disappointment. The austere form in which this emotion clothes itself (influenced of course by the epic) thus tends to confirm the view that the similar style in Homer is also the vehicle of deep pathos.

A last epigram: the famous epitaph of Phrasiclea (68 Peek), Attic, sixth century.

σῆμα Φρασικλείας· κόρē κεκλέσομαι αἰεί,
ἀντὶ γάμο παρὰ θεῶν τοῦτο λαχōσ' ὄνομα.

'The grave of Phrasiclea. I shall be called for ever maiden; instead of marriage the gods gave me this name.' No words of lamentation were felt necessary in this simple and perfect statement. The death of an unmarried girl is one of the 'intrinsically emotional' things. It has often been pointed out that the epic avoids the violent gestures and wild cries of passionate woe which are admitted in Attic tragedy. They appear in Homer only as ὣς ἔφατο κλαίουσ', ἐπὶ δὲ στενάχοντο γυναῖκες, 'So she spoke, weeping, and the women groaned after her.' No doubt in the real world such shrieks were to be heard at funerals,[70] but they were banished from the epigrams, as the frightful powers of the malignant dead were banished, the necromancers,[71] and the Erinyes.[72] The effort of stylization can be seen to be closely related in the two genres.

But though the grave epigram was not effusive, it is clear that it was expected to produce an emotion in the wayside reader, and that the emotion was pity. Peek collects (Nos. 1223 ff.), those epigrams which make this explicit. στῆθι καὶ οἴκτιρον, 'stop and feel pity', is a repeated phrase. No. 1223 (Attic, *c.* 550 BC):

παιδὸς ἀποφθιμένοιο Κλεοίτο τō Μενεσαίχμο
μνῆμ' ἐσορōν οἴκτιρ', ὃς καλὸς ὂν ἔθανε.

'Seeing the tomb of Cleoetus son of Menesaechmus, who is

---

[69] *Von altgriechischen Kriegergräbern*, *NJbb*. 18 (1915), 8 = *Das Epigramm*, ed. G. Pfohl (1969), 47.

[70] Cf. Nilsson, *Geschichte der griechischen Religion*, i², 714, for the funerals of the archaic period and the attempts of legislators to curb them.

[71] W. Burkert in *Rh. Mus.* 105 (1962), 36.

[72] H. Lloyd-Jones, *The Justice of Zeus* (1971), 75.

dead, pity him, who was so beautiful and died.' Here again a further comparison suggests itself with the epic. H. Fränkel[73] has well shown that, within the epics, narrators of stories say they relate 'sufferings', κήδεα, ἄλγεα. We have observed that the *Iliad* has as its subject suffering and death, and must have been listened to from an interest in that subject. Suffering is what produces song, says Helen; [74] if the song of Athene's anger and the suffering of the Achaeans is bitter to hear, says Telemachus to Penelope, *Odyssey* i.353,

$$\sigma o i \ \delta' \ \epsilon \pi \iota \tau o \lambda \mu \acute{a} \tau \omega \ \kappa \rho a \delta \acute{\iota} \eta \ \kappa a \grave{\iota} \ \theta \upsilon \mu \grave{o} s \ \acute{a} \kappa o \acute{\upsilon} \epsilon \iota \nu$$

'Let your heart and mind endure to hear it'—others, too, have suffered. That is to say: by listening to tragic song and reflecting on it, understand what the world is like, and what is the position of man within it.[75]

This tragic and consistent view of human life is what makes the epic so great. The 'obituaries' and the other passages of austere pathos are vitally important for it. The *Iliad* is a poem of death; actual duels in it are short, and the greater hero shows his greater stature by killing his opponent, who for his part is usually killed with ease, sometimes without resistance.[76] A contrast with the duels, for instance, in Malory's *Morte Darthur*, where knights hew and hack at each other for hours with periods of rest, brings this out clearly.[77] Fate, not fighting technique, is what interests the *Iliad*; the hero, splendid and vital, going down into death. A long poem consisting of such encounters could easily become gruesome, or boring, or unbearable; what prevents this is the light in which the warriors are seen. The device, like the conception it serves, is not an obvious or universal one. In the *Iliad* the lesser heroes are shown in all the pathos of their death, the change from the brightness of life to a dark and meaningless existence, the grief of their friends and families; but the style preserves the poem from sentimentality on the one hand and sadism on the other. Stripped of the sort of passages here discussed, it would lose not merely an ornament, but a vital part of its nature.

[73] *Dichtung und Philosophie*[2], 15 ff.
[74] *Iliad* 6.357.
[75] Strikingly argued by W. Marg, *Homer über die Dichtung* (1957), 14.
[76] Cf. G. Strasburger, *Die kleinen Kämpfer*, 50.
[77] Cf. M. M. Willcock in *BICS* 17 (1970), 1 ff.

V

GODS AND GODDESSES

Really we can hardly avoid taking Homeric religion seriously—W. Marg[1]

The divine, presented with such clarity in the Homeric poems, is manifold in form and yet everywhere consistent. A lofty spirit, a noble content, is expressed in all of its forms—W. F. Otto[2]

Ach, was wollt ihr euch verwöhnen
In dem Hässlich-Wunderbaren!—Goethe

THE Homeric poems are pervaded from end to end by an elaborate polytheism. The *Iliad* begins with the anger of Apollo and ends with the gods conducting Priam to Achilles and ordering Achilles to yield to him the body of Hector. The *Odyssey* begins on Olympus and ends with the intervention of Athena which makes peace between Odysseus and the kinsmen of the slaughtered Suitors. Action on earth is accompanied by action, decision, and conflict in heaven, and gods and goddesses intervene in the human world. In the case of the *Iliad* the plot is held together by the constant agency of the divine,[3] while Odysseus is brought home and defended by the goddess Athena; without her help he could not leave Calypso in the beginning, nor slay the Suitors in the end. In both poems the central characters draw what is, at least at one level, the moral of the whole story in terms of the gods. 'That is the destiny which the gods have devised for mortal men, to live in suffering, while they are free from care', says Achilles to Priam; 'These men the fate of the gods and their own sin have destroyed', says Odysseus over the corpses of the Suitors.[4] If the poems are to be taken seriously at all, then it would seem that

---

[1] *Gnomon* 28 (1956), 2: 'Es ist eigentlich kaum zu umgehen, Homer religiös ernst zu nehmen.'

[2] *The Homeric Gods* (Eng. trans., 1954), 16.

[3] 'Was die Ilias zur Einheit bildet, ist nicht nur das Motiv des Zornes, sondern vor allem diese Allengegenwart des Olymps', U. Hölscher, *Untersuchungen zur Form der Odyssee* (1939), 49.

[4] Achilles, 24.525; Odysseus, xxii.413.

the gods who preside over them must be taken seriously, too. And it is clear that gods are not taken seriously if they can be treated as an entertaining but essentially literary device, either to avert monotony and vary the atmosphere, or to produce situations for the human characters in the poems which are not specifically divine or religious but simply represent, in striking form, conflicts of ordinary secular life.

In this chapter I criticize two approaches which appear in important recent works on Homer, and suggest that the ways in which they deal with the gods and the divine are inadequate to a central feature of the poems. I hope not to be aridly polemical; the point is not to criticize each other, but to do justice to the unique Homeric vision, and if these scholarly works were not important it would be a waste of time to criticize them. And they are representative of approaches which have in common the minimizing of the divine. The gods of Homer must be faced as gods, and then we must see what we can make of them. I think it will be seen that the poems cannot be understood if we do not allow them a crucial role in our interpretation; the role, in fact, which the Greeks themselves ascribed to them when they read the poems. How we, as people living with different traditions and other beliefs, are to find it possible to give such a significance to an ancient polytheistic religious system—that is another question, and not, I hope, an unanswerable one.

Professor J. M. Redfield, in his interesting book *Nature and Culture in the Iliad* (1975), applies to the *Iliad* an essentially sociological and anthropological approach. He concentrates his attention upon the role of the hero in an ancient society like that depicted in the poem and considers its paradoxes and dilemmas, especially for Hector, who on the one hand must fight and expose his life, and on the other must, if Troy is to have a future, survive; who can defend his society from violence only by accepting violence himself.[5] The characters are seen as reacting to the pressure of their society, and understood in that light; and the values of possible human societies are not merely arbitrary. They must produce a result which can exist in the real world, in the light of the existence of the fundamental and unalterable facts of nature such as the existence of two

[5] On Hector see now H. Erbse, 'Ettore nell' Iliade', in *Studi Classici e Orientali* 28 (1978), 13–34.

sexes, the production of children, and the universality of death.
A work of fiction illuminates the society within which it is produced, because it makes sense in terms of the attitudes of that
society and shows how they work. Stories which, like heroic
epics, deal with exceptional events, show the conventions of the
society as they work in exceptional circumstances and under
strain; the *Iliad* thus 'accepts the heroic ethic and yet inquires
into its limitations and self-contradictions' (p. 85).

No short summary of a long book can be satisfactory, and
this is summary indeed. But I think it brings out the sort of
approach Redfield follows, especially when we add that he is
led by it to make rather unexpected statements. We have
already seen him argue that when Achilles in Book 9 rejects the
overtures of the Achaean envoys he is 'the victim of his own
ethic', and what he does is 'not a departure from the heroic
pattern but an enactment of that pattern'; he is 'trapped by his
self-definition as a warrior, which permits him neither reconciliation nor retreat' (104–5).[6] We now find that the gods in the
poem are not really gods.

Most important, the gods of the *Iliad* are lacking in *numen*; they are in fact
the chief source of comedy in the poem. We can, I think, explain this difference most easily by assuming that the gods of the *Iliad* belong to the conventional world of epic and were understood as such by the audience. Just
as the epic tells, not of men, but of heroes, so also it tells stories, not of gods
conceived as actual, but of literary gods (76).

And in fact a scene like that in which Athena appears to
Achilles and persuades him not to kill Agamemnon is not really
about 'the relation between man and god as the audience would
normally understand that relation'; what happens is that we
see an instance of the situation, well known in real life, of a
man driven to an act of rebellion against an authority, but
being prevented by a higher authority which, though able to
prevent his revolt, is yet unable to remedy his grievance. 'The
essential scene, thus, is the man between two authorities; one of

[6] Cf. p. 74. Redfield finds that in the poem 'error is forced upon the hero by his
culture.' I have made clear my view that Achilles is not forced into error by anything other than his own temperament, which is disapproved by the other heroes;
Hector, too, as Erbse rightly argues (cf. n. 5 above), takes decisions which turn
out to be mistaken, not because of his 'culture', but because he is the commander
of the weaker side and so must take risks, and also because he is mortal and so does
not understand the plan of Zeus.

the authorities is divine, but "divine" is merely a specific version of "higher" ' (78).

He also, consistently, applies the same treatment to the gods of the dead and the importance of burial for the hero. Homer describes the *psyche* of a slain warrior, at the moment of his death, 'flying out of the body and going down to Hades, bewailing its lot, leaving its strength and youth',[7] but Redfield regards the *psyche* as something which does not exist for the owner, but only for other people. An unconscious man, whose *psyche* has temporarily left him, 'exists only for others. The *psyche*, I wish to assert, is a self that exists for others, one aspect of the social soul' (177 f.). The dead do not continue to exist, in any real sense: 'So the existence of the *psyche* in Hades is not a continuation of the personal life but rather a kind of monument to the fact that personal life once existed' (181). Of the funeral for which Hector begs with his last breath, and which makes Achaeans and Trojans fight like wolves over the body of Patroclus, it 'may be thought of as a ceremony by which a definite social status is conferred upon the dead ... He has done what he could, and his community declares that it can expect nothing more of him. Since he can no longer be among them, he is entitled to the status of the departed. They thus release him' (175). As for the gods of the dead, 'Hades' world is a non-world' (181).

Such an account reduces the specifically divine element in the poem, and also the unambiguously supernatural aspect of death and its survival, for practical purposes to nothing; action and significance are to be understood on the level of social facts, and there is nothing else. Hardly less dismissive, in a different way, is Professor Kirk. His many valuable writings on Homer show little interest in the gods, and we find him saying, of the scene in which Athena checks the murderous impulse of Achilles, that 'certain divine actions (for example Athena tugging Achilles' hair in the first book of the *Iliad* to stop him losing his temper with Agamemnon) may be little more than *façons de parler*.'[8] In his fullest treatment of the divine scenes, he gives this general account of their effect:

---

[7] 16.856, 22.363.

[8] G. S. Kirk, *The Nature of Greek Myths* (1974), 292. The rather facetious style of this passage suggests the writer's impatience with the convention, and, as so often,

The gods provide other forms of diversion: often the description of battle is suddenly interrupted, and the scene shifts to Olympus or Ida where the gods plan to help their favourites, or where Zeus weighs fate in the scales. These divine scenes successfully avert the threat of monotony, because they provide a total change of atmosphere and behaviour—domesticity and humour and all sorts of not very heroic qualities are allowed to enter the lives of the gods. Yet such scenes are not objectionably irrelevant or structurally heavy-handed . . .[9]

It is certainly true that the existence of the divine plane enables the poet to vary his narrative, although we remind ourselves that Penelope and Andromache show us something of domesticity, and Irus and Thersites something of humour, without needing to invoke the gods. But it also does far more. To see how much, we shall first need to ask whether it is true that the gods lack *numen* and are not to be taken seriously as anything more than 'literary gods'.

We observe at once that Homeric men are pious. Prayers, vows, and sacrifices occur throughout the poems, and high points in the plot are regularly marked by such utterances. We recall for instance the prayer of Hector for his son, which half consoles his wife as he leaves her side, the prayer with which Achilles sends Patroclus into battle, and the prayer which Odysseus addresses to the Phaeacian river as he struggles out of the sea. Before shooting an arrow at a formidable enemy, one prays to Apollo; of a defeated contestant in a chariot race one says, 'He should have prayed to the immortals; then he would not have come last.' Before going on a dangerous expedition it

---

impatience is not good for accuracy. Athena comes, not to 'stop Achilles losing his temper with Agamemnon'—she bids him 'Yea, with words indeed revile him'—but to prevent killing. Nor, surely, can an Athena who is but a figure of speech for Achilles changing his own mind say, 'Thus I shall speak, and it shall be fulfilled: in time thrice as many noble gifts shall come to you in recompense for this injury; restrain yourself, and be guided by us.' The same reductive explanation in Eustathius, 81.27: Ἀθηνᾶ δὲ οὐρανόθεν ἐλθοῦσα κωλύει, τουτέστιν ἡ παρ' αὐτῷ ἀγχίνοια. With the style, compare *The Songs of Homer*, 379, 'When Patroclus is knocked silly by Apollo . . .'. *ibid.*, 76 (on Olympus), 'Zeus comforts and upbraids, or mulls over his female conquests . . .' *Myth: its Meaning and Functions*, 240, 'Aphrodite prodding Helen into the bedroom . . .'

[9] G. S. Kirk, *The Songs of Homer* (1962), 345. So for instance Gilbert Murray wrote, 'The gods are patronised, conventionalised, and treated as material for ornament . . .' (*Rise of the Greek Epic*[3], 265). Boileau, we are told, believed that 'Homère avoit crainte d'ennuyer par le tragique continu de son sujet', and consequently 'il avoit voulu égayer le fond de sa matière aux dépens des dieux mêmes . . . il les fait jouer la comédie dans les entr'actes de son action.'

is natural to pour a libation to Zeus and ask him for a favourable omen. Agamemnon bitterly claims that on his journey to Troy he did not pass a single altar of Zeus without making an offering upon it. Penelope prays constantly and is told by her son to 'vow to offer acceptable hecatombs to all the gods, if Zeus will grant us vengeance'; 'all men need the gods', says the excellent Pisistratus, son of Nestor.[10] These references could be multiplied, but the point is obvious. The poems are full of substantial scenes of religious activity: the propitiation of Apollo at Chryse, the truce and oaths for which both sides invoke the gods and make offerings, the prayers and services in Troy which Hector orders in the sixth book of the *Iliad*, the worship of Poseidon which Telemachus finds going on when he comes to Pylos, and the sacrifice in honour of Athena which Nestor conducts there before they leave.[11] Both sides at Troy have regular experts to interpret the will of the gods. In the *Odyssey* the wandering Theoclymenus belongs to a celebrated family of seers and gives proof of his inherited skill.[12] In each house the hearth is sacred and can be invoked to witness an oath. Gods move among men in disguise, we are told, testing them for vice or virtue, so that one should be very careful in dealing with a stranger.[13]

Nor is this all. Actions of cult are made into the vehicles for expressing psychology and emotion. Thus Achilles, sending Patroclus into battle, takes out a special cup, reserved for his own use among men, and for libations to Zeus among gods; from that cup he pours a libation to Zeus and utters his moving prayer for his safe return. When Patroclus is dead, Achilles' grief expresses itself in gestures suggested by ritual: fasting, abstinence from bathing, cutting off the lock of hair which he had vowed to the River Spercheius on his return home, human sacrifice at Patroclus' pyre, and finally the desire to be buried

---

[10] Hector, 6.476; Achilles, 16.233; Odysseus, v.445; prayer to Apollo, 4.101; 'you should have prayed', 23.546; asking for an omen, 24.287; Agamemnon, 8.238; Penelope, xvii.50; Pisistratus, iii.48. 'Und fromm sind diese Menschen', H. Schrade, *Götter und Menschen Homers*, 153.

[11] Chryse, 1.430–87; truce, 3.264–354; prayers in Troy, 6.263–312; Poseidon, iii.31–67; Athena, iii.418–63.

[12] xv.223–55, xvii.152, xx.345–57. Theoclymenus is defended from the harsh criticisms of Page, *The Homeric Odyssey*, 83 ff., by H. Erbse, *Beiträge zum Verständnis der Odyssee*, 42 ff.

[13] Hearth, xiv.159, xvii.156, xix.304, xx.231; gods among men, xvii.484.

in the same urn with his ashes.[14] Nothing could show more clearly the depth and pervasiveness with which ritual and cult possess the minds of the characters of the poems.

When we turn from the men to the gods, we find that they are by no means always lacking in dignity or stature. The first god we see in the *Iliad* is Apollo, invoked to avenge his dishonoured priest by smiting the Achaeans.

> ὣς ἔφατ' εὐχόμενος, τοῦ δ' ἔκλυε Φοῖβος Ἀπόλλων,
> βῆ δὲ κατ' Οὐλύμποιο καρήνων χωόμενος κῆρ,
> τόξ' ὤμοισιν ἔχων ἀμφηρεφέα τε φαρέτρην.
> ἔκλαγξαν δ' ἄρ' ὀιστοὶ ἐπ' ὤμων χωομένοιο,
> αὐτοῦ κινηθέντος· ὁ δ' ἤιε νυκτὶ ἐοικώς.
> ἕζετ' ἔπειτ' ἀπάνευθε νεῶν, μετὰ δ' ἰὸν ἕηκε·
> δεινὴ δὲ κλαγγὴ γένετ' ἀργυρέοιο βιοῖο·
> οὐρῆας μὲν πρῶτον ἐπῴχετο καὶ κύνας ἀργούς,
> αὐτὰρ ἔπειτ' αὐτοῖσι βέλος ἐχεπευκὲς ἐφιεὶς
> βάλλ'· αἰεὶ δὲ πυραὶ νεκύων καίοντο θαμειαί (1.43–52).

'So he prayed, and Phoebus Apollo heard him, and came down from the peaks of Olympus with anger in his heart, bearing on his shoulders his bow and covered quiver. The arrows clanged on his shoulders in his anger as he moved, and he came like night. Then he sat far off from the ships and let fly a dart at them; terrible was the clang of his silver bow. The mules he struck first, and the nimble dogs; then he aimed his piercing shaft at the men and struck them, and ever there burned many pyres for the dead.' This description surely presents a god who must be taken seriously. The style combines elaborate repetition and variation of the important words ('anger', 'clang', 'bow', 'arrows', 'dart'), and also a most impressive brevity: 'He came like night.' And this is a god who must be appeased by the orthodox procedures of ritual after a personal injury of the classic type. We find the same pattern, of an injured deity exacting vengeance, in the episode of the Cattle of the Sun; Artemis sent the monstrous boar to ravage Calydon because Oeneus omitted her when all the other gods received hecatombs; Aeneas wonders whether Diomede, who is slaughtering

---

[14] Fasting, 19.154 ff.; bathing, 23.40; hair, 23.141; human sacrifice, 23.175; burial, 23.83. Cf. on this E. Samter, *Homer* (1923), 165 ff.

many Trojans in battle, is not a god, 'angry with Troy, in wrath because of sacrifices'.[15]

It is true that Apollo's appearance is unusual in representing so faithfully, in a high poetical style, the popular conception of a god bringing plague.[16] But there is no shortage of passages which offer really impressive gods. Gods manifest themselves with superhuman speed and in spectacular ways: Athena darts down to earth like a shooting star, 'and amazement seized on those who saw'; Thetis rises from the sea 'like a mist'; Athena comes down among the Achaeans 'like a rainbow'.[17] They may depart in non-human form; Athena leaves Pylos

in the likeness of a sea-eagle, and amazement seized on those who saw. The old man was amazed, seeing it; he took the hand of Telemachus and addressed him: 'My friend, I fancy you will not be a coward or a weakling, if, young as you are, gods escort you as your guides. This is none other of the dwellers on Olympus but the daughter of Zeus, the conqueror, Tritogeneia, she who honoured your noble father among the Argives. O goddess, be gracious, and grant me fair fame, to me and to my sons and to my queen; and I will offer to you a heifer' . . .[18]

Athena comes to the hut of Eumaeus in the form of a woman; Telemachus cannot see her 'for by no means do the gods appear manifest to all', but Odysseus sees her, and so do the dogs, which do not bark but whimper and slink away. When Odysseus and his son remove the weapons and armour from the hall,

Pallas Athena made bright light before them, holding a golden lamp. Then Telemachus at once addressed his father: 'My father, I see a great marvel; to my eyes at least the walls, the main beams, the cross-beams and the pillars are bright as if with burning fire. In truth some god is here, one of those who keep the wide heaven.' To him in answer spoke wily Odysseus: 'Be silent and keep your thoughts in check and ask no questions. This is the way of the gods who dwell on Olympus.'[19]

[15] Cattle of the Sun, xii.260 ff.; Artemis, 9.536; Diomede, 5.177.

[16] Cf. Deut. 32:23, 'I will heap mischiefs upon them; I will spend my arrows upon them: they shall be wasted with hunger, and devoured with burning heat', and Ezek. 5:16.

[17] Athena, 4.75; Thetis, 1.359; rainbow, 17.547. On these similes see T. Krischer, *Formale Konventionen der hom. Epik* (1971), 19 ff.

[18] iii.371 ff. Birds, as at iii.371, xxii.239, despite the arguments of F. Dirlmeier, 'Die Vogelgestalt homerischer Götter', *SB Heidelberg*, 1967, 2. What Dirlmeier finds himself obliged to admit in the case of 20.224 (p. 24), seems to me to undermine his argument about iii.371.

[19] Athena and the dogs, xvi.157–63; and the lamp, xix.33–42, cf. R. Pfeiffer, *Ausgewählte Schriften*, 1–7.

It is perhaps worth emphasizing that in each of these last three episodes we see not only the god behaving like a real god, mysteriously, but also the characters who are present at the moment of revelation responding to it in what can only be called a religious way: adoration or reverent silence. Even animals are aware of the special quality of the presence of a god.

We have already seen the shattering effect which a god produces on men by the use of the terrifying aegis or a supernatural shout; in the *Iliad* Apollo, his shoulders wrapped in a cloud, so that he is invisible, shakes the aegis in the face of the Achaeans and utters a mighty shout: 'He bewitched their heart in their breasts, and they forgot their fighting spirit'; they take to flight like a herd of cattle or a flock of sheep, panicked by two lions. When Athena holds up the aegis against the Suitors, 'their wits were scattered'; fleeing like a herd stampeded by the gadfly they are slaughtered without resistance.[20] But there are other divine revelations no less terrible, though simpler. Apollo strikes Patroclus, at the height of his heroic exploits:

ἀλλ' ὅτε δὴ τὸ τέταρτον ἐπέσσυτο δαίμονι ἶσος,
ἔνθ' ἄρα τοι, Πάτροκλε, φάνη βιότοιο τελευτή·
ἤντετο γάρ τοι Φοῖβος ἐνὶ κρατερῇ ὑσμίνῃ
δεινός·[21] ὁ μὲν γὰρ ἰόντα κατὰ κλόνον οὐκ ἐνόησεν·
ἠέρι γὰρ πολλῇ κεκαλυμμένος ἀντεβόλησε,
στῆ δ' ὄπιθεν, πλῆξεν δὲ μετάφρενον εὐρέε τ' ὤμω
χειρὶ καταπρηνεῖ, στρεφεδίνηθεν δέ οἱ ὄσσε.
τοῦ δ' ἀπὸ μὲν κρατὸς κυνέην βάλε Φοῖβος Ἀπόλλων ...
τὸν δ' ἄτη φρένας εἷλε, λύθεν δ' ὑπὸ φαίδιμα γυῖα,
στῆ δὲ ταφών (16.786 ff.).

'But as he rushed on the fourth time like a god, then, Patroclus, did the end of your life appear to you, for Phoebus met you in the strong battle, and he was terrible. Now Patroclus had not

[20] Apollo, 15.328 ff.; Athena, xxii.297 ff.

[21] I remark upon this splendidly effective use of enjambement, one weighty word standing alone and receiving heavy emphasis. Something quite similar in 1.52, the carrying over of the powerful verb βάλλε. See the remarks, perhaps excessively cautious, of M. W. Edwards in *TAPA* 97 (1966), 139 f: 'It seems to me wise to think it possible that any literary effect that may be felt in this and other cases may have been meant by the poet himself . . .' Discussion of the question whether such words carry special emphasis: references in M. N. Nagler, *Spontaneity and Tradition* (1974), 92 n. 29.

marked him as he came through the press, for hidden in thick mist did he meet him, and stood behind him and struck his back and broad shoulders with the flat of his hand; and his eyes rolled round. From his head Phoebus Apollo knocked his helmet . . .' (broke his spear, unfastened his corslet, and cast down his shield), 'and blindness seized his mind, and his bright limbs lost their strength, and he stood in confusion . . .' What makes the passage powerful is, first, the silent approach of the god, hidden from mortal eyes, his arrival meaning death for the hero, 'like a god' though he is. Second, it is the contrast between the effortless gesture of Apollo, a blow with the flat of the hand, and its shattering effect upon Patroclus. We see vividly the gulf in power that separates even a mighty man from a god. The combination of mystery, power, and effortlessness, marks this as a divine intervention; there can be no question here, surely, of arguing that 'the "divine" is merely a specific version of "higher."' [22]

As even the dogs of Eumaeus recognized Athena's divinity and were frightened, so does old Priam, mourning for his son, when Iris the divine messenger comes to him with the command of Zeus. She finds Priam lying on the ground, wrapped up closely in his cloak, defiled with the droppings of cattle in which he rolled in the ecstasy of grief:

στῆ δὲ παρὰ Πρίαμον Διὸς ἄγγελος, ἠδὲ προσηύδα
τυτθὸν φθεγξαμένη· τὸν δὲ τρόμος ἔλλαβε γυῖα·
'θάρσει, Δαρδανίδη Πρίαμε, φρεσί, μηδέ τι τάρβει·
οὐ μὲν γάρ τοι ἐγὼ κακὸν ὀσσομένη τόδ' ἱκάνω
ἀλλ' ἀγαθὰ φρονέουσα . . .' (24.169 ff.)

'And the messenger of Zeus stood beside Priam and spoke to him in a little voice. Trembling seized on his limbs. "Let not your heart be troubled, Priam son of Dardanus, nor be afraid. I am not come hither to bode evil to you, but with good will." '
Let not your heart be troubled, neither let it be afraid; who does not recognize here the language of supernatural visitors to terrified humanity, or needs to be reminded how often in the Bible

---

[22] I do not, however, find convincing the idea of H. Schrade, *Götter und Menschen Homers*, 145, that the poet means us to imagine Patroclus struck by a hand emerging from a cloud, a representation of the divine which is familiar in Israelite and other Eastern sources (see his *Der verborgene Gott*, 132 ff.).

trembling comes upon those brought face to face with the divine?

Zeus is capable of rising to the full dignity of supreme godhead, as he does when we see him with the nod of his head which shakes mighty Olympus, the eternal locks waving on the immortal head of the god, confirm as immutable his promise to Thetis to glorify her son and oppress the Achaeans. And we do not fail to observe that in this scene the poet combines the mythological god who repays a favour done by Thetis and intervenes in human affairs in a fully anthropomorphic way, with the elemental god of the sky, thunderer, gatherer and scatterer of the clouds, who is at home far away on the peak of the highest mountain, and who, if he moves, shakes it to its foundations. The bridge between the two is constructed with perfect elegance and conviction, and crowned with one of the most powerful images of the divine ever created by a Greek.[23]

Hardly less grand is the moment when Zeus holds up the scales which are to decide the issue of Achilles' duel with Hector:

> ἀλλ' ὅτε δὴ τὸ τέταρτον ἐπὶ κρουνοὺς ἀφίκοντο,
> καὶ τότε δὴ χρύσεια πατὴρ ἐτίταινε τάλαντα,
> ἐν δὲ τίθει δύο κῆρε τανηλεγέος θανάτοιο,
> τὴν μὲν Ἀχιλλῆος, τὴν δ' Ἕκτορος ἱπποδάμοιο,
> ἕλκε δὲ μέσσα λαβών· ῥέπε δ' Ἕκτορος αἴσιμον ἦμαρ,
> ᾤχετο δ' εἰς Ἀίδαο· λίπεν δέ ἑ Φοῖβος Ἀπόλλων (22.208 ff.).

'But when the fourth time they reached the springs, then the Father held out his golden scales, and set in them two fates of death that brings long woe, one for Achilles, the other for horse-taming Hector; and he held them by the middle and poised. Down sank Hector's fated day and fell down to Hades; and Phoebus Apollo left him.' Again we find the impressive brevity of description in Zeus' fateful act; and as Apollo in the first book 'came like night', so here the same god, who has alone given Hector the strength which has enabled him to run from Achilles, is the subject of the massive and pregnant half-line, 'and Phoebus Apollo left him.' Such a scene, so described,

---

[23] Zeus nods, 1.528–30. On the connection of the wrath-theme with the divine machinery by means of Thetis, which makes it possible for the *Iliad* to be a poem of cosmic scope, cf. R. Friedrich, *Stilwandel im homerischen Epos* (1975), 104.

is worthy to decide the fate of mighty heroes, and if that is true, then these gods must be worthy to be gods indeed.

Apollo, attacked in battle by a hero, utters the classic statement of Greek wisdom, 'Know yourself':

ἀλλ' ὅ γ' ἄρ' οὐδὲ θεὸν μέγαν ἅζετο, ἵετο δ' αἰεὶ
Αἰνείαν κτεῖναι καὶ ἀπὸ κλυτὰ τεύχεα δῦσαι.
τρὶς μὲν ἔπειτ' ἐπόρουσε κατακτάμεναι μενεαίνων,
τρὶς δέ οἱ ἐστυφέλιξε φαεινὴν ἀσπίδ' Ἀπόλλων.
ἀλλ' ὅτε δὴ τὸ τέταρτον ἐπέσσυτο δαίμονι ἶσος,
δεινὰ δ' ὁμοκλήσας προσέφη ἑκάεργος Ἀπόλλων·
'φράζεο, Τυδείδη, καὶ χάζεο, μηδὲ θεοῖσιν
ἶσ' ἔθελε φρονέειν, ἐπεὶ οὔ ποτε φῦλον ὁμοῖον
ἀθανάτων τε θεῶν χαμαὶ ἐρχομένων τ' ἀνθρώπων' (5.434 ff.)[24].

'Yet Diomede did not even reverence the great god, but was eager still to slay Aeneas and strip his famous armour. Thrice did he leap on him, lusting to slay him, and thrice Apollo beat back his glittering shield. But when he sprang at him a fourth time like a god, then Apollo the Archer addressed him with a terrible shout: "Reflect, son of Tydeus, and fall back; think not to match your spirit with that of gods, for there is never equality between the race of immortal gods and of men who walk the earth." ' Reflect, says the god; think what you are and what I am, and realize how futile it is for you to measure yourself against me. He uses no weapon, he simply pushes Diomede back, and then makes it clear to the hero that his patience is exhausted. His voice is 'terrible', the same epithet as described the god himself when he came to smite Patroclus, and the clang of his silver bow when he shot the arrows of plague. There is no arguing with such a god, and Diomede falls back, abandoning his attempt on Aeneas.

In the *Odyssey*, Telemachus expresses doubt that he and his father will be able alone to tackle all the Suitors, and urges him, if he can think of any helper they could call on, to name him. Odysseus replies, 'Yes, I shall speak: do you listen to me and tell me, whether Athena with Father Zeus will suffice for us, or shall I think of another helper?' 'Those are good helpers whom you name', replies Telemachus, 'though they sit high in the clouds; they rule over men and over immortal gods.'[25] Tele-

[24] Cf. also 16.705 and F. Dirlmeier in *ARW* 36 (1939), 280.
[25] xvi.256 ff.

machus has just reckoned up the total number of the Suitors to be one hundred and eight; even against such odds Odysseus is confident that the aid of the two mighty gods will be with him, and that with them he will prevail.

It cannot of course be maintained that all the appearances and allusions to the gods in the poems show them in this sort of light, and we shall go on to try to do justice to the variety and complexity of the Homeric gods as a whole. The point which has been made here, and which could be made at greater length, is that, among other things, we do find terrible and 'numinous' gods, and human characters who react to them in a way appropriate to their serious divinity. Reductionist accounts which try to deny this element in the poems are denying something which is vital for their nature and meaning. Even a goddess like Aphrodite, who is anything but a favourite and suffers personal indignity in both epics, can on occasion show her formidable side. Having rescued Paris, her protégé, from death at the hands of Menelaus, she deposits him in his bedroom and goes off, disguised as an old maidservant, to bring Helen to him. Helen sees through the assumed identity and bitterly reproaches the goddess for taking her from her home and husband in Greece, and declares that she will not go to Paris' bed: she could not face the women of Troy, and she is cruelly unhappy.

> τὴν δὲ χολωσαμένη προσεφώνεε δῖ' Ἀφροδίτη·
> 'μή μ' ἔρεθε, σχετλίη, μὴ χωσαμένη σε μεθείω,
> τὼς δέ σ' ἀπεχθήρω ὡς νῦν ἔκπαγλα φίλησα,
> μέσσῳ δ' ἀμφοτέρων μητίσομαι ἔχθεα λυγρὰ
> Τρώων καὶ Δαναῶν, σὺ δέ κεν κακὸν οἶτον ὄληαι.'
> ὣς ἔφατ', ἔδεισεν δ' Ἑλένη Διὸς ἐκγεγαυῖα,
> βῆ δὲ κατασχομένη ἑανῷ ἀργῆτι φαεινῷ
> σιγῇ, πάσας δὲ Τρῳὰς λάθεν· ἦρχε δὲ δαίμων (3.413 ff.).

'Divine Aphrodite answered her in wrath. "Do not provoke me, wretch, lest I abandon you in anger, and hate you even as I have exceedingly loved you; lest I devise cruel hatred between both sides, Trojans and Achaeans, and you come to an evil end." So she spoke, and Helen daughter of Zeus was afraid; she went, wrapping herself in her bright shining garment, in silence; the Trojan women did not see. The goddess led the way.' Helen is the offspring of Zeus,[26] and her defiance of the goddess was the desperate cry of a human creature struggling to regain her self-respect. Aphrodite silences her with threats, and the intimidated woman has no choice but to follow. The scene is concluded with another of those phrases unsurpassed in brevity and power: 'the goddess led the way',[27] and we see not only the tableau of the two moving figures but also the significance of what is happening. Helen tried to resist, but Aphrodite is a goddess, and her resistance is futile. We are fortunately able to compare this episode with a real instance of an authority which is 'higher' but not 'divine'.

After his quarrel with Agamemnon, Achilles withdraws to his ships, and Agamemnon sends two heralds to take away his captive Briseis. The heralds approach 'unwillingly'; in respect and awe of Achilles they stand before him in silence, preferring not to utter their distasteful errand, 'and Achilles did not rejoice to see them.' He tells Patroclus to bring the girl out, saying that he does not blame them but their arrogant master. He calls on the heralds as his witnesses in the sight of gods and men, and of the harsh king himself, against the day when there will come need of Achilles to rescue them all from disaster. Agamemnon, he says, is mad and unable to look prudently to future and past and so preserve his people. With that he lets Briseis go, and in tears calls on his goddess mother to hear him in the depths of the sea.

Achilles, as we see, does not only make a most formal protest against Agamemnon's action, he also threatens him and does what he can to punish him and bring him to disaster; yet Agamemnon, king of men, is the highest human authority. By contrast, a man confronting a god is helpless and can do nothing but obey. As Achilles must bitterly confess to Apollo when the god has deceived him, 'You have robbed me of great glory and

---

[26] Cf. also iv.569, and K. J. Reckford in *GRBSt.* 5 (1954), 19.

[27] See also 1.530, 'And he made mighty Olympus shake'; 2.41, Agamemnon woke, 'and the divine voice was shed about him.' In another tradition, one thinks of such passages as Gen. 5:24, 'And Enoch walked with God: and he was not; for God took him.' Isa. 9:7, 'Of the increase of his government and peace there shall be no end . . . The zeal of the LORD of hosts will perform this.' Matt. 4:11, the end of the temptation of Christ: 'Then the devil leaveth him, and, behold, angels came and ministered unto him.' Of the words 'and Phoebus Apollo left him', B. C. Fenik observes, 'There is scarcely a weightier half line in the *Iliad*' (*Homer: Tradition and Invention* (1978), 81).

saved the Trojans easily, since you had no retribution to fear afterwards. How I would pay you out, if I had the power' (21.15–20). The greatest of heroes, at the peak of his prowess and his career, has no means even to hope for satisfaction from a god like that which he immediately begins to plan against his king. Above all, the atmosphere is different. On the one hand, a long quarrel, movement, the sending of heralds, formal denunciation, everything clear and intelligible: on the other, the dark threat of Aphrodite and instant, silent obedience; or Apollo wrapped in darkness striking one supernatural blow; or the god coming like night to kill irresistibly until he is appeased; or Father Zeus, far away from gods and men, making one superhuman movement which shakes the mountain and determines the future.

It will be well to conclude this discussion by turning back to that scene which both Redfield and Kirk, in their different ways, treat as not really supernatural: the appearance of Athena to Achilles, at the moment when the furious hero has half drawn his sword and is deciding whether to cut Agamemnon down.

ἧος ὁ ταῦθ᾽ ὥρμαινε κατὰ φρένα καὶ κατὰ θυμόν,
ἕλκετο δ᾽ ἐκ κολεοῖο μέγα ξίφος, ἦλθε δ᾽ Ἀθήνη
οὐρανόθεν· πρὸ γὰρ ἧκε θεὰ λευκώλενος Ἥρη,
ἄμφω ὁμῶς θυμῷ φιλέουσά τε κηδομένη τε.
στῆ δ᾽ ὄπιθεν, ξανθῆς δὲ κόμης ἕλε Πηλείωνα
οἴῳ φαινομένη· τῶν δ᾽ ἄλλων οὔ τις ὁρᾶτο·
θάμβησεν δ᾽ Ἀχιλεύς, μετὰ δ᾽ ἐτράπετ᾽, αὐτίκα δ᾽ ἔγνω
Παλλάδ᾽ Ἀθηναίην· δεινὼ δέ οἱ ὄσσε φάανθεν (1.193 f.).

'While he was debating this in heart and soul, and drawing his great sword from its sheath, Athena came from heaven. White-armed Hera sent her, who loved and cared for both men in her heart. She stood behind the son of Peleus and took him by his golden hair, appearing to him only; of the others no man saw her. And Achilles was amazed, and he turned about, and at once he knew Pallas Athena: terrible was the shining of her eyes.'

We have already seen some reason to feel discontented with the interpretation of this passage as 'little more than a figure of speech' for a simple change of mind on the part of Achilles.[28]

[28] Above, n. 8.

In deciding whether it is adequately described as simply the intervention of higher but not necessarily divine authority, we need to consult not merely the 'content' of what is said, but also the style. We see that the intervention of the goddess is sudden; the line which describes Achilles beginning to draw his sword, the action which if completed would be irreparable, takes an unexpected turn before its conclusion when the goddess intervenes.[29] The four lines which show us her intervention and the hero's response to it consist of a series of short phrases, with no less than seven verbs. The hero feels the same amazement as seized on those who saw Athena dart down to earth like a meteor; no words are wasted as he turns and recognizes the goddess, seeing the shining eyes which characterize Athena, γλαυκῶπις, the goddess of the clear blue eyes.[30] Her eyes shine and are terrible, as Apollo is terrible when he acts against Patroclus, and they are described in the same style of compression and power as Apollo leaving Hector, or Aphrodite leading Helen. She is invisible to all but the chosen hero, and her coming halts even Achilles. Since other scholars have given such different accounts of the scene, it is clear that its interpretation is subjective. To me it seems that what we have here is a supernatural incident, the appearance and action of a god, which is robbed of its nature if it is reduced to any sort of purely human terms. We see both the divine origins of such a scene, and also the characteristic way in which the Homeric

---

[29] ἦλθε δ' Ἀθήνη, 'and Athena came', makes an unusually abrupt rhythm. Rather surprisingly, the only exact parallel in the poems would be the false version of the last line of the *Iliad*: ὡς οἵ γ' ἀμφίεπον τάφον Ἕκτορος· ἦλθε δ' Ἀμαζών—an invention to allow the *Aethiopis* to be linked directly to the poem. More normal rhythms: 22.131 (cf. 21.64), ὡς ὥρμαινε μένων, ὁ δέ οἱ σχεδὸν ἦλθεν Ἀχιλλεύς; ii. 267, ὡς ἔφατ' εὐχομένη, σχεδόθεν δέ οἱ ἦλθεν Ἀθήνη, cf. also xiii.221, xx.30. At iii.435 the arrival of Athena is expected, as the scene is of preparations for a sacrifice to her: ... οἷσίν τε χρυσὸν εἰργάζετο· ἦλθε δ' Ἀθήνη | ἱρῶν ἀντιόωσα. That passage therefore, the closest in the poems to ours, differs in the important respect that the arrival of the goddess is not, as here, sudden and dramatic; nor does anybody see her.

[30] This word is a notorious puzzle. I give the meaning after P. Chantraine, *Dictionnaire étymologique de la langue grecque* (1968–). At 1.200 it is occasionally argued that the eyes are those of Achilles, not Athena; see H.-W. Norenberg in *Hermes*, 100 (1972), 251–4. The invention of pronouns was the beginning of ambiguity, but the eyes of the goddess, not those of the hero, are in point here. 'Achilles erkennt Athena sofort danach, dass ihre Augen schrecklich leuchten', W. Burkert, *Griechische Religion* (1977), 289.

poems refine and civilize, when we compare an Ugaritic text (*ANET*³, 130), about the god Baal.

Athena pulls Achilles' hair and reasons with him: 'I have come to check your wrath, if you will be guided by me.' When the monstrous Yamm sends messengers to the gods demanding the surrender of Baal, the infuriated god seizes a cudgel to attack the 'lads' who have brought the message; he is restrained by two goddesses: 'Now Prince Baal was wroth. Seizing a cudgel in his hand, a bludgeon in his right hand, he reached to strike the lads. His right hand Anath[31] seizes, Ashtoreth seizes his left hand', and they expostulate with him, pointing out that messengers are only agents, not principals, and should not be attacked. By comparison with this lively episode, we see that the *Iliad* has made Achilles' anger more heroic. He is moved to draw his sword against Agamemnon himself, and we remember that when the king sends heralds to enforce his will Achilles treats them with urbanity. We see, too, that the intervention of Athena is less forceful and more serene. She does not seize his hands and physically prevent his action, but rather she appeals courteously to his reason. We are still moving in a world which contains real gods, but while retaining their reality they have changed and elevated their style.[32]

Turning from the gods of the upper world to the realm of the dead, we find again that an approach which treats the soul of the dead man as something which 'exists only for others', and an 'aspect of the social soul', while the realm of Hades is 'a non-world',[33] turns out to be shallow when confronted with the text itself. We have seen[34] that the corpse of the dead man continued, in a sense, to be the man himself, the object of passionate hatred in his enemies, who desire to dishonour it and deprive if of burial, and of passionate desire in his friends, who fight, risk their lives, and even come alone by night into the presence of the hated slayer in order to secure it for proper funeral. The intensity of these feelings, productive in Books 16 and 17 of the

[31] So C. H. Gordon, *Ugaritic Literature* (1949), 14.

[32] Compare the fighting of Athena with the battle-fury of Anath, vividly described in the Ugaritic text quoted at *ANET*³, 136: 'She binds the heads to her back, fastens the hands in her girdle. She plunges knee-deep in knights' blood, hip-deep in the blood of heroes', and the very strange scene which follows.

[33] J. M. Redfield, *Nature and Culture in the Iliad*, 177, 181. See above, p. 147.

[34] Above, pp. 44 ff.

most terrible and desperate fighting in the *Iliad*, cannot be reconciled with the conception of the soul of the dead man as
merely 'a kind of monument to the fact that personal life once
existed', and of the funeral as simply a marking of the fact that
'he has done what he could, and his community declares that
it can expect nothing more of him'. Why should the Trojans
proclaim their desire to fight on over Patroclus' corpse, 'even if
it is fated that all alike should die beside him' (17.421), if all
that they can achieve is to prevent an edifying and harmless
ceremony of that nature? The soul of the dead goes down
lamenting to the other world; if he does not receive burial,
then 'The spirits keep him far from Hades' gates, the phantoms
of men outworn, nor do they suffer him to mingle with them
across the river, but vainly he wanders along the wide-gated
dwelling of Hades.' So says the ghost of Patroclus, begging
Achilles to 'bury me at once, let me pass through the gates of
Hades'. Nor is it only one's own community which marks the
conclusion of a satisfactory civic career by dismissing its dead
with honour. Achilles, we hear, when he had slain Andromache's father, 'did not strip off his armour, for reverence restrained him, but he burned him with his inlaid armour and
heaped a cairn over him'. After Patroclus' death Achilles
changed, in this as in other respects, and the glimpse of his old
behaviour contrasts all the more tellingly with his refusal of
burial to Hector.[35]

The dead are not only 'strengthless heads', ἀμενηνὰ κάρηνα,
they are also 'the famous nations of the dead', κλυτὰ ἔθνεα νεκρῶν.
The god of the lower world is called Aidoneus, lord of the dead,
famous horseman, strong doorkeeper, who rules with his hound
and his wife Persephone over a realm of decay which the gods
abhor.[36] By it flow the River of Fire and the River of Lamentation, Pyriphlegethon and Cocytus. The dead have no substance
and cannot speak to the living unless they are given fresh blood

[35] Fate of the unburied, 23.71–4. It is consistent with this that Elpenor, being unburied, is not among the other shades, and that he begs for burial, xi.52 ff. Achilles
buries Eetion, 6.416; contrast the horrific treatment (flaying, impaling, and so on)
meted out to defeated kings by the Assyrians: Luckenbill, *Records*, 290, 292, 298,
etc. Agamemnon wishes to destroy the Trojans utterly: 'may they be destroyed
uncared for and unknown', 6.60, that is, without tendance after death.
[36] Lord of the dead, 20.61; πυλάρταο κρατεροῖο, 13.415; κλυτόπωλος, 5.654;
the hound of hateful Hades, 8.368; gods abhor, 20.65.

to drink; but when they are given an opportunity they long to hear of the fortunes of those they have left behind.[37] Their gods are invoked by the living to guarantee oaths, and they punish perjurers under the earth. Althaea, cursing her son, knelt and beat on the earth with her hands, 'calling on Hades and dread Persephone to grant death for her son'; Phoenix was cursed by his father, who 'invoked the hateful Furies', and the gods fulfilled his prayer, 'Zeus of the Underworld and dread Persephone'. When Odysseus has fulfilled his dreadful task of going to consult the dead at the edge of the world, he leaves the place in sudden terror: 'the countless tribes of the dead thronged up at me with a mighty shriek. I was seized by fear that turned me pale, lest Queen Persephone be sending against me the head of the Gorgon, that dread monster, up from Hades.' The lower world is more than a non-world, it is a place of horrors which the battle of the gods might reveal, breaking open the earth, to the disgust of gods and men; and the queen of the dead has terrors at her command just as surely as the queen of the sea has monsters in the deep.[38]

The importance of the argument is this. The Homeric epics are poems about the actions and doom of heroes, but we see everything in them falsely if we do not see it against the background of the gods and of the dead. The gods are at home in the radiant brightness of Olympus, the dead in eternal darkness; men live between them in a world in which light and dark succeed each other. Gods enjoy eternal youth and energy, the dead are without power or activity; men are capable of rising to heroism and may be 'god-like', but for all men old age and death are the eventual doom. Gods can be irresponsible in action and need fear no disastrous consequences; men are so placed that the end of all their actions is the departure of the soul, lamenting, leaving its youth and strength.

[37] 'The other souls of the dead stood sorrowing, and each of them asked of those that were dear to him', xi.541.

[38] 'You gods who under the earth punish perjurers', 3.278, 19.259; Althaea, 9.569; Phoenix, 9.454; Odysseus, xi.632, cf. v.421, his fear that Amphitrite might send a sea monster against him. Hades' kingdom to be revealed, 20.61 ff., cf., in the Akkadian myth of the descent of Ishtar to the Nether World (*ANET*³, 107), the fear of Ereshkigal, queen of the dead, at the approach of the goddess Ishtar. She fears the loss of her power and privileges; in the *Iliad* the fear of the lord of the dead seems to be the 'aesthetic' one, that his horrors will be universally seen and loathed.

In terms of the story, without the gods the abduction of Helen would be what it already is in Herodotus and what it remains for Offenbach: an essentially frivolous tale of a lively wife, a lusty lover, and a cuckold. The agency of Aphrodite, her protection of the man who 'has the gifts of Aphrodite', her compulsion of Helen, make the story a significant and tragic one. The contrast of Achilles with Hector depends upon the divine background. Achilles has real foreknowledge of his own fate, and this is brought out in a crescendo of increasing detail and exactness throughout the poem;[39] he knows he will die, and he accepts his death. Hector, by contrast, passes from despair of the future to hope in successive speeches, and mis-interprets the prophecies he receives from Zeus, falling into disastrous over-confidence. When the dying Hector warns Achilles of his approaching fate, Achilles replies, 'I shall accept my fate whenever Zeus wills to accomplish it, and the rest of the immortal gods.' Hector, however, when the dying Patroclus foretells his death, replies, 'Patroclus, why do you predict death for me? Who knows whether Achilles, son of fair haired Thetis, may first be smitten by my spear and lose his life?' Achilles knows, because he is the son of a goddess, and she has told him; Hector is ignorant, because he is only a man.[40]

Achilles' knowledge transforms the nature of his rage and suffering in the last books, and also his access to the divine world, which enables him to secure the help of Zeus in his struggle with Agamemnon, places him eventually in the tragic position of one who has had his prayers granted, and who sees that he has ruined himself and his friend. As he says to his mother, 'The Olympian has indeed granted my prayer; but what pleasure have I in that, since my dear comrade is dead, Patroclus, whom I honoured above all my comrades, like my very self? Him have I lost ...'[41] Without this background,

[39] Achilles will have 'a short life', 1.352, 416, 505; choice of two destinies, 9.411; 'after Hector', 18.95; 'a god and a man will slay you', 19.417; 'by Apollo, near the wall', 21.275; 'Paris and Apollo at the Scaean Gates', 22.359.

[40] Hector in despair, 6.464; hopeful, 6.476; disregards the limitation on Zeus' promise, 18.292; over-confidence, 8.538, 13.53, 13.825, 17.201 ff.; Achilles to Hector, 22.365, repeating what he said to his mother at 18.115; Hector to Patroclus, 16.859; 'I shall not run from Achilles', 18.305-9.

[41] 'The Olympian has granted my prayer', 18.79. 18.82, τὸν ἀπώλεσα. Some translate this 'I have destroyed him'. So Bowra, *Tradition and Design*, 17, C. Moulton, *Similes in the Homeric Poems*, 104. Most scholars prefer 'lost'. The former

Achilles would be in a different position; his outburst of killing in Books 20 and 21 would lack the tragedy which gives it its resonance, and the story of his wrath would not be, as it is, that of a man whose stature enables him to carry his human passions on to the level of the divine will, but who finds in the end that no man can understand or control its workings.[42]

The theodicy of the *Odyssey* is, in its different way, equally pervasive and important. In that poem human suffering, as Zeus explains in his opening speech, is the result of human disregard of divine instructions. Aegisthus was warned by the gods not to murder Agamemnon; he ignored their advice, and 'now he has paid for it all.' The companions of Odysseus were warned not to touch the Cattle of the Sun, but they eventually disobeyed and so 'they perished by their own reckless folly.' The return of the Achaeans from Troy was disastrous, and many of them lost their lives, because they committed sins at the sack of the city: 'Zeus planned a cruel return for the Argives, since not all of them were prudent or righteous.' The Suitors are repeatedly warned, and the message is underlined by divine signs, of the wrongness of their actions; Athena brings about their destruction, and their fate is seen as the working of divine justice.[43] The poem is not meant to be simply an adventure story. The hero is helped through his tribulations by a goddess, and the justice of his actions goes with divine favour and with eventual success. So it is more than simple poetic convention which explains why the whole action begins with divine intervention, both to release Odysseus from his detention by

---

translation would have its implications for the plot of the whole poem, if Achilles proclaimed himself guilty of Patroclus' death. Parallels such as ii.46, of Telemachus losing his father, and iv.724, of Penelope losing her husband, I think show that this is how the verb must be translated here, but at a passage like 22.107, Ἕκτωρ ἧφι βίηφι πιθήσας ὤλεσε λαόν, where we should perhaps say 'lost' (Hector has not 'destroyed' his people in the sense in which an enemy does, 5.758), the sense of 'culpably lost' is clearly present. It is best not to press the translation of 18.82 too hard, nor to build too much on so difficult a word.

[42] It is in accord with his disregard of this side of the poem that Redfield speaks of Achilles' 'absolute incapacity for illusion' (p. 28). In fact, as Achilles has in the end to admit, he misunderstood the implications of Zeus' plan and his own will; cf. also 16.61, 17.401, 18.9.

[43] Aegisthus, i.35; Odysseus' men, i.6, xii.320 ff.; return of the Achaeans, iii.132; divine signs to the Suitors, ii.146, xx.345; divine justice of their destruction, xx.393, xxii.39, xxii.413, xxiii.63, xxiv.351.

Calypso, and to start Telemachus on his career as a man; and why Athena intervenes again to make Telemachus leave Sparta and start out for home, and, when he reaches Ithaca, to go first not to his own house but to the hut of Eumaeus, where he will meet his father.

In the *Odyssey* what appears to the characters to be chance is seen by the audience to be divine planning, as with Nausicaa's impromptu suggestion of laundry and a picnic. Even the incident which wakes the sleeping hero, just in time to be discovered and saved, is planned by the goddess, Nausicaa throwing the ball to a maid, missing her, and dropping it into the sea: 'they all raised a piercing cry', and Odysseus woke up.[44] Even that, says the poet, was devised by Athena, as it was when Odysseus on his raft found a favourable wind, or Penelope enjoyed a refreshing sleep, or the Suitors insulted the disguised Odysseus, or one Suitor thought of leaving Odysseus' house in time but did not do so, or the spears thrown at Odysseus by the Suitors missed their mark. The world of the *Odyssey* is a world in which there is no place for chance, and the poem cannot be understood unless that point is seen as important; and the divine is constantly at work, leading men and shaping their destiny—whether or not they are aware of it.[45]

The divine is all-pervasive in the Homeric poems. It also has a distinct character, quite different in vital respects both from the imagination of other early peoples and from what we know about other early Greek epics. The magical, the miraculous, and the uncanny, are confined within far stricter limits than we find elsewhere. Zeus in the *Iliad* tells Hera that he feels more desire for her than he felt for Europa or for Danae, but there is no suggestion that he came to the one as a bull, to the other in a shower of gold. Originally the armour of Achilles, made by a god, was impenetrable; that was why it had to be struck from him before he could be killed. The *Iliad* avoids this, preferring to

---

[44] vi.113–17.
[45] Wind, v.382; Penelope sleeps, xviii.187; Suitors insult Odysseus, xviii.346; Suitor thinks of leaving, xviii.155; Suitors' weapons miss, xxii.256. 'The entire *Odyssey* . . . is filled with the same purpose—to justify the ways of god to man', W. Jaeger, *Paideia*, i.54. On the 'new form of religious belief' expressed in the divine leading of the *Odyssey*, U. Hölscher, *Untersuchungen*, 85; I should prefer not to be so confident in assigning the difference to a religious change, outside the poem, which is of a different kind; cf. H. Lloyd-Jones, *The Justice of Zeus*, Ch. 2.

say only, with pregnant irony, that it is 'not easy' for mortal men to break the handiwork of gods.[46] The uniqueness of Achilles' armour is its beauty alone. No warrior can have impenetrable armour or be invulnerable, and the old may not be restored to youth, nor the dead to life. Greek mythology knew of invulnerable heroes like Caeneus, and early epics said that Ajax was invulnerable; Medea knew how to make the old young, and in epics outside Homer Achilles was brought back to life and settled happily on the White Island. In ordinary Greek thought Heracles was a god, and the Dioscuri, Castor and Polydeuces, were immortal and active in the world. But the austere teaching of the *Iliad* is that 'not even mighty Heracles escaped death, who was dearest to Zeus', and the Dioscuri are dead and buried in their homeland of Sparta.[47] As for Achilles, in the *Odyssey* he is truly dead, and bitterly does he deplore his lot. Superhuman powers, like the miraculous eyesight of Lynceus, who could survey the whole Peloponnese at a glance, or the winged sandals of Perseus, or the winged horse of Bellerophon, or the real wings of Calais and Zetes, are all inconceivable in Homer. Only in the tales told by Odysseus do we find monsters and magic, and the poet prefers not to vouch for their truth himself, as Aristotle pointed out;[48] and even there the achievements and powers of the hero himself do not exceed the limits of humanity. Swift-footed Achilles, whose tread was so mighty that it produced, according to a later poet, a fountain where he first leapt ashore,[49] pursues Hector at the pace at which a man runs. When gods intervene they do so in fully human fashion. At the moment of highest exaltation the hero performs feats beyond the normal strength of a man, but not wildly in excess of it; he does not massacre countless

---

[46] Amours of Zeus, 14.319 ff.; Achilles' armour, P. J. Kakridis, 'Achilles' Rüstung', *Hermes* 89 (1961), 288–97, *Iliad* 20.265.

[47] Ajax invulnerable, cf. A. Severyns, *Le Cycle épique*, 328; Heracles, 18.117; Dioscuri, 3.243.

[48] Aristotle *fr.* 163 R. King Alcinous pays Odysseus a rather two-edged compliment when he tells him, 'We do not think you a liar, like so many deceivers on earth ... You have told your story like a rhapsode', that is, like a professional singer. Amazons, like the Chimaera, are also kept by Homer to allusions in speeches made by the characters in the poems, like the shape-changing of Proteus, the petrifaction of Niobe, and the weird stories of the daughters of Pandareus.

[49] Antimachus *fr.* 84 Wyss.

thousands, like Roland at Roncesvalles or Dionysus in Nonnus.[50]

Now, many of these wilder and less human stories did feature prominently in the other epics of Greece. The Argonaut story featured a speaking ship, the supernatural music of Orpheus (contrast, in the *Iliad*, Achilles singing of the glorious deeds of men, on a lyre captured when he sacked a city), the winged sons of the North Wind, fire-breathing bulls, a dragon guarding the Golden Fleece, and so on. Even in the sombre *Thebaid* Athena was bringing immortality to her wounded protégé Tydeus (contrast the 'gentle death' in store for her protégé Odysseus), when his conduct made her change her mind. In the other epics on the theme of Troy, Memnon was given immortality after being slain by Achilles, and Achilles himself taken to the White Island by his mother; the Dioscuri were given by Zeus 'immortality on alternate days', a bizarre notion; Iphigeneia was made immortal by Artemis; and all the main characters in the *Telegony*, including Penelope and Telemachus, were made immortal by Circe.[51]

This is an absolutely central characteristic. In the *Iliad* an unkillable warrior would be an absurdity; every man must face death, and no magical armour can be allowed to exempt him from that terrible prospect. And that death must be a real death, not one which is to be blurred or evaded by allowing the hero to be presented with immortality instead. That their mightiest heroes were really dead was an idea which, in general, the Greeks found very hard to bear. Even the *Odyssey* flinches from the stern Iliadic view to the extent of allowing Menelaus to claim that he is fated not to die.[52] But in general the Homeric poems insist that all men are alike subject to that necessity.

The Homeric gods are calculated to bring out the nature of Homeric man. 'Blessed gods', 'gods who live at ease', they confront 'miserable mortals', 'wretched mortals'. 'Deathless and ageless', they look on at men doomed to age and death. By contemplating men, the gods understand their own

---

[50] On all this see, for instance, W. R. Paton in *CR* 1912, 3, H. Fränkel, *Dichtung und Philosophie*, 79, A. Lesky, *Gesammelte Schriften*, 428 ff., J. Griffin, 'The Epic Cycle and the Uniqueness of Homer', in *JHS* 97 (1977), 39–53.

[51] References in *JHS* 97 (1977), 42.

[52] iv.561 ff.

nature,[53] and their home on radiant Olympus can be described only by the negative of the features of this world:

> ἡ μὲν ἄρ' ὣς εἰποῦσ' ἀπέβη γλαυκῶπις Ἀθήνη
> Οὔλυμπόνδ', ὅθι φασὶ θεῶν ἕδος ἀσφαλὲς αἰεὶ
> ἔμμεναι· οὔτ' ἀνέμοισι τινάσσεται οὔτε ποτ' ὄμβρῳ
> δεύεται οὔτε χιὼν ἐπιπίλναται, ἀλλὰ μάλ' αἴθρη
> πέπταται ἀννέφελος, λευκὴ δ' ἐπιδέδρομεν αἴγλη·
> τῷ ἔνι τέρπονται μάκαρες θεοὶ ἤματα πάντα (vi. 41 ff.).

'So spoke bright-eyed Athena and departed to Olympus, where they say is the seat of the gods, unmoved for ever. Not by winds is it shaken, nor ever wetted with rain, nor does the snow come near it, but bright air is spread about it cloudless, and white radiance plays upon it. There the blessed gods live in delight all their days.'[54] At the same time it is by contemplating the gods and seeing in them a nature like their own, but delivered from the restrictions which hamper and limit them, that men understand what they are themselves.

'Remember that you are not a god' was the most regular and most typical of all expressions of Greek wisdom; it would not have been, if Greeks had not been tempted to forget it, and to think that they were, or could be, gods. A god has the power, the stature, and the freedom from death and from fear of consequences, which a man would like to have. We shall draw some more of the particular consequences of the divine existence and observation of human actions, in the last chapter, but now what concerns us is the general situation, in a world which contains both men and also gods. We have seen that men aspire to be god-like and are dignified with that title, which is not without pathos. Men even try to fight with gods, and in very special circumstances, with the immediate aid of another god, may for once prevail, as Diomede does over Aphrodite and Ares; but in the next book he is made to explain elaborately that without such aid he would not think of attacking a god. Lycurgus, who attacked Dionysus, was blinded and killed by the gods who live at ease. Eurytus, who challenged Apollo at

[53] μάκαρες θεοί, θεοὶ ῥεῖα ζώοντες, and δειλοῖσι βροτοῖσι, ὀιζυροῖσι βροτοῖσι. A god is ἀθάνατος καὶ ἀγήρως. Gods need men to understand themselves: W. F. Otto, *The Homeric Gods*, 129, 'It is only by contrast with mankind that the gods become fully aware of their grandeur and their oneness.'

[54] Cf. R. Spieker in *Hermes*, 97 (1969), 136–61.

archery, and Thamyris, who challenged the Muses at song, both came to grief; Niobe, who claimed to equal Leto, saw all her children slain by Artemis and Apollo and, at last turned to stone, still broods over her sufferings at the gods' hands. Otus and Ephialtes who tried to attack Olympus, were slain in their youth by Apollo, though they were 'the fairest and biggest of men, after famous Orion'. 'He does not live long who fights with the immortals, nor do his children prattle about his knees as he returns from the dread slaughter of battle', says Dione, consoling her daughter Aphrodite in heaven.[55] The stature of man is defined by both facts: men can aspire even to contend with gods—but such aspiration must end in disaster. The god returns to his blessedness, but the man is destroyed.

Gods need fear no consequences, and they are free to grant or to reject the prayers of men. Agamemnon prayed to Zeus for victory over Troy, but the god 'accepted his offerings, but made his painful toil increase'. Achilles prays to Zeus that Patroclus may drive the Trojans back from the ships and return in safety: 'So he spoke in prayer, and Zeus the Counsellor heard him. One part he granted, the other he refused.' The women of Troy pray to Athena for deliverance, 'but Pallas Athena denied the prayer.' Even grimmer, when both sides pray for a just outcome to the duel between Paris and Menelaus, 'So they spoke, but Zeus did not yet grant their prayer.'[56] The plans and purposes of gods can thus be inscrutable. Athena in the *Odyssey* is constantly disguised and mysterious. Not even Zeus can make Hera tell why she is resolved on the destruction of Troy. Athena, who has a shrine and receives offerings and prayers on the acropolis of Troy, is determined to destroy the city. The plan of Zeus is a mystery, first to Agamemnon, who believes that the god plans to glorify him and permit Troy's fall, and then to Hector, who thinks the god is assisting him to destroy the Achaeans altogether; even Achilles turns out to have misunderstood in the end. Gods practise deception, from the false dream sent to Agamemnon and the temptation of Pandarus by Athena, to the deadly deceit with which the goddess ensnares Hector. Apollo, in the *Iliad*, has two levels of hostility towards the Achaeans; they arouse and assuage, in the first book, an anger whose passing leaves him still their enemy, despite the ceremony in which 'all day long they worshipped the god with music, singing the lovely paean to the Archer, while his heart delighted to hear them'.

The complex plan of Zeus, which involves helping Troy but not actually routing the Achaeans, leads to ambiguities. Nestor prays to him for succour, and Zeus, hearing his prayer, thunders mightily; but the Trojans are encouraged by the sign to attack all the more, taking it to themselves. The darkness which Zeus sheds over the corpse of Patroclus as a mark of his affection for him becomes such a horror and encumbrance to the Achaeans who are trying to rescue the body that Ajax utters his moving prayer, 'Father Zeus, at least deliver the sons of the Achaeans from the darkness and gives us clear sky and let us see; and in the light slay us, since that is your will.'[57] At a more general level, the poet offers no explanation for the fact that once there were heroes, and now there are not, but only the inferior men of today. Hesiod tried to fit their appearance and disappearance into a universal scheme of human history, but for Homer it is simply an unexplained fact. We are told only that Hera gave full permission to Zeus, in pursuit of her own unexplained hatred of Troy, to sack at will her favourite cities, Argos and Sparta and Mycenae of the broad ways. No doubt by Homer's time they had been sacked, in the period of the invasions; this inscrutable divine will is all that can be found as a reason for such disasters. Still less can we ask for an explanation of human suffering. Zeus allots good and evil as he pleases, giving to no man good unmixed; that is how the gods have devised human life, a life of suffering, while they are themselves free from care.[58] Their carefree existence is necessary, to throw into relief and make us see human life as it is.

---

[57] Hera, 4.30 ff.; Athena, 6.286–311, 20.314; Agamemnon's dream, 2.6 ff.; Pandarus, 4.71 ff.; Hector, 22.214–99. Cf. K. Deichgräber, *Der listensinnende Trug des Gottes* (1952). Ceremony to Apollo, 1.472–4; ambiguous thunder, 15.372–80; darkness over Patroclus, 17.268, 375, 643 ff., cf. Schadewaldt, *Iliasstudien*, 117.

[58] Hesiod, *Works and Days*, 156 ff., cf. F. Codino, *Introduzione a Omero* (1965), 64–7. Hera's cities, 4.50–4; human suffering, 24.524–33, and T. B. L. Webster, *From Mycenae to Homer*, 164. Hera's motive, suppressed by Homer on the surface, was the Judgement of Paris, see p. 195.

And the mysteriousness of gods can itself be a numinous quality. Zeus is both god of the bright sky and god of the dark clouds and thunder. He can be addressed as both at once, as he is at 22.178, ὦ πάτερ ἀργικέραυνε κελαινεφές, 'O Father, lord of the bright lightning, lord of the dark cloud'; and we find the same contrast developed more fully and with greater power in such a passage as this, describing how Hector went to avenge the death of a comrade and with the help of Zeus put the Achaeans to flight.

ὣς φάτο, τὸν δ' ἄχεος νεφέλη ἐκάλυψε μέλαινα,
βῆ δὲ διὰ προμάχων κεκορυθμένος αἴθοπι χαλκῷ.
καὶ τότ' ἄρα Κρονίδης ἕλετ' αἰγίδα θυσσανόεσσαν
μαρμαρέην, Ἴδην δὲ κατὰ νεφέεσσι κάλυψεν,
ἀστράψας δὲ μάλα μεγάλ' ἔκτυπε, τὴν δ' ἐτίναξε,
νίκην δὲ Τρώεσσι δίδου, ἐφόβησε δ' Ἀχαιούς (17.591 ff.).

'So he spoke, and a black cloud of grief fell on Hector, and he went through the forefront of the battle, harnessed in flashing bronze. Then also the son of Cronos took up the tasselled aegis, glittering, and shrouded Mount Ida in clouds, and made lightning and mighty thunder, and shook the mountain; and he gave victory to the Trojans, and turned the Achaeans to flight.' The aegis of the god is glittering, but he hides the mountain in clouds; from the darkness emerge his lightnings. Even the mortal hero, raised and urged on by the god, combines darkness and splendour in the same way.[59] It is not inappropriate to recall the God of the Old Testament, who went before his people alternately as a pillar of cloud and a pillar of fire, and who also could be both at once. Exodus 14:19–20: 'And the pillar of the cloud went from before their face, and stood behind them: And it came between the camp of the Egyptians and the camp of Israel; and it was a cloud and darkness to them, but it gave light by night to these: so that the one came not near the other all the night.'[60] Such a comparison makes

---

[59] I am indebted here to D. Bremer, *Licht und Dunkel in der frühgriechischen Dichtung* (1976), 67.

[60] Cf. also Deut. 4:11, 'And ye came near and stood under the mountain; and the mountain burned with fire unto the heart of heaven, with darkness, cloud, and thick darkness.' Ps. 18:11, 'He made darkness his hiding place, his pavilion round about him . . . At the brightness before him his thick clouds passed, hailstones and

again the point, that such a passage possesses both the style and the substance of a real description of the divine.

The emphasis in this chapter has been upon the numinous and sublime side of the Homeric gods. It has been one-sided; every reader of Homer is aware that the gods are often seen very differently, as frivolous, cynical, and all too human. It is the serious aspect which needs to be emphasized, because it is that which, it seems, is often missed. In the last chapter we shall see more of the other side, but first the moment has come to look at another opinion which is abroad among students of Homer, and which also seems to call for a reply. We have said that the gods of Homer manifest themselves in human and superhuman form, not monstrous or bestial, avoiding the bizarre and irrational. They act through human personality and renounce the wildly miraculous, they speak with men and appear to them in the guise of men and women. This vision of the world was one of crucial importance for the whole of Greek civilization and its vision both of god and man, not only in literature[61] but in religion and art; one thinks for instance of classical sculpture, which raises men almost to divinity and represents gods almost as transfigured men, and so of the continued power of the idea in the Renaissance and beyond.

Such a vision, however, is not sufficiently savage for some tastes. In 1929 W. F. Otto wrote of it:[62]

The clear definiteness of the natural form was accepted as a genuine manifestation of the divine, and hence deity itself must be presented in the noblest of all natural forms—the human. Such views of the divine the modern philosophers of religion refuse to recognize ... They must even prefer the monstrous images which we encounter in the religions of many peoples, because by bursting the bounds of natural forms and limits they suggest the unexampled, ineffable, incomprehensible, and overwhelming ...

---

coals of fire.' Isa. 45:7, 'I form the light, and create darkness: I make peace, and create evil: I the LORD do all these things.' Ps. 97:2-4, Isa. 4:5, Ezek. 1:4, 'A great cloud, and a fire infolding itself, and a brightness was about it.'

[61] 'Gar nicht hoch genug kann der quasi-geschichtsschöpfende Impuls veranschlagt werden, der von der Ilias auf die Ordnung und die Neuschöpfung der griechischen Götter-und Heldensage ausging', H. Strasburger, 'Homer und die Geschichtschreibung', *SB Heidelberg* 1972, 1.15.

[62] *Die Götter Griechenlands*, 213. I quote from the English translation by Moses Hadas, p. 165.

Since those words were written, scholars have begun to take seriously the bizarre myths of primitive peoples, full of 'monstrous images', and the revolt from classicism makes them seem deeper and truer than the human scale and coherent logic of the myths of Homer. Professor Kirk, whose varied and important works on Homer entitle him to a respectful hearing, will serve as a representative figure. 'Greek mythology', he writes, 'is seriously short of the qualities of imaginative unreason that are normally associated with myths', and he speaks of its 'rarity of deeply imaginative fantasy', and can only suggest that this cannot always have been true. 'I suggest in all seriousness that Greek myths were not always so bland, so devoid of real unexpectedness. They cannot always have lacked that crude power and ecstatic dislocation of ordinary life that may be an essential element in the formation of a truly creative culture.'[63] Greek myths are remarkable for the small part that animals play, in the sense of creatures existing and being prominent who are ambivalent in status between animals and man, like Coyote in the Winnebago trickster cycle or Spider in many African tales. In Greek terms, such figures are nearer to the 'lower' form of fable than that of myth. This, on such a view, becomes something to deplore: 'The anthropomorphism of the Greeks was severe. They missed something thereby, I believe.'[64] Nor are these points unimportant: 'The point can hardly be emphasized too often: Greek myths are limited in fantasy', and 'most Greek myths ... have a thematic simplicity, almost shallowness.'[65]

The admirer of Homer, especially if at all favourably inclined to the sort of account given here of Homeric religion as a serious one capable of giving a profound description of the nature and position of man in the world, cannot fail to be stirred by such words. It was surely above all the Homeric poems which created for later Greece the heroic and human mythology which is being criticized. Myths remained, like those of Perseus, or the succession Uranus–Cronos–Zeus, which

[63] G. S. Kirk, *Myth: its Meaning and Functions* (1970), 241, 240; idem, *The Nature of Greek Myths* (1974), 91.
[64] *The Nature of Greek Myths*, 51. A curious connection on p. 50: 'They are half men, these creatures; Coyote in the Winnebago trickster cycle has a huge penis that he has to carry in a box slung over his shoulder.'
[65] Ibid., 215; *Myth: its Meaning and Functions*, 187.

were full of weird things, but they were characteristically driven into the background by fully human heroic stories; and the animal fable which we associate with the name of Aesop was generally *déclassé*. What is it that Homeric myths lack so seriously, this imaginative unreason, this ecstatic dislocation, this deeply imaginative fantasy? Fortunately we are not left without examples of what we are missing. Thus, an 'eerie, almost poetical quality' is possessed by the following myth of the Bororo of Brazil:

Long ago a young man called Geriguiaguiatugo followed his mother into the forest, where she was going to collect special leaves for the initiation of young men after puberty. He raped her, and his father, discovering by a trick that his son was the culprit, sent him on a deadly mission to fetch various kinds of ceremonial rattle from the lake of souls. The young man's grandmother advises him to enlist the help of a humming-bird, which obtains for him the object of his quest. Other missions aided by other kinds of bird are also successful, so that eventually his father takes him on a parrot-hunting expedition and strands him half-way up a cliff, hanging on only by a magic stick given him by his grandmother. Father goes away, but son manages to climb the cliff. On the isolated plateau above he kills lizards and hangs some of them round his belt as a store of food; but they go rotten, and their smell makes the young man faint, then attracts vultures who devour his posterior as well as the maggoty lizards. The sated vultures turn friendly and convey him to the foot of the cliff. The young man is now hungry again, but the wild fruits he eats go straight through him, devoid as he now is of fundament. Remembering a tale of his grandmother's, he fashions a new posterior out of a kind of mashed potato. He returns to his village, which he finds abandoned; but eventually discovers his family, after taking the form (according to the main version) of a lizard. He appears to his grandmother in his own shape; during the night a terrible storm extinguishes all the fires except hers; the other women, including the father's new wife, come for embers the next day. Father pretends that nothing has happened between him and his son, but the son turns into a stag and casts him with his antlers into a lake, where the father is devoured by cannibal piranha fish. His lungs rise to the surface and become the origin of a special kind of floating leaf. The young man then kills his mother and his father's second wife.[66]

And again:

In another Bororo myth a young man refuses to leave his mother's hut and frequent the men's hut, as he should do just before puberty. His grandmother punishes him with her intestinal vapours, crouching over him as he sleeps. The youth becomes ill, but eventually finds the trouble and kills his grandmother by thrusting an arrow up her anus; he secretly buries her under her hammock with the aid of four species of armadillo. Now there is an expedition to catch fish by suffocating them—a method used by the Indians—and on the following day the women of the village return to the river to collect the final victims. The young man's sister wants to leave her child with the grandmother so that she can accompany the other women, but when she cannot find her she places the child in a tree, where he turns into an anteater. The sister stuffs herself with dead fish, suffers horribly, and exhales evil vapours that are the origin of all diseases; her brothers kill her and throw pieces of her into two particular lakes.

A last example, this time from the mythology of ancient Mesopotamia, 'the most fascinating of all surviving Sumerian myths, "Enki and Ninhursag" ':

The action takes place, before the creation of man, in the paradise-land of Dilmun, imagined as lying to the south of Sumer, either at the mouth of the great rivers or in the Persian Gulf. Dilmun is 'clean' and 'bright', and that is somehow associated with Enki's lying with his wife Ninsikilla, 'pure lady' —an epithet, probably of Ninhursag, that may explain the emphasis on Dilmun's purity. In spite of this purity and the absence of old age and death, Dilmun is still short of water. Ninsikilla asks Enki, the god of sweet water, to supply it, and he does so by calling on the sun- and moon-gods for help, as well as by making it come up from the earth and by 'causing his phallus to water the dikes'. Then (or perhaps as part of this same water-supplying sequence) Enki impregnates Nintu, 'the mother of the land', who is definitely Ninhursag; she bears a daughter after nine days. Enki has forbidden anyone to walk in

---

[66] I quote both stories from Kirk, *Myth: its Meaning and Functions*, 64–5, who draws them from C. Lévi-Strauss, *Mythologiques*.

the marshes, but this young daughter, Ninmu, does so; Enki catches sight of her, crosses the river in his boat, and impregnates her. She too bears a daughter, Ninkurra, who also lurks around in the marshland with the inevitable consequences; her daughter is called Uttu. But now Nintu–Ninhursag decides to intervene; she tells Uttu to require that Enki bring her, out of the desert, cucumbers, grapes, and some other fruit. Enki irrigates the uncultivated places to the delight of an unnamed gardener, who gives him the fruit. Uttu receives it and now at last allows Enki to impregnate her. But along comes Ninhursag and removes Enki's seed from within Uttu—or so it seems from a fragmentary text; next we are told that eight different plants are growing, and it is probable that Ninhursag has placed Enki's seed within herself—in the earth—to make them grow. Enki catches sight of them and eats each in turn, apparently so that he may know their name and nature and decree their fate. Ninhursag is infuriated; she curses Enki and withdraws from him 'the eye of life', so that he sickens. She disappears, and because of this and the watergod's illness there is a drought. The great gods are in despair, but the fox says that he can bring Ninhursag back and does so. Ninhursag now seats the dying Enki in her vagina. Enki is diseased in eight different parts, presumably corresponding to the eight different plants he has so destructively eaten; and Ninhursag causes to be born eight deities, one to heal each part. The deities are a miscellaneous lot, chosen solely because their names happen to resemble, superficially, those of the different diseased parts of the body. And so, with Ninhursag's assignment of functions to these deities, the myth ends.[67]

It is of course clear that we have here something very different from Homer. Coherence and rationality are frankly abandoned in favour of shape-changing, incest, friendly animals, and a sequence of events which appears arbitrary and inconsequential. Sophisticated structural analysis decodes the Bororo stories as being concerned with 'an immoderate conception of family relationships' and a theme of excrement and decay which attempts to show how 'corruption is a mediator between nature and culture'. The Sumerian tale turns out to be

---

[67] Quoted from Kirk, *Myth: its Meaning and Functions*, 91–3. The Sumerian original is translated by S. N. Kramer in *ANET*³, 38 ff.

concerned with extending the area made fertile by irrigation, and also with the theme of sexual irregularity causing disasters, with the implication that human fertility and natural fertility are strictly interrelated. All this may well be true, although I cannot pretend that I find the stories, as stories, 'poetical' in any degree.

Now, although the Greek myths, as we find them in Homer and after, are so seriously lacking in the sort of quality which this view desires, the undeniable fact remains that the Greeks did not find them unsatisfying. From Homer to Tragedy, their literature was ceaselessly concerned with the myths, and so were their visual arts and their music. As Kirk himself puts it, 'no other important western civilization has been so controlled by a developed mythical tradition.'[68] There is therefore a paradox about our condemning them, at this late date, for being insufficiently creative and imaginative, unless we are prepared to condemn Greek culture, too, as deficient in these qualities. If we are not, then it may be worth asking what the Greeks did look for and find in their myths, if it was not this exuberant and grotesque play of fantasy.

The answer is not hard to find. Greek mythology is distinguished from others above all by the dominant position within it of myths about heroes.[69] Heroes do not, in general, turn into anteaters, or make themselves buttocks out of mashed potatoes, or impregnate three generations of their own female descendants; nor are they half-animals. They illuminate, by their actions and their nature, not the Lévi-Straussian problems of the relationship between nature and culture, but the position, the potential, and the limitations of man in the world. In the noble speeches and tragic insights of a Sarpedon, a Hector, an Achilles, we see both the terrible and unalterable laws of life and death, and also the greatness which man can achieve in facing them. The loyalty of Penelope, the endurance and resolution of Odysseus, the self-sacrifice of Patroclus, even the tragic dignity of the guilty Helen: all show us that amid suffering and disaster human nature can remain noble and almost god-like. Even the folly of Agamemnon and Achilles'

---

[68] Kirk, *Myth: its Meaning and Functions* 250.
[69] Kirk, *op. cit.*, 179: 'The Greeks are a special case. In the mythology of most other peoples, heroes ... are either inconspicuous or altogether absent.'

passionate rage are raised, by this perspective, to significance and a kind of glory.

It is by the contrast and interplay of gods and heroes that the Homeric poems create and maintain this significance. The Greeks found the result so satisfying that it tended to eclipse the unreason of nature myths. Like them, we may feel that the questions of life and death, the meaning of action and suffering, and the significance and limits of human stature, are not less interesting or less fundamental than those of the contrast between civilization and the state of nature. If we do, then we may perhaps understand why they found their myths, in their humanized form, capable of sustaining and nourishing the passionate attention of a highly creative people.

THE DIVINE AUDIENCE AND THE RELIGION OF THE ILIAD

Eternity is in love with the productions of time—Blake.

W E have been discussing the importance of the gods in the Homeric epics. It is clear that of all the devices which are used to enhance the significance of action, none can be more pervasive or more profound than the existence of a pantheon of gods who are deeply concerned with the deeds and sufferings of the heroes, and who themselves constantly intervene among them. We have seen that no account of the poems can be adequate which fails to take the gods seriously. In this last chapter we shall turn our attention in greater detail to one important aspect of the divine: the role of the gods as an audience.[1] It will again be argued that this is much more than a mere 'divine apparatus', that it stands in a peculiar and identifiable relation to real religion, and that it is of the greatest importance both for the *Iliad* and for later Greek poetry.

The idea that gods look down and witness human action is of course an ancient one and extremely widespread. The very learned work of R. Pettazzoni, *The All-Knowing God* (English trans. by H. J. Rose, 1956), assembles a mass of evidence from cultures all over the world, and his general interpretation of an impressive body of material seems hard to evade. Among Indo-Europeans, Semites, Hamites, Ugro-Finns, Ural-Altaic peoples, and others, we find the idea of a sky-god who knows everything. This conception is surprisingly constant, allowing Pettazzoni to sum up his findings in these words:

We now find that we have a clear picture of the original ideological complex of Divine omniscience. Its subject is not primarily deity in general, but a determinate category of divine beings. Its object is not the whole range of knowledge, but man and his doings. The manner in which Divine omniscience comes about is quite definite, for it is founded upon a power of

---

[1] A longer treatment of this subject appeared in *CQ* 28 (1978), 1–22.

universal vision, completed on occasion by similar powers of hearing, by omnipresence and the like. This Divine omniscience is not merely passive and contemplative but gives rise to a sanction, generally punitive (p. 22).

The 'determinate category of divine beings' is described: 'It is mostly sky-gods and astral gods, or gods somehow connected with the heavenly realms of light, to whom omniscience is ascribed'; and sight is the vital sense: 'Divine omniscience is a visual omniscience.'

Zeus, the far-seeing god of the sky, is pre-eminently a god to fit with Pettazzoni's account, and Indian parallels make it pretty certain that in this role he continues an ancient Indo-European belief.[2] We observe however that there is one important difference. Sometimes Zeus is indeed presented as a moral and punishing god, but often he is presented, and the other gods with him, simply 'looking on', as if human action were a show put on for the divine diversion.[3] Sometimes, again, it is a tragedy which is watched in heaven with tears. I give three examples of each. After the failure of the duel between Paris and Menelaus, on earth both sides try to find the vanished Paris and so put an end to the war, and Agamemnon demands the surrender of Helen; but in heaven:

οἱ δὲ θεοὶ πὰρ Ζηνὶ καθήμενοι ἠγορόωντο
χρυσέῳ ἐν δαπέδῳ, μετὰ δέ σφισι πότνια "Ηβη
νέκταρ ἐῳνοχόει· τοὶ δὲ χρυσέοις δεπάεσσι
δειδέχατ' ἀλλήλους, Τρώων πόλιν εἰσορόωντες (4.1–4).

'The gods sat by Zeus, assembled on the golden floor. Among them the lady Hebe poured out their nectar; they pledged each other with golden goblets, gazing on the city of Troy.' Again, at 7.61 Apollo and Athena, having arranged a duel between Hector and an Achaean champion, sit in a tree to watch, 'delighting in the warriors'. Finally at 8.51 Zeus, having forbidden any god to intervene in the battle, sits exulting to watch the spectacle:

αὐτὸς δ' ἐν κορυφῇσι καθέζετο κύδεϊ γαίων,
εἰσορόων Τρώων τε πόλιν καὶ νῆας Ἀχαιῶν.

[2] εὐρύοπα is used only of Zeus: its archaic form confirms its high antiquity. An Avestan parallel, Durante in *Indogermanische Dichtersprache*, ed. R. Schmitt (1967), 298, and see M. L. West's Commentary on Hesiod, *Works and Days* 267.
[3] 'Es lässt sich m. E. zeigen, wie in der Ilias bisweilen die irdischen Ereignisse als ein Schauspiel für die Götter empfunden werden', H. Fränkel, *Die hom. Gleichnisse* (1921), 32 n.1. See also P. Vivante, *The Homeric Imagination* (1970), 28–32.

'He himself sat on the mountain peak exulting in his splendour, gazing on the city of Troy and the ships of the Achaeans.' On the other side, 16.430: as Sarpedon and Patroclus come together in a duel which will end with Sarpedon's death,

> τοὺς δὲ ἰδὼν ἐλέησε Κρόνου πάϊς ἀγκυλομήτεω,
> Ἥρην δὲ προσέειπε κασιγνήτην ἄλοχόν τε·
> 'ὤ μοι ἐγών, ὅ τέ μοι Σαρπήδονα, φίλτατον ἀνδρῶν,
> μοῖρ' ὑπὸ Πατρόκλοιο Μενοιτιάδαο δαμῆναι . . .'

'Seeing them the son of Cronos felt pity, and he spoke to Hera, his sister and wife: "Woe is me, for Sarpedon, best beloved of men to me, is doomed to be vanquished by Patroclus son of Menoetius." ' As the Achaeans are routed by Hector, 'the goddess Hera of the white arms beheld them and felt pity' (8.350). Lastly, Achilles pursues Hector, running for his life,

> θεοὶ δ' ἐς πάντες ὁρῶντο·
> τοῖσι δὲ μύθων ἦρχε πατὴρ ἀνδρῶν τε θεῶν τε·
> 'ὤ πόποι, ἦ φίλον ἄνδρα διωκόμενον περὶ τεῖχος
> ὀφθαλμοῖσιν ὁρῶμαι· ἐμὸν δ' ὀλοφύρεται ἦτορ
> Ἕκτορος . . .' (22.166–70).

'And all the gods looked on. To them spoke the father of gods and men: "Alas, I see a man I love pursued round the wall; and my heart laments for Hector." '

These passages suffice to show that the gods do watch human actions as a spectacle. They do also retain, in other places, the ancient and universal function of watching in order to intervene, to defend, and to punish. When two sides make a truce, they invoke 'Father Zeus, who rulest from Mount Ida, most glorious, most great, and thou, O Sun, who dost see all things and hear all things' (3.276, xiv. 393); gods go about in disguise, 'gazing upon the sin and righteousness of men' (xvii. 481); Hecuba urges Priam to pray to Zeus as his patron, 'Zeus of Mount Ida, who looks upon all the land of Troy' (24.290).

It would be easy to trace the same connection, of the divine observation and divine protection or punishment, through Greek literature.[4] The 'eye', ὄπις,[5] of the gods generally has

---

[4] Cf. *CQ* 28 (1978), 3.
[5] In Homer ὄπις 'always means vengeance of visitation of the gods for transgressing divine laws,' *LSJ s.v.*; cf. Frisk, *Griech. etym. Wörterbuch s.v.*, for the development from 'Aufsicht' to 'animadversio, Strafe'. Divine eyes and punishment, Plutarch, *Adv. Colotem* 30 = *Moralia* 1124 ff.

this meaning, of an eye to punishment, as when Zeus inflicts storm and flood upon a country of unrighteous rulers, 'who give crooked judgments by violence in the assembly and drive out justice, without regard for the eye of the gods'.[6]

So true was this that it is a regular and bitter reproach to a god to say of him that he 'does not see', meaning that he does not prevent or avenge some terrible happening, or to ask him 'Do you see?' In the *Iliad*, Ares says this to Zeus: 'Father Zeus, do you not grow angry, seeing these acts of violence?'

Of men, too, it is expected that shameful or pathetic sights will produce action. Agamemnon reproaches the Athenian leaders and Odysseus for hanging back and allowing others to fight before their eyes: 'But now you would look on gladly, if ten columns of the Acheans before you were fighting with the pitiless sword.' Athena says that any good man would be outraged to see the shocking behaviour of Penelope's suitors, while Achilles fears that at the sight of Hector's corpse Priam would not be able to contain his grief and anger.[7]

It seems clear enough from all this that the notion of Zeus as observing human action with a view to defence of his own and punishment of wrongdoers is already familiar to Homer, as it was to the ancient Indo-European tradition and to many other comparable early societies. In the *Iliad*, however, it is often replaced by a different one, that of the sky-god and the other gods with him looking on without any necessary implication of action; of the gods, in fact, watching men like spectators of a drama or a sporting competition.

The two conceptions are not of course in reality as sharply opposed to each other as I have here made them. The Zeus who sits 'exulting in his splendour' to watch the fighting at 8.51 has just made a great speech forbidding any god or goddess to intervene in defiance of his general plan for the future shape of the war; and when he looks down and 'pities' the disastrous position into which Hera and Poseidon have brought the Trojans and Hector at 15.12—'seeing him the father of gods and men felt pity'—he at once goes on to outline the future and to enforce obedience to his will. There may be an overlap between gods

---

[6] 16.384. On this passage see H. Lloyd-Jones, *The Justice of Zeus* (1971), 6 n. 27 and reff.: add W. Elliger, *Landschaft in gr. Dichtung* (1975), 78.

[7] 5.782; 4.347; i.228; 24.585.

'looking after' heroes and cities, and 'looking on' at their sufferings; but in some important passages the second idea emerges clearly. The ancient commentators were shocked by the apparent heartlessness of some of them. We have quoted the beginning of *Iliad* 4: the gods drinking toasts to each other from golden cups and gazing at the city of Troy. On this one comment reads:[8] 'People say it is unseemly that the spectacle of war should delight the gods.' Rather touchingly, its author has a solution to offer to the difficulty: 'It is brave actions which delight them.' A similar explanation is offered at 21.389, a vivid and memorable passage. As the gods come together in mutual combat, Zeus laughs for pleasure:

σὺν δ' ἔπεσον μεγάλῳ πατάγῳ, βράχε δ' εὐρεῖα χθών,
ἀμφὶ δὲ σάλπιγξεν μέγας οὐρανός. ἄιε δὲ Ζεὺς
ἥμενος Οὐλύμπῳ· ἐγέλασσε δέ οἱ φίλον ἦτορ
γηθοσύνῃ, ὅθ' ὁρᾶτο θεοὺς ἔριδι ξυνιόντας.

'They rushed together with a mighty crash: the wide earth groaned, and the whole heaven rang like a trumpet. Zeus heard it, seated on Olympus, and his heart laughed for joy, as he saw the gods come together in conflict.' 'Zeus is pleased because he sees them competing in martial virtue', says one hopeful scholiast. This edifying theory can hardly withstand comparison with such passages as the delighted laughter of the Achaeans at the beating-up of Thersites, and Agamemnon 'rejoicing at heart' at a quarrel between Odysseus and Achilles, and the laughter of the Suitors ('holding up their hands they died laughing') at Odysseus' chastisement of Irus.[9] The 'inextinguishable laughter' with which the gods see Hephaestus bustling about in incongruous substitution for Hebe or Ganymede, and with which they enjoy the sight of Aphrodite and Ares detained *in flagrante*, also must fit here, and the 'sweet laughter' which arises when Aias falls in the cow-dung.[10] This mirth proceeds from a delighted sense of one's own superiority; at ease oneself, one enjoys the spectacle of others struggling or humiliated for

---

[8] *ΣT* in 4.4.
[9] 2.270; viii. 78; xviii.100.
[10] 1.599, viii. 326, 23.786. P. Friedländer, *Lachende Götter*, in *Die Antike* 10 (1934), 209–26 = *Studien zur ant. Lit. und Kunst*, 3–18.

one's pleasure. It is a short step to the hateful laughter which is dreaded by the heroes and heroines of Tragedy and which, we must remember, was in certain circumstances allowed by Attic law at the expense of criminals undergoing execution.[11]

In this way we are brought face to face with the question: what is the attitude of the gods towards men in the *Iliad*? I think it will turn out that the conception here discussed provides an important clue to the answer. The question is a vital one, because only in the light of the nature and perspective of the gods is human life intelligible, and the conception of life and death which characterizes the *Iliad* is the poetic heart of the poem and of its greatness.

The subject of heroic song is given by Penelope as 'the deeds of men and gods, which poets sing of' (1.338). Both gods and men have mighty deeds, which can form epic songs;[12] in the *Iliad* a number of stories are alluded to of the battles and sufferings of the gods in the old days, as when Hera was wounded by Heracles, Hephaestus was flung from Heaven, and Cronos and the Titans were ousted and imprisoned in the distant depths of Tartarus.[13] It has often been pointed out[14] that in the *Iliad* such serious sufferings by the gods belong to the past and no longer actually happen. Once, Zeus hung up Hera between Heaven and Earth with anvils tied to her feet; now, he reminds her of it, and at her apology he smiles. Once, Zeus flung gods from Heaven to Earth;[15] but now a tactful piece of clowning by Hephaestus or a climb-down by Hera restores good humour. Lines like those which in the *Theogony* of Hesiod form part of the tremendous struggle between Zeus and Typhoeus (847 ff.)—heaven, earth, and sea all shake, Hades leaps from his throne in fear—serve in the *Iliad* (20.56 ff.) only

---

[11] Aeschines 2.181, cf. Dem. 23.69. The motif of pleasure in watching others in distress, 'suave mari magno', is both exploited and softened by Lucretius, Book 2, *init.*

[12] The attempt of W. Kullman, *Das Wirken der Götter*, to argue that originally there were on the one hand songs purely about gods, and on the other songs purely about men, seems to me to be built in the air. See the review by W. Burkert, *Gnomon* 29 (1957), 166, who points out that the *Song of Gilgamesh* and similar works add to the *a priori* unlikelihood that heroic song ever existed in which the gods played no part. Perhaps Tolkien's *Lord of the Rings* is the first heroic epic to be wholly without gods or religion.

[13] 5.392; 1.590, 18.395; 15.187 ff., 5.898, 8.478.

[14] Eloquently by K. Reinhardt, *Tradition und Geist*, 24 ff.

[15] 15.18; 15.47; 1.590, 15.23, 18.395.

to introduce the abortive Battle of the Gods, which ends not with the overthrow of a mighty god, but with Apollo declining battle sententiously, Hermes declining it with a witty compliment, and Artemis having her ears boxed and going home in tears.[16]

The poet of the *Iliad* even invents archaic-sounding myths of divine conflict in the olden days, such as the story which Achilles 'often heard Thetis tell', of the conspiracy against Zeus by Hera, Poseidon, and Pallas Athena. This tale, isolated and inexplicable as a serious myth, was seen by Aristarchus to be an Homeric invention[17]—the three gods who favour the Achaeans in the *Iliad*, and who have nothing else in common, are combined as those from whose evil plans Thetis rescued Zeus, and whose hostility to Troy should now be frustrated by Zeus in gratitude granting Thetis' prayer for a great Trojan victory. The *Theogony* gives us an idea of the deadly serious poems about War in Heaven, and that they were numerous is confirmed by Xenophanes, fr. 1.21 ff., which tells of songs about the 'battles of Titans, Giants, and Centaurs', all alike, in the opinion of the poet, out of place at the festive board. In those days gods fought with each other, and the losers might be castrated or hurled into Tartarus, never to emerge; but now Zeus reigns secure on Olympus, and immortal battles are soon and easily composed.

Thus Ares, hearing of the death of his son, cries that he will go off to avenge him and defy the thunderbolt of Zeus (15.115), but he is consoled with a cliché ('better men have died before and will again', 15.139–41), and takes his place again at table. In a moment of anger Zeus threatens Ares that 'If you were not my son, you would be lower than the Titans in Tartarus' (5.898)—but since he is, he must be cured of his hurt and dressed in splendour among the gods—

> τὸν δ' Ἥβη λοῦσεν χαρίεντα δὲ εἵματα ἕσσεν·
> πὰρ δὲ Διὶ Κρονίωνι καθέζετο κύδεϊ γαίων,

---

[16] 21.462, 498, 492. See Reinhardt, *Die Ilias und ihr Dichter*, 446, on the transposition of the Titanomachy into frivolity, *Unernst*, in Book 21.

[17] ΣA in *Il.* 1.400, ἐπίτηδες τοὺς τοῖς Ἕλλησι βοηθοῦντας: cf. Σ in 1.399–406, τί ποτε βουλόμενος ταῦτα ἔπλασε; W. Bachmann, *Die aesthetischen Anschauungen Aristarchs* (1901), 18: M.-L. von Franz, *Die ästhetischen Anschauungen der Iliasscholien* (Diss. Zürich, 1943), 17 ff.: M. M. Willcock in *CQ*, N.S. 14 (1964), 144. W. Kullmann on the other hand (*Das Wirken*, 14) believes the story is really ancient.

'Hebe bathed him and dressed him in lovely garments, and by the side of Zeus, son of Cronos, he sat exulting in his splendour.'

A great attempt is made in the *Iliad* to depict all the gods as living together on Olympus with Father Zeus, although it emerges here and there that gods actually have separate local homes, which indeed correspond more accurately to the realities of local cult: Poseidon at Aegae, Aphrodite on Paphos, and Athena at Athens, while Hera has three favourite cities, Argos and Sparta and Mycenae of the broad streets.[18] The conception of a unified divine society is alien to later Greek religion, and it seems that it was a creation of the epic,[19] influenced ultimately by the religious ideas current in the Aegean and Near East in the second half of the second millennium BC. In that period we find such striking resemblances over a wide area, from Crete to Mesopotamia, that scholars can speak of a 'common religious language', Walter Burkert for instance writing, 'A pantheon of anthropomorphic gods who speak and act among themselves in human fashion, who love, suffer, and feel anger, and who are mutually related as husbands and wives, parents and children, obviously belonged to the common language of the Aegean and Near East. So did assemblies of gods . . .'[20] The device had the effect of uniting and contrasting the gods as a whole with the human world as a whole; no longer is it only Zeus the sky-father who looks down from heaven at our sins, but all the gods together turn their eyes upon human doings. The gods who would be irreconcilably out of place in the society of Olympus

---

[18] 13 *init.*, viii. 363, vii.81, 4.52.

[19] M. P. Nilsson, *The Mycenaean Origins of Greek Mythology* (1932), 221 ff., W. K. C. Guthrie in *CAH*[3], 2[2], 905: 'The epic tradition welded into a single family of deities, with clear cut human characters, a strange collection of divine beings of widely diverse origins and nature.' See also B. C. Dietrich, *Origins of Greek Religion* (1974), 43; G. S. Kirk, *Songs of Homer*, 328; L. A. Stella, *Tradizione micenea e poesia dell' Iliade* (1978), 83 ff., who thinks a real Mycenaean 'myth of a divine kingship' lies behind it.

[20] *Griechische Religion der archaischen und klassischen Epoche* (1977), 282. Cf. also C. H. Gordon, *Ugaritic Textbook* (1965), 2, L. R. Palmer, *Interpretation of Mycenaean Texts* (1963), 256, M. C. Astour in *AOAT* 22 = *Essays C. H. Gordon* (1973), 19 ff., E. B. Smick, ibid., 178, and the references above, p. xvii n. 4. Divine assemblies: *ANET*[3], 85, 99, 111, 114, 128, 130, 458. There are those who deny Eastern influence on Homer; thus C. G. Starr, *Origins of Greek Civilisation* (1961), 165–9, J. Muhly in *Berytos* 19 (1970), 44 ff., who accepts that the *Theogony* of Hesiod shows Oriental influence but argues that this is 'simply too late' to explain anything about Homer—a difficult couple of propositions to maintain simultaneously.

—fertile Demeter, raging Dionysus—are as far as possible stylized out of the poem and the world. The gods, together in heaven, are intensely aware of their difference from men, who are repeatedly raised almost to divine height and then thrust crushingly back into their mere mortality. All men need the gods, says Nestor's prudent son;[21] the poet avoids showing the gods eating (only in the *Odyssey* do they eat ambrosia), and they do not, it seems, feed on the smoke of sacrifices offered by men,[22] in the age-old conception, but they still demand these offerings, and it seems that in some sense the gods need men. It is in the mutual reflection of men and gods that each understands not only the other but also itself.[23]

It is the existence of age and death which forms the great difference between the two. The gods are 'for ever deathless and ageless'. All their belongings, too, are superior to those of men, because they are immortal. Achilles' horses are supreme, 'for they are immortal'. Mortals cannot harm the armour made by gods; Hephaestus' handiwork is such as a god should make, not a mortal man. Achilles, son of an immortal mother, can manage horses intractable to other mortal men. Gods are more beautiful than men, and Ganymede is abducted from earth, 'because of his beauty, to live with the immortals'.[24]

Priam pathetically boasts that his son Hector was so splendid that he seemed a god among men, or the child of a god, not of a mortal man (24.258). That is the view on earth: Hector is 'god-like', he is in battle 'the equal of man-slaying Ares', in Troy he is honoured like a god—but in heaven he is seen very differently. Even the proposal that his body be buried is in Hera's view an offence to the superiority of heaven:

εἴη κεν καὶ τοῦτο τεὸν ἔπος, ἀργυρότοξε,
εἰ δὴ ὁμὴν Ἀχιλῆι καὶ Ἕκτορι θήσετε τιμήν.
Ἕκτωρ μὲν θνητός τε γυναῖκά τε θήσατο μαζόν·
αὐτὰρ Ἀχιλλεύς ἐστι θεᾶς γόνος (24.56).

[21] iii.48.
[22] 9.535, 'the gods feasted on the hecatombs offered by Oeneus', is set in the past, in the mouth of Phoenix. The poet prefers expressions such as 'the goddess came to meet the offering', ἱρῶν ἀντιόωσα, iii.436.
[23] cf. H. Schrade, *Götter und Menschen Homers* (1952), 58.
[24] Achilles' horses, 23.277; armour, 20.265; Hephaestus' handiwork, 19.22; Achilles, 10.403 = 17.76; Ganymede, 20.235.

'Your saying might be true, Lord of the Silver Bow, if you will give the same honour to Achilles and to Hector. Hector was mortal and was nursed at the breast by a woman; but Achilles is the son of a goddess.' And Zeus replies that there is no question of equal honour for the two. Gods hate death and have nothing to do with it. Gods have immortal clothes, and immortal armour, their everyday possessions are made of imperishable gold.[25] When they are seen to eat they feed on 'immortality', ambrosia; they drink nectar, which may have the same etymological meaning; goddesses anoint themselves with 'immortality', and with 'immortal beauty'. Menelaus sums up by saying that no man can compete in possessions with Zeus, 'for his house and his treasures are immortal.'[26]

Gods are also distinguished from men in power. Their prowess and honour and strength are greater, and this is regularly brought out by their being able to do all things easily. Aphrodite rescues Paris 'easily, like a god'; just so does Apollo save Hector. The will of Zeus puts a valiant man to flight and robs him of victory, when he chooses, 'easily'. Athena sends back Hector's spear when he casts it at Achilles, blowing it very gently; Apollo kicks down the Achaean wall as a playful child kicks down a sand-castle.[27] Even more than being easy, their actions are irresponsible; gods have no consequences to fear. So Thetis says to Zeus, as he is silent on hearing her prayer:

νημερτὲς μὲν δή μοι ὑπόσχεο καὶ κατάνευσον,
ἢ ἀπόειπ', ἐπεὶ οὔ τοι ἔπι δέος (1.515).

'Truly now, promise and nod assent; or else refuse, since there is nothing for you to fear.' So too Achilles storms at Apollo:

νῦν δ' ἐμὲ μὲν μέγα κῦδος ἀφείλεο, τοὺς δὲ σάωσας
ῥηιδίως, ἐπεὶ οὔ τι τίσιν γ' ἔδεισας ὀπίσσω.
ἦ σ' ἂν τεισαίμην, εἴ μοι δύναμίς γε παρείη (22.18).

[25] Gods hate death, 20.65; Apollo leaves Hector, 22.213; immortal clothes, 16.670 etc.; armour, 17.194 etc.; gold, 8.41–4 = 13.23–6. Ambrosia, 14.170; immortal beauty, xviii.193; Zeus' house, iv.77.

[26] Frisk, *Griechisches etymologisches Wörterbuch s.v.* νέκταρ, Chantraine, *Dict. étymologique de la langue grecque, s.v.*, set out but regard as uncertain the old derivation, which would give the word the meaning 'deliverer from death'.

[27] Aphrodite, 3.381; Apollo, 20.444; Zeus' will, 16.689 = 17.178; Hector's spear, 20.440; sand-castle, 15.362. Also 10.556, 13.90, 14.245, 16.846; iii.231, x.573, xiv.348, xvi.197, 211, xxiii.185.

'Now you have robbed me of a great victory and rescued them easily, since you had no retribution to fear afterwards. How I would punish you, if I had the power.'

Such 'easiness' is a complaint, a criticism, on the lips of the victim;[28] the god has no need to justify what he does, and the ease which is part of the praise of the power of the god has another aspect when the sufferer feels the action to have been unjust. Here the line is a straight one to the criticisms of the gods in Euripides. The dying Hippolytus says to his patron goddess as she leaves him:

χαίρουσα καὶ σὺ στεῖχε, παρθέν' ὀλβία·
μακρὰν δὲ λείπεις ῥᾳδίως ὁμιλίαν (*Hipp.* 1441).[29]

'Farewell to you in turn, blessed virgin; easily do you leave our long intimacy.' The contrast between human misery and the radiant unconcern of the gods is like that in Creusa's bitter aria in the *Ion*, where after accusing the god of rape and of abandoning his child to death she goes on, 'but you play on your lyre, chanting paeans' (905).[30] But what Euripides makes an attack on the divine is in Homer something different, a statement of the nature of the world and human life, terrible but dispassionate.

All the actions of the gods are easy; so then is their whole life. They are 'blessed gods' and 'gods who live at ease'.[31] Their physical circumstances are those of delight; on Olympus, 'there the blessed gods enjoy pleasure for ever', vi.46. There they feast and drink, and have to entertain them the music of Apollo and the Muses (1.603). To complete their bliss they need only one thing more: a subject to interest them. They hate to look at Hades and the realm of the dead; the subject is provided by the existence of mortal men and their sufferings. The

[28] Cf. H. L. Ahrens, '*Pa. Beitrag zur gr. Etymologie und Lexikographie* (1873), 11.

[29] 'No word of rebuke in this: only his yearning for her and a resigned acceptance of his mortal lot', W. S. Barrett, ad loc. But such an objective statement—she is a goddess, and so this action, like all others, is easy to her—inevitably carries an emotional weight; to him it is life and death, to her something 'easy'. It is not 'the puritan's ideal' which is criticized here. 'There is hardly another scene which under the cloak of the holy and the pathetic makes such an accusation', is the perceptive comment of Reinhardt, *Tradition und Geist*, 234.

[30] Cf. also *H.F.* 1115, 1127.

[31] See Wilamowitz, *Glaube der Hellenen*, 1,332 ff.; W. Burkert in *Rh. Mus.* 103 (1960), 140; R. Spieker in *Hermes*, 97 (1969), 149 ff; W. Burkert, *Griechische Religion der arch. und klass. Epoche* (1977), 195.

nature of men and of gods is exactly calculated to set off and define that of each other. Thus as the life of gods is blessed, so that of men is miserable; as they are typically so in a Homeric phrase for 'men'.[32]

Zeus states the rule that 'of all the things which breathe and move on the earth, not one is more miserable than man' (17.446), and the context in which he says it adds, if possible, yet more point; he is moved to pity by the unhappiness of Achilles' immortal horses, which are mourning for Patroclus. The horses belong to heaven, and their grief seems to move Zeus more than Patroclus' death.

The only comfort for death is that all must die, and that truth has a different ring according as it is spoken on earth or in Heaven. Among the gods Zeus laments for the imminent death of Hector, who is 'a man I love' and a generous maker of offerings: 'And all the gods looked on. To them spoke the Father of gods and men: "Alas, I see a man I love pursued round the wall, and my heart laments for Hector, who has burned me many thighs of oxen . . . Shall we save him from death?"' (22.166.) Athena replies shortly that Hector is a mortal and doomed to die; and Zeus at once says, 'I didn't mean it, my dear child, and I want to be kind to you. Act as you please.'

For the children of gods, a little more concern is shown. We have seen how readily Ares is consoled for the death of a son; that of Sarpedon, son of Zeus, is indeed more tragic, and Zeus honours him with a supernatural fall of rain like blood. But Sarpedon is not mentioned again on Olympus, and the contrast is great with the shattering effect of Hector's death upon those who love him, or with that of Patroclus' death on Achilles. The god who mourns as a mortal mourns is Thetis,[33] who has entered by her marriage into human life; and she of course is not at home on Olympus. The only time she is shown entering its bright society makes the point with all the clarity imaginable, for when she is summoned by Zeus she is grieving for her son and reluctant to come among the immortals—'Why has he summoned me, that mighty god? I shrink from mingling with

---

[32] Olympus, vi.46; music, 1.603. μάκαρες θεοί: δειλοῖσι βροτοῖσι, ὀιζυροῖσι βροτοῖσι.

[33] 18.51–96, 24.83–102, xxiv. 47–64.

the immortals; I have countless woes in my heart.' Dressed in
the blackest of garments, 'so dark that there was no blacker
raiment', she comes among the gods, who receive her with a
golden cup and cheering words. 'Hera put a fair golden goblet
in her hand and addressed her with words of cheer, and
Thetis drank and gave back the cup.'[34] Among these gods, even
a mourner must drink and be of good cheer.

With Thetis we have come to men and their acceptance of
mortality. When Achilles tells Lycaon that 'all must die', the
words take on a deep and tragic significance; 'Patroclus is
dead, who was a much better man than you; even I shall be
killed, for all my strength and my mother the goddess; come,
my friend, you must die too. Why all this lamentation?' It is
one thing for a god to say 'All men must die'; it is another for a
great hero to say '*I* must die', knowing that it will be soon.
Achilles' own acceptance of death is the source of the power of
the passage.[35] So too when Achilles speaks to Priam he gives
the same personal application to the terrible generalization that
'the gods have allotted to miserable mortal men a life of
suffering, while they themselves are free from care' (24.525).—
'So to Peleus, too, the gods have given much suffering, and I his
son shall not live long, but here I sit in Troy, far away from
him, a grief to you and to your children.' Achilles' acceptance
of death transforms a cliché into a truly tragic insight, just as
it is also that acceptance which ennobles and makes bearable his
slaughter of Trojans in the last books.[36]

But the gods live at ease and are strangers to death. Consequently they do not possess the heroic qualities which men
must learn by accepting destiny,[37] and their 'life of ease' has a
sinister side. Three times the phrase appears, and twice the
'gods who live at ease' are described as killing a mortal who has
overstepped his limits and trespassed on the divine world.[38] In

---

[34] Sarpedon, 16.459; Thetis, 24.83–102.

[35] Cf. W. Marg in *Die Antike*, 18 (1942), 177: W. Schadewaldt, *Von Homers Welt und Werk*[4] (1965), 260 ff.: and *CQ* N.S. 26 (1976), 186.

[36] Otherwise they would be, I suppose, merely repulsive or meaningless, like the massacres of Indians by an invulnerable Dionysus in Nonnus. Virgil had the insight to see that since Aeneas could not be killed in the fighting in the *Aeneid*, his fate must be made tragic by other means.

[37] The point is well made by H. Erbse, *A und A* 16 (1970), 110.

[38] 6.138, Lycurgus; v. 122, Orion.

the *Odyssey*, where the gods are morally on the defensive as they are not in the *Iliad*, and in which Zeus' first words are a justification of the ways of heaven to men, it is notable that the nearest approach to the life of the gods ascribed to any mortals is given to the wicked Suitors,

τούτοισιν μὲν ταῦτα μέλει, κίθαρις καὶ ἀοιδή,
ῥεῖ᾽, ἐπεὶ ἀλλότριον βίοτον νήποινον ἔδουσιν (i. 159).

'These men care for such things as these, the lyre and singing, at ease, for they devour another's livelihood without paying the price.' Leisure, music, a life of ease, no price: all this is the divine existence presented as an evil. And a cynical view of the joys of heaven seems to underlie the passage where we hear of the throne of Alcinous, 'on which he sits and drinks wine like an immortal' (vi. 309). We seem to be well on the way to that conception of the divine blessedness so elegantly expressed in the Homeric *Hymn to Apollo*: the gods dance as the Muses sing of their own immortal happiness and the misery of men.

Μοῦσαι μέν θ᾽ ἅμα πᾶσαι ἀμειβόμεναι ὀπὶ καλῇ
ὑμνεῦσίν ῥα θεῶν δῶρ᾽ ἄμβροτα ἠδ᾽ ἀνθρώπων
τλημοσύνας, ὅσ᾽ ἔχοντες ὑπ᾽ ἀθανάτοισι θεοῖσι
ζώουσ᾽ ἀφραδέες καὶ ἀμήχανοι, οὐδὲ δύνανται
εὑρέμεναι θανάτοιό τ᾽ ἄκος καὶ γήραος ἄλκαρ (H. Apoll. 182ff.).

'The Muses in turn with lovely voices sing of the gods' immortal gifts and the sufferings of men, the things they get at the hands of the immortal gods as they live helpless and defenceless, unable to find a cure for death and a remedy for old age'; and the gods and goddesses dance, and Apollo plays his lyre among them, stepping high, and a shining is all about him; and Zeus and Leto are delighted as they watch their son dancing among the immortal gods. Such a passage, in which divine gaiety has become wholly an end in itself and mortal misery is actually the subject of the singing of the gods (contrast in the *Iliad* 1.604),[39] leads to the serenely self-absorbed gods of Epicurus.[40]

[39] We are not told the subject of the Muses' song in the *Iliad* passage. The divine archer Apollo who slew the Achaeans from heaven in the early part of Book 1 is in heaven the divine musician who reflects order and beauty. Cf. W. Marg, *Homer über die Dichtung*, 10.

[40] *Comprehende igitur et propone ante oculos deum nihil aliud in omni aeternitate nisi Mihi pulchre est, et Ego beatus sum, cogitantem*—Cicero's cruel portrayal of the gods of Epicurus, *de Nat. Deorum* 1.114. ('Imagine and see in your mind's eye a god who for all eternity has no thoughts except "I am happy" and "I am well off." ')

In the *Iliad* the blessedness of the gods never quite topples over into mere self-indulgence of this sort.[41] The gods look on and delight in the spectacle, but they are not shown as resembling a bloodthirsty audience at a gladiatorial orgy of carnage, but in a complex light. The idea of the divine watcher of whom justice and indignation are expected is sometimes applied to them, but sometimes they resemble the spectators at a sporting event, and sometimes they are the audience of a tragedy. The Achaean heroes themselves are keen watchers of sporting contests, as we see from *Iliad* 23, and Homer's audience is expected to share this universal aristocratic taste. The excitement among the watchers of the Funeral Games of Patroclus, vividly recorded in the poem, with the quarrelling about who is winning in the chariot race and the lively partisanship in other events, forms a parallel to this aspect of the divine audience. It is one of the ways in which the gods themselves form an aristocratic society which reflects and glorifies the human society for which the poem was composed.[42] This is brought out with especial clarity at a high point of the poem, when gods and men watch Achilles' pursuit of Hector. 'Not an ordinary prize was at stake, such as men compete for in foot-races; they were running for the life of Hector, tamer of horses. As when race-horses compete for a prize, a tripod or a woman, at some funeral games: even so did they run three times round the city of Priam; and all the gods looked on.' That is to say, it almost *was* an athletic spectacle of the conventional sort—except that the gods were among the audience, and the stake was the life of Hector. The poet must explicitly tell us what were the points of difference.

It is a remarkable fact that in the Funeral Games of Patroclus a real duel is envisaged, which Achilles announces in language

---

[41] Despite such assertions as that of Rachel Bespaloff, *On the Iliad*, trans. Mary McCarthy (1947), 68: 'The one sin condemned and explicitly stigmatized by Homer: the happy carelessness of the Immortals'. 'Explicitly' here seems to mean 'implicitly'. By contrast, another short work translated by Mary McCarthy, *The Iliad: or, The Poem of Force*, by Simone Weil (n.d.), seems to me a profound and true account of the poem, and of other things besides (reprinted, in a different translation, in: *Intimations of Christianity among the Ancient Greeks*, ed. E. C. Geissbuhler (1957, 1976)).

[42] 'The gods are, so to speak, an aristocratic society which is immortal', W. Jaeger, *Paideia*, i, 32. See W. Kullmann, *Das Wirken der Götter*, 84–6; P. Cauer, *Grundfragen der Homerkritik*, 358.

which means a fight to the death: 'Whichever of the two shall first reach the other's fair flesh and touch the inward parts through the armour and the dark blood, to him I shall give . . .' (23.805). Scholars both ancient and modern have been horrified by this reckless plan, and it is fair to add that the Achaeans took a similar view, halting the contest before blood was shed. But passages which refer to fighting as 'dancing' and 'dancing to Ares', as when Hector says to Ajax, 'I know how to dance to furious Ares in close battle,'[43] make one think of a non-rational conception of fighting, in which it is a game,[44] and one which is watched with keen and critical interest and delight. And indeed just as gods look on, 'delighting in the warriors', we find that a god 'would not criticize' the ferocity with which, at a particular moment, men are fighting. As the battle rages over the body of Patroclus, 'about him the fray grew wild; not Ares who musters armies nor Athene might scorn the sight of it, however great their martial rage.'[45] Men, too, have the same taste:

> ἔνθα κεν οὐκέτι ἔργον ἀνὴρ ὀνόσαιτο μετελθών,
> ὅς τις ἔτ' ἄβλητος καὶ ἀνούτατος ὀξέϊ χαλκῷ
> δινεύοι κατὰ μέσσον,[46] ἄγοι δέ ἑ Παλλὰς Ἀθήνη
> χειρὸς ἑλοῦσα . . .

'And now no man might enter that battle and scorn it, if he could whirl through the midst unhurt and unwounded, Pallas Athene leading him by the hand', for many Trojans and Achaeans were killed that day.

---

[43] 7.241, cf. H. Usener, *Kleine Schriften*, iv, 186; Schrade, *Götter und Menschen Homers*, 110; E. K. Borthwick in *Hermes*, 96 (1968), 64 and 97 (1969), 388. Σ in 7.241: 'War is the dance and the sport of brave men.' Cf. Eustath. 926.3, 939.65. Von der Mühll regards the single combat in the Games for Patroclus as 'very archaic'.

[44] J. Huizinga, *Homo Ludens*, Ch. 5: 'Play and War'. The chapter, 'Jeux meurtriers' in A. Severyns, *Homère*, III: *L'Artiste* (1948), 106–15, is not concerned with this aspect. For another side, see K. Meuli, *Der griechische Agon*, and W. Burkert, *Homo Necans* (1972), 65.

[45] 17.397; 4.539.

[46] Cf. 18.604, in the dance depicted on the shield:
> δοιὼ δὲ κυβιστητῆρε κατ' αὐτοὺς
> μολπῆς ἐξάρχοντες ἐδίνευον κατὰ μέσσους,

'Two tumblers whirled through the midst of them, leading the dance.' Again the similarity of dancing and fighting; and here too a crowd of spectators stand watching the dance, 'delighting in it' (604).

The gods, then, in this aspect of their contemplation of human fighting, do no more than share the taste of the heroes themselves and the poet's own audience. But the last aspect remains: the tragic. The gods in Book 22 look on at the pursuit of Hector, which is so like a sporting event, but the feelings which Zeus expresses are different. Hector, we are repeatedly told, is 'dear to Zeus' (e.g. 6.318, 8.493, 10.49, 13.674), but Zeus plans his death[47] and must watch him die; Sarpedon is Zeus' own son, and he too must be allowed to meet his death at Patroclus' hands, though he is 'dearest of men' to his father, who looks on in pity but does not save.[48] Sarpedon is indeed honoured with a supernatural sign of the grief of Zeus, a fall of bloody rain, and is given posthumous honours in Lycia; but this is such cold comfort that the hero's friend Glaucus cries bitterly: 'The best of men is dead, Sarpedon, the son of Zeus; he does not even help his own child' (16.521). A god, even a god who 'lives at ease', feels passionate emotions as he watches his favourites on earth in triumph or defeat. We have already seen the 'pity' they feel for their sufferings; no less common is anger. And the two goddesses defeated in the Judgment of Paris[49] feel for Troy an implacable hatred which nothing can satisfy but its destruction.[50] *Tantaene animis caelestibus irae?* Blake said that 'Eternity is in love with the productions of Time'; the eternal gods suffer and rejoice because of their involvement with men, who pass away like the leaves and are gone. Such passions are the unavoidable consequence of blood relationships between gods and men.

The divine watching can thus be tragic, and all the gods, not

[47] Esp. 15.68; 15.596 ff., 610–14; 17.207. Zeus also causes the reckless impulse which leads to the death of Patroclus, 16.688 ff., whom he describes (17.204) as Achilles' 'comrade gentle and brave'. Cf. above pp. 86 ff.

[48] 'Dearest', 16.433; pity, 16.431.

[49] Notoriously the Alexandrians were concerned to deny that Homer 'knew' this story, cf. *ΣA* in 24.25, *ΣT* in 24.31. The demonstration by Karl Reinhardt that it does underlie the *Iliad* (*Das Parisurteil* (1938) = *Tradition und Geist*, 16–36) is, or should be, a landmark in Homeric studies. Regarded as certain in some quarters ('Man hat längst erkannt', Erbse in *A und A*, 16 (1970), 106: see also, independently, J. A. Scott in *CJ* 14 (1919), 226–30, E. Drerup, *Das Homerproblem* (1921), 360 n. 1; V. Magnien in *REG* 37 (1924), 145, and G. M. Calhoun in *AJP* 60 (1939), 10 n. 23), it is still by some denied (F. Focke in *Hermes*, 82 (1954), 274: G. Jachmann, *Homerische Einzellieder* (1949), 16 ff.). See T. C. W. Stinton, *Euripides and the Judgement of Paris* (1965), 1–4.

[50] Esp. 4.28; 7.31 ff.; 18.367; 20.313.

least Zeus, are shown to us at times suffering as they look on; their presence and attention also serves as a device to heighten for us the emotional significance of terrible events.[51] But the men in the poem do not know of this suffering. 'He does not even help his own child', says Glaucus of Zeus, and even the favourites of the gods must struggle and die. No wonder that they reproach Heaven, as Menelaus does, with its indifference.[52] The same cry comes also in the *Odyssey*:

Ζεῦ πάτερ, οὔ τις σεῖο θεῶν ὀλοώτερος ἄλλος·
οὐκ ἐλεαίρεις ἄνδρας, ἐπὴν δὴ γείνεαι αὐτός,
μισγέμεναι κακότητι καὶ ἄλγεσι λευγαλέοισι (xx. 201.)

'Father Zeus, no other god is more baneful than you; you have no compassion on men when you yourself begat them, but you plunge them into suffering and bitter pains.'[53]

The men of the *Iliad* are greater than we are, and they do concern the gods. Poseidon asks Zeus if he has summoned the gods because of the Trojans and the Achaeans. 'You have divined my purpose', he replies: 'I care for them, though they perish. But for my part I will stay here, in a fold of Olympus, where I will delight my heart with gazing' (20.19–23). They move him, but he takes pleasure in watching them struggle, and they do not touch him as deeply as did his son Heracles, as Hera points out to Hypnos: 'Do you think Far-seeing Zeus will help the Trojans, as much as he was angry for the sake of Heracles, his own son?' (14.265). And even Heracles had to suffer a life of toil and humiliation, as he bitterly tells Odysseus in the World of the Dead: 'Poor wretch, do you too lead such a life of evil doom as I endured beneath the rays of the sun? I was the son of Zeus, and yet I had suffering without end . . .' (xi.618). No wonder that Zeus is prepared to surrender Troy, 'consenting but against my will', although he admits that 'I honoured it above all mortal cities.' In return he claims the right to destroy any favourite city of Hera; and she agrees,

---

[51] *ΣA* in 22.201, 'In order to produce greater emotion now, as in a theatre'; cf. *ΣT* in 1.541, 'He has invented a spectator for his fighting.'

[52] 3.365, 13.631.

[53] Here we have the original of the passages in Tragedy which criticize Zeus for his indifference to the sufferings of his offspring, especially the *Trachiniae* and the *Heracles*.

saying that he can destroy Argos, Sparta, and Mycenae when he chooses. 'For I too am a god as well as you', says Hera, and so she has a right to have her will respected: Troy must fall. 'Come now, let us give way to each other in this; I shall yield to you and you to me.' And Zeus agrees: 'Do as you will; let us two not quarrel over the destiny of Troy.' This scene,[54] which immediately precedes the outbreak of fighting in the *Iliad*, is a nightmare picture for men. Punctilious service of the gods, even divine affection, is no defence; the will of another god ('for I too am a god') overrules any human claim. 'What has Troy done to you?' Zeus asks Hera, and she need not even answer. Justification is not the point, and the gods are not limited to a tragic attitude towards the sight of human suffering: they can always change their viewpoint and enjoy the spectacle. Finally, they can turn away their attention altogether.

At the beginning of Book 13 Zeus has brought Hector and the Trojans up to the Achaean ships. He then turns away his shining eyes,

> Ζεὺς δ' ἐπεὶ οὖν Τρῶάς τε καὶ "Εκτορα νηυσὶ πέλασσε,
> τοὺς μὲν ἔα παρὰ τῆσι πόνον τ' ἐχέμεν καὶ ὀιζὺν
> νωλεμέως, αὐτὸς δὲ πάλιν τρέπεν ὄσσε φαεινώ,
> νόσφιν ἐφ' ἱπποπόλων Θρῃκῶν καθορώμενος αἶαν . . .
> ἐς Τροίην δ' οὐ πάμπαν ἔτι τρέπεν ὄσσε φαεινώ (13.1).

'When Zeus had brought the Trojans and Hector to the ships, he left them there to toil and endless suffering. He turned away his shining eyes and looked upon the land of the horse-breeding Thracians . . . to Troy he turned no more his shining eyes . . .' The plot requires Zeus not to be on the watch; but the passage[55] is far more than a mere hinge necessary for the action. Zeus can turn his shining eyes on to what happens at Troy, if he chooses, or he can look away and leave men to their misery, strikingly juxtaposed with his serenity.

Again, as battle rages in Book 11, only Eris is present to

---

[54] Presumably this corresponds to the fact that in the poet's time these cities had in fact been sacked. Their patron goddess allowed this to happen, in a gruesome bargain with Zeus. Cf. F. Codino, *Introduzione a Omero* (1965), 66. By contrast, the pleas of the goddess Ningal to the gods to avert the destruction of her city of Ur, and her lamentations after it: *ANET*[3], 458–63. The Homeric conception is by no means 'natural'.

[55] Cf. above p. 131, and H. Fränkel, *Dichtung und Philosophie*, 61.

enjoy the sight; all the other gods are at ease, at home in their lovely houses on Mount Olympus:

> οἱ δὲ λύκοι ὣς
> θῦνον· Ἔρις δ' ἄρα χαῖρε πολύστονος εἰσορόωσα·
> οἴη γάρ ῥα θεῶν παρετύγχανε μαρναμένοισιν,
> οἱ δ' ἄλλοι οὔ σφιν πάρεσαν θεοί, ἀλλὰ ἕκηλοι
> σφοῖσιν ἐνὶ μεγάροισι καθῆατο, ἧχι ἑκάστῳ
> δώματα καλὰ τέτυκτο κατὰ πτύχας Οὐλύμποιο (11.72).

'They were raging like wolves; cruel Discord looked on and was glad. She alone of the gods was present as they fought; the other gods were away, seated at ease within their houses, where each had a lovely dwelling built on the folds of Olympus.' At other times the gods go off in a body to be entertained by the Aethiopians, and the world must get on without them.

From God the All-Knowing Watcher we have thus reached the god who is *not* watching, and who by not watching defines the position of mortals still more crushingly. The gods, it seems, have other things to do, apart from watching the struggle even of great heroes, in which when they choose they immerse themselves with passion; to such an extent that Nestor in the *Odyssey* says that he never saw gods 'loving' men so openly as Athena helped Odysseus at Troy.[56] The gods are involved in human life, they love and pity men; but also they enjoy the spectacle, and at will they can turn away from it. There is no contradiction here, just as we must accept everywhere in Homer that aspects of the divine which seem to us disparate or irreconcilable are in fact inseparable. It is difficult for us to see the dread Zeus on the mountain, whose nod shakes Olympus, as identical with the henpecked head of a jovial society; but for Homer he is both.[57]

---

[56] iii.221. It is no doubt more than a coincidence that striking effects are produced in the *Iliad* also both by the presence and by the absence of human watchers. Helen is brought out to watch the duel of Paris and Menelaus; Patroclus cannot bear to watch the disasters of the Achaeans; Priam and Hecuba watch Hector's death—and Andromache, yet more pathetically, is ignorant of it. The other Achaeans imagine Achilles to be looking on at their sufferings with pleasure, 14.140.

[57] Cf. H. Schrade, *Götter und Menschen Homers*, 70. The puzzle about Homer's gods is their 'Protean qualities', the 'curious intermingling of the sublime with the vulgar', says G. M. Calhoun, *TAPA* 68 (1937), 11; he thinks to resolve the difficulty by distinguishing the crude old myths on the one hand, and the progressive

Thetis finds Zeus sitting alone, away from the other gods, on the highest peak of Olympus, a grand figure; his answer to her supplication is anxiety about the trouble he will have with his wife, and the hope that she will not observe what is happening —an unimpressive response, until he adds the terrific nod of his head which marks his promise to Thetis as irrevocable. This was the scene which tradition said inspired the Olympian Zeus of Phidias, the greatest of all Greek representations of the divine. At his return to the other gods, they all rise to greet him; but the expected row with Hera at once breaks out, leading Zeus to threats of violence, and the harmony of heaven is restored only by Hephaestus' tactful praise of his father's irresistible power, with a plea that they should not quarrel over mortals, as this will spoil the pleasure of the feast, 'since baser things are prevailing'. Hera smiles, and the gods laugh as Hephaestus bustles about in the role of Ganymede or Hebe.[58] This bald summary gives an idea of the utter impossibility of separating 'higher' and 'lower' ideas of the gods in the *Iliad*, or serious ones from frivolous ones. Men are of enough importance to make Zeus incur trouble for their disputes; at the same time they are beneath the serious notice of the gods, who apply to them the words which the haughty Suitors use when their princely banquet is disturbed by the quarrels of beggars.[59] And gods pass with all imaginable abruptness from sublimity to frivolity; neither is truer or more vital than the other, and neither is true without the other. Reinhardt coined the phrase 'a sublime frivolity', *ein erhabener Unernst*, for the gods of the *Iliad*, and he was right.[60]

The rest of the *Iliad* shows that the greatest humiliations and disgraces of the gods are intimately and regularly linked with the greatest exaltations of their power and splendour. Amid the startling scenes of *Iliad* 5, where the mortal Diomede attacks and wounds two gods, we find on the lips of Apollo the most impressive statement of the unbridgeable gulf between gods

---

views of the poet on the other. This is not only a doomed enterprise but also a profoundly wrong one; it is the coexistence of both aspects which makes Homer's gods what they are. Not every compound is the better for being resolved into simple elements—even if it were possible to agree on the means of doing so.

[58] 1.498–600.

[59] xviii.404.

[60] K. Reinhardt, *Das Parisurteil*, 25.

and men: 'Reflect, son of Tydeus, and fall back; do not try to make your spirit equal to the gods. Never is the race of the immortal gods like that of earth-bound men.' It is Apollo again who refuses to join in the undignified fighting of the gods in Book 21, replying to a challenge from Poseidon:[61] 'Earthshaker, you would no longer call me wise, if I were to fight with you over mortals, wretched creatures . . .'[62] Here again the same calm and absolute superiority and dignity are set amid the most undignified scenes; and the lines which introduce the Theomachy were singled out by 'Longinus' for their sublimity (*On the Sublime* 9.6). Amid the seduction and fooling of Zeus in Book 14, we yet find that the union of guileful goddess and gullible god is also the Sacred Marriage which invigorates all nature; and when Zeus awakes, what follows is a reassertion of his invincible power, and the longest and most explicit enunciation of his whole plan for the Trojan war and the eventual fall of Troy.[63] When Zeus insults his son Ares, telling him that he is the most hateful god on Olympus and but for the family connection would long since have been lower than Tartarus (5.889–98), the immediate consequence is that Ares is healed of his wound, bathed, and dressed in lovely garments: 'and he sat by the side of Zeus exulting in his splendour.' In the *Odyssey*, too, the mortification of Ares and Aphrodite, exposed to view by Hephaestus and mocked by all the gods, is followed by Aphrodite's departure for Paphos, where she assumes all the splendour of her divinity:

ἡ δ' ἄρα Κύπρον ἵκανε φιλομμειδὴς Ἀφροδίτη,
ἐς Πάφον, ἔνθα τέ οἱ τέμενος βωμός τε θυήεις.
ἔνθα δέ μιν Χάριτες λοῦσαν καὶ χρῖσαν ἐλαίῳ
ἀμβρότῳ, οἷα θεοὺς ἐπενήνοθεν αἰὲν ἐόντας,
ἀμφὶ δὲ εἵματα ἕσσαν ἐπήρατα, θαῦμα ἰδέσθαι (viii. 362).

---

[61] 5.440; 21.462. On this Apollo see W. F. Otto, *The Homeric Gods*, 66–7.

[62] 'Over mortals', βροτῶν ἔνεκα, cf. 1.574, ἔνεκα θνητῶν, 8.428.

[63] 14.346–61; 15.33; 104–9; 15.56–71. The Near East provides us with divine scenes of love and seduction very different in character. In the Hittite myth of Hebamma, the goddess Ishtar lures the giant by appearing to him naked, *Studien zu den Bogazköy-Texten*, 14 (1971), 55 ff. In the Ugaritic myth of the union of Baal and Anath, 'He seizes and holds her womb' (or 'vagina': C. H. Gordon, *Ugaritic Literature* (1949), 53), 'she seizes and holds his stones,' *ANET*[3], 142. It is worth looking again at *Iliad* 14 in the light of such stories. Anath adorns and perfumes herself before going to speak to the god El, but what she says to him is a series of crude threats—to smash his skull, make his beard flow with blood, and so on: *ANET*[3], 137.

'She went to Cyprus, laughter-loving Aphrodite, to Paphos, where she has a grove and fragrant altar. There the Graces bathed her and anointed her with oil imperishable, such as is used by the everlasting gods, and upon her they put lovely garments, a marvel to behold.'[64]

The gods can always reassert their divinity, show their superiority to men, and retire from the realm of suffering and passion into their blessedness. Now that they no longer have serious wars in heaven, their divine energy might be at a loss without the interest which human history has for them. Their attitude can lead them to suffer, and they watch at times as spectators of a tragedy, rather than a comedy, feeling pity and sorrow, though not of course terror; but their concern cannot rival in intensity that felt by such human watchers as Priam or Achilles. The divine audience both exalts and humbles human action. It is exalted by being made the object of passionate concern to the gods, and at the same time it is shown as trivial in the sublime perspective of heaven.[65]

It seems perhaps most natural to us to think of all this as being far more a matter of literature than of real religion; but the ancients thought of Homer as one of those who formed their theology. So it may be less bizarre than might at first sight appear, to point out that this aspect of the *Iliad* could be described in the words used of his own religion by so passionate a religious thinker as Pascal:

It is dangerous to let a man see too clearly how much he has in common with the animals, without at the same time making him realize his greatness. It is also dangerous to let him see his greatness too clearly, without realizing his baseness. It is more dangerous still to leave him in ignorance of both. But it is very advantageous to draw attention to both.[66]

Both the baseness and the greatness of man are vital to the *Iliad*, and they are brought out with equal force and emphasis. The poet could say of his poem what Pascal says of his own

[64] See W. Burkert, in *Rh. Mus.* 103 (1960), 130–44.

[65] 'Das tief Ergreifende erscheint, aus dem Abstand des Göttlichen gesehen, auch wieder als gleichgültig', Schadewaldt, *Von Homers Welt and Werk*[4], 393.

[66] Blaise Pascal, *Pensées*, ed. Pléiade, 1170: 'Il est dangereux de trop faire voir à l'homme combien il est égal aux bêtes, sans lui montrer sa grandeur. Il est encore dangereux de lui trop faire voir sa grandeur sans sa bassesse. Il est encore plus dangereux de lui laisser ignorer l'un et l'autre. Mais il est très avantageux de lui représenter l'un et l'autre.' Trans. M. Turnell (1962). And again: 'Si l'homme se vante, je l'abaisse; s'il s'abaisse, je le vante.'

work: 'If man exalts himself, I abase him; if he abases himself, I exalt him.' Pascal means that men are like animals because of sin and the Fall, Homer that they are like leaves because of their insignificance and lack of divinity; that is a difference which it would be flippant to minimize. But I think the comparison helps to show that the Iliadic presentation is compatible with a view of the world and human life which is both tragic and truly religious. If the poem did not rest on such a view, one both universal and serious, it could hardly be the great and profound work which it is.

That the gods, especially Zeus, observed human actions, was a natural and universal idea. That they contemplated them as a moving but also entertaining spectacle was not; and the gods had to pay a certain price for the great benefits it gave the poem in literary terms. Already in Homer it is at moments on the point of becoming a reproach to them that they 'look on' at injustice or suffering; but that is another story. It remains here to consider the sort of effects made possible by the Iliadic conception. Sometimes dramatic, sometimes small and inconspicuous, they are of great importance for the poem.

We have already discussed the opening of *Iliad* 13, Zeus turning away his shining eyes and leaving men to their unending labour and pain. Similar is the contrast, all the more effective for being unstressed, in a passage like this, of the partisanship of Zeus and Poseidon for the two warring sides:

> τὼ δ' ἄμφις φρονέοντε δύω Κρόνου υἷε κραταιὼ
> ἀνδράσιν ἡρώεσσιν ἐτεύχετον ἄλγεα λυγρά (13.345).

'Those two mighty sons of Cronos, their wills in conflict, were contriving pain and suffering for heroic men.'

In the eleventh book Zeus 'stretched the lines of battle level, gazing down from Mount Ida, and they slaughtered each other' (11.336). Apollo destroys the Achaean wall as a child destroys a sand-castle:

> ὥς ῥα σύ, ἤιε Φοῖβε, πολὺν κάματον καὶ ὀιζὺν
> σύγχεας Ἀργείων ... (15.365).[67]

---

[67] Cf. 12.29, the eventual complete effacement by the gods of the wall, τὰ θέσαν μογέοντες Ἀχαιοί, 'which the Achaeans toiled to build'.

'So did you, Phoebus, shatter much labour and sweat of the Argives . . .' Again, Zeus sits by himself, ignoring the hostility of the other gods,

εἰσορόων Τρώων τε πόλιν καὶ νῆας Ἀχαιῶν
χαλκοῦ τε στεροπήν, ὄλλυντάς τ᾽ ὀλλυμένους τε (11.82).

'Gazing on the city of Troy and the Achaean ships, and the flash of bronze, and men slaying and being slain'. Such details bring out the full complexity of human and divine action and suffering: the frightful impact on men of the intervention of immeasurably superior gods. For men, suffering, labour, and death; for the gods, serene observation and easy action. We have seen this again in passages which bring out the difference between a man who is 'god-like' and a real god.[68]

These passages derive their power from the existence of the divine audience. The gods look on, and under their shining gaze human achievements and human suffering are seen in a certain unique way. We are able to share their viewpoint and to see human life as they see it, in its double aspect of greatness and littleness. And the gods themselves acquire not least from their role of watchers their own complex nature: sublime heavenly witnesses and judges, and at the same time all-too-human spectators and partisans. The development of the real and simple religious conception into a complex literary device was momentous for the later literature and religion of antiquity.

This conception of the gods as an audience, constantly present, and by turns serenely contemplative and passionately emotional, proved to be very hard to maintain. Outside the *Iliad* the divine onlooker, if he does not intervene for justice, tends either to be criticized as immoral, or to become detached altogether from human life in Epicurean idleness. Already in the *Odyssey* the gods can be seen pointing the two possible ways. In general they observe human sin and righteousness (xvii.487), moving among men in disguise, an unambiguously moral idea; or else they look on, in the spicy Lay of Demodocus, at a scene of immorality, and roar with laughter (viii.321 ff.), Hermes even saying that he would be glad to sleep with golden Aphro-

---

[68] Pp. 83 ff. above.

dite, 'even if all the gods and all the goddesses were looking on'. But in the *Iliad* this device, like the others we
have been studying, is used, in its complexity, to bring out
and to underline the nature and significance of human life and
death.

BIBLIOGRAPHY

Abert, H., *Mozart*, 2 vols., Leipzig, 1919–21.

Ahrens, H. L., '*Pa. Ein Beitrag zur griechischen Etymologie und Lexikographie*, Hanover, 1873.

Ameis, K. F., and Hentze, C., *Anhang zu Homers Ilias*, Leipzig, 1882.

Ancient Near Eastern Texts related to the Old Testament, ed. J. R. Pritchard, Princeton, 3rd edn., 1969.

Astour, M. C., 'Ugarit and the Aegean', *AOAT* 22 = *Essays C. H. Gordon* (1973), 17–27.

Auerbach, E., *Mimesis*, trans. W. R. Trask, Princeton, 1953.

Austin, N., 'The Function of Digressions in the Iliad', *GRBSt.* 7 (1966), 295–312.

Bachmann, W., *Die aesthetischen Anschauungen Aristarchs*, Diss. Nürnberg, 1901.

Bassett, S. E., 'The Pursuit of Hector', *TAPA* 61 (1930) 130–49.

Bassett, S. E., *The Poetry of Homer*, Berkeley, 1938.

Battle of Maldon, The, in *Anglo-Saxon Poetry*, trans. R. K. Gordon, London, 1926, 329–34.

Beck, G., 'Beobachtungen zur Kirke-Episode', *Philologus* 109 (1965), 1–30.

Beowulf, A translation into modern English Prose, by J. R. Clark Hall, rev. edn., London, 1940.

Bespaloff, R., *On the Iliad*, trans. M. McCarthy, New York, 1947.

Bethe, E., *Thebanische Heldenlieder*, Leipzig, 1891.

Bethe, E., *Homer*, I, Leipzig, 1914.

Beye, C. R., *The Iliad, the Odyssey, and the Epic Tradition*, London, 1966.

Bonner, Campbell, 'The κεστὸς ἱμάς and the Saltire of Aphrodite', *AJP* 70 (1949), 1–6.

Bowra, C. M., *Tradition and Design in the Iliad*, Oxford, 1930.

Bremer, D., *Licht und Dunkel in der frühgriechischen Dichtung*, Bonn, 1976.

Bricriu's Feast, ed. G. Henderson, *Irish Text Society*, 2 (1899).

Bruck, E. F., *Totenteil und Seelgerät im griechischen Recht*, Munich, 1926.

Buffière, F., *Les Mythes d'Homère et la pensée grecque*, Paris, 1956.

Burkert, W., 'Das Lied von Ares und Aphrodite', *Rh. Mus.* 103 (1960), 130–44.

—— 'Γόης. Zum griechischen Schamanismus', *Rh. Mus.* 105 (1962), 36–55.

—— *Homo Necans*, Berlin, 1972.

—— 'Von Amenophis II zur Bogenprobe des Odysseus', *Grazer Beiträge*, 1 (1973), 69–78.

—— 'Rešep-Figuren', ibid., 4 (1976), 51–80.

—— *Die griechische Religion der archaischen und klassischen Epoche*, Stuttgart, 1977.

—— 'Das hunderttorige Theben und die Datierung der Ilias', *WS* 10 (1978), 5–21.

Caithe Maige Turedh, ed. W. Stokes, in *Revue Celtique* 12 (1891).

Cambridge History of the Bible, I, ed. P. R. Ackroyd and C. F. Evans, Cambridge, 1970.

Campanile, E., 'Indo-European Metaphors and non-Indo-European Metaphors', *Indo-European Studies* 2 (1974), 247–58.

Cauer, F., 'Homer als Charakteristiker', *NJbb.* (1900), 597–610.

Cauer, F., *Grundfragen der Homerkritik*, 3rd edn., Leipzig, 1923.

Cid, Song of My, trans. W. S. Merwin, London, 1969.

Clarke, W. M., 'Achilles and Patroclus in Love', *Hermes* 106 (1978), 381–95.

Codino, F., *Introduzione a Omero*, Rome, 1965.

Deichgräber, K., *Der listensinnende Trug des Gottes*, Göttingen, 1952.

Deichgräber, K., 'Der letzte Gesang der Ilias', *SB Mainz*, 1972.

Dihle, A., *Homerprobleme*, Opladen, 1970.

Dirlmeier, F., 'Θεοφιλία und φιλοθεία', *Philologus* 90 (1935), 57–77, 176–93.

—— 'Apollon, Gott und Erzieher des hellenischen Adels', *ARW* 37 (1939), 277–99.

—— 'Die Vogelgestalt homerischer Götter', *SB Heidelberg*, 1967.

—— 'Die schreckliche Calypso', *Festschrift R. Sühnel*, 1967, 20–6.

—— 'Das serbokroatische Heldenlied und Homer', *SB Heidelberg*, 1971.

Drerup, E., *Das Homerproblem*, Würzburg, 1921.

Edda: L. M. Hollander, *The Poetic Edda*, 2nd edn., Austin, 1962.

Edwards, W. M., 'Some Features of Homeric Craftsmanship', *TAPA* 97 (1966), 115–79.

Elliger, W., *Die Darstellung der Landschaft in der griechischen Dichtung*, Berlin, 1975.

Erbse, H., 'Betrachtungen über das 5. Buch der Ilias', *Rh.M.* 104 (1961), 156–89.

—— 'Zeus und Hera auf dem Idagebirge', *Antike und Abendland* 16 (1970), 93–112.

—— *Beiträge zum Verständnis der Odyssee*, Berlin, 1972.

—— 'Ettore nell' Iliade', *Studi classici e orientali* 28 (1978), 13–34.

Faust, M., 'Die künstlerische Verwendung von κύων "Hund" in den homerischen Epen', *Glotta* 48 (1970), 9–31.

Fenik, B. C., *Typical Battle Scenes in the Iliad*, 1968 = *Hermes*, Einzelschriften, 21.

—— *Studies in the Odyssey*, 1974, = *Hermes*, Einzelschriften, 30.

—— ed., *Homer, Tradition and Invention*, Leiden, 1978.

Fianagecht, ed. K. Meyer, Royal Irish Academy, Todd Lecture Series, Vol. XVI, 1910.

Finnegan, R., *Oral Poetry*, Cambridge, 1977.

Finley, Sir Moses, *The World of Odysseus*, London, 1956.

Finsler, G., *Homer*, 3rd edn., Leipzig 1924.

Fränkel, *Die homerischen Gleichnisse*, Göttingen 1921.

—— *Dichtung und Philosophie des frühen Griechentums*, New York, 1951.

—— *Wege und Formen frühgriechischen Denkens*, 2nd edn., Munich, 1970.

Franz, M.-L. von, *Die aesthetischen Anschauungen der Iliasscholien*, Diss. Zurich, 1943.

Friedländer, P., *Studien zur antiken Literatur und Kunst*, Berlin, 1969.

Friedrich, R., *Stilwandel im homerischen Epos*, Heidelberg, 1975.

Friedrich, W. H., *Verwundung und Tod in der Ilias*, Göttingen, 1956.

Gernet, L., *Anthropologie de la Grèce antique*, Paris, 1968.

Gordon, C. H. *Ugaritic Literature*, Rome, 1949.

—— *Ugaritic Textbook*, Rome, 1965.

—— 'Homer and Bible', *Hebrew Union College Annual*, 26 (1955), 43–108.

Görgemanns, H., and Schmidt, E. A., *Studien zum antiken Epos*, Meisenheim, 1976.

Gould, J., 'Hiketeia', *JHS* 93 (1973), 74–103.

Griffin, J., 'Homeric Pathos and Objectivity', *CQ* 26 (1976), 161–85.

—— 'The Epic Cycle and the Uniqueness of Homer', *JHS* 97 (1977), 39–53.

—— 'The divine Audience and the Religion of the *Iliad*', *CQ* 28 (1978), 1–22.

Gundert, H., 'Charakter und Schicksal homerischer Helden', *NJbb.* (1940), 225–37.

Hainsworth, J. B., 'The Criticism of an oral Homer', *JHS* 90 (1970), 90–8.

Harder, R., *Kleine Schriften*, Munich, 1960.

Hedammu, myth of, J. Siegelova, *Studien zu den Boğazköy-Texten* 14 (1971), 35–84.

Heinze, R., 'Von altgriechischen Kriegergräbern', *NJbb.* 18 (1915), 1–7, reprinted in: *Das Epigramm*, ed. G. Pfohl, 1969.

Herter, H., 'Der weinende Astyanax', *Grazer Beiträge*, 1 (1973), 157–64.

Heubeck, A., *Die homerische Frage*, Darmstadt, 1974.

Hirzel, R., *Der Eid*, Leipzig, 1902.

Hölscher, U., *Untersuchungen zur Form der Odyssee*, 1939 = *Hermes*, Einzelschriften, 6.

—— 'Das Schweigen der Arete', *Hermes* 88 (1960), 257–65.

—— 'Penelope vor den Freiern', *Festschrift R. Sühnel*, 1967, 27–33.

Huizinga, J., *Homo Ludens*, Eng. trans., London, 1949.

Jachmann, G., *Homerische Einzellieder*, Cologne, 1949.

—— *Der homerische Schiffskatalog und die Ilias*, Cologne, 1958.

Jacoby, F., *Kleine philologische Schriften*, 2 vols., Berlin, 1961.

Jaeger, W., *Paideia*, trans. G. Highet, 3 vols., Oxford, 1945.

Kakridis, J. T., *Homeric Researches*, Lund, 1949.

—— 'Dichterische Gestalten und wirkliche Menschen bei Homer', *Festschrift W. Schadewaldt* (1970), 51–64.

—— *Homer Revisited*, Lund, 1971.

—— 'Neugriechische Scholien zu Homer', *Gymnasium* 78 (1971), 505–24.

—— 'Poseidons Wunderfahrt', *WS Beiheft* 5 (1972) = *Festschrift W. Kraus*, 188–97.

Kakridis, P. J., 'Achilles' Rüstung', *Hermes* 89 (1961), 288–97.

Kirchhoff, A., *Die homerische Odyssee*, 2nd edn., Berlin, 1879.

Kirk, G. S., *The Songs of Homer*, Cambridge, 1962.

—— ed., *Language and Background of Homer*, Cambridge, 1964.

—— *Myth, its Meaning and Functions*, Berkeley, 1970.

—— *The Nature of Greek Myths*, Harmondsworth, 1974.

208 BIBLIOGRAPHY

Kirk, G. S., *Homer and the Oral Tradition*, Cambridge, 1978.
Klingner, F., *Studien zur griechischen und römischen Literatur*, Zurich, 1964.
Knott, E., and Murphy, G., *Early Irish Literature*, London, 1967.
Köhnken, A., 'Die Narbe des Odysseus', *Antike und Abendland* 22 (1976), 101–14.
Krischer, T., *Formale Konventionen der homerischen Epik* = *Zetemata* 56, Munich, 1971.
Kullmann, W., *Das Wirken der Götter in der Ilias*, Berlin, 1956.
Latte, K., *Kleine Schriften*, Munich, 1968.
Lesky, A., *Gesammelte Schriften*, Bern, 1966.
—— *Homeros*, RE Supplement XI, 1967.
Lewis, D. M., *Sparta and Persia*, Leiden, 1977.
Lloyd-Jones, H., *The Justice of Zeus*, Berkeley, 1971.
Lohmann, D., *Die Komposition der Reden in der Ilias*, Berlin, 1970.
Luckenbill, D. D., *Ancient Records of Assyria and Babylonia*, 2 vols., Chicago, 1926–7.
Magnien, V., 'La discrétion homérique', *REG* 37 (1924), 147–63.
Maniet, A., 'Pseudo-interpolations et scène de ménage dans l'Odyssée', *Ant. Class.* 10 (1947), 37–46.
Marg, W., 'Kampf und Tod in der Ilias', *Die Antike* 18 (1942): revised, *Würzburger Jahrbücher* 2 (1976), 7–19.
—— 'Das erste Lied des Demodokos', *Navicula Chiloniensis*, 1956, 16–29.
—— *Homer über die Dichtung*, 2nd edn., Münster 1971.
—— 'Zur Eigenart der Odyssee', *Antike und Abendland* 18 (1973), 1–14.
Meister, K., *Die homerische Kunstsprache*, Leipzig, 1921.
Michel, C., *Erläuterungen zum N der Ilias*, Diss. Heidelberg, 1971.
Moulton, C., *Similes in the Homeric Poems* = *Hypomnemata* 49, Göttingen, 1977.
Mühlestein, H., 'Jung Nestor jung David', *Antike und Abendland* 17 (1971), 173–90.
Mühll, P. Von der, *Kritisches Hypomnema zur Ilias*, Basel, 1952.
Muhly, J. D., 'Homer and the Phoenicians', *Berytos* 19 (1970), 19–64.
Murray, G., *The Rise of the Greek Epic*, 3rd edn., Oxford, 1924.
Nägelsbach, C. F. von, *Homerische Theologie*, 2nd edn., Nuremberg, 1861.
Nagler, M. N., *Spontaneity and Tradition*, Berkeley, 1974.
Neumann, G., *Gesten und Gebärden in der griechischen Kunst*, Berlin, 1965.
Nibelungenlied, Penguin translation by A. T. Hatto, 1965.
Nilsson, M. P., *The Mycenaean Origins of Greek Mythology*, Berkeley, 1932.
Njal, Saga of, Penguin translation by M. Magnusson and H. Pálsson, 1960.
Norden, E., *Kleine Schriften*, Berlin, 1966.
Notopoulos, J. A., 'Parataxis in Homer: a new Approach to Homeric literary Criticism', *TAPA* 80 (1949), 1–23.
Otto, W. F., *The Homeric Gods*, trans. M. Hadas, London, 1954.
Page, D. L., *The Homeric Odyssey*, Oxford, 1955.
—— *History and the Homeric Iliad*, Berkeley, 1959.
Parry, A., 'The Language of Achilles', *TAPA* 87 (1956), 1–7, reprinted in *The Language and Background of Homer*, ed. G. S. Kirk, 1964.
—— 'Have we Homer's Iliad?', *YCS* 20 (1966), 175–216.

Parry, A., 'Language and Characterization in Homer', *HSCP* 76 (1972), 1–22.
Parry, A. A., 'Blameless Aegisthus' = *Mnemosyne*, Suppl. 26, Leiden, 1973.
Parry, M., *The Making of Homeric Verse*, ed. A. Parry, Oxford, 1971.
Patzer, H., 'Dichterische Kunst und poetisches Handwerk im homerischen Epos', *SB Frankfurt*, 1971.
Peek, W., ed., *Griechische Vers-Inschriften I: Grabepigramme*, Berlin, 1955.
Petersmann, G., 'Die monologische Totenklage der Ilias', *Rh. Mus.* 116 (1973), 3–16.
Petersmann, G., 'Die Entscheidungsmonologe', *Grazer Beiträge* 2 (1974), 147–69.
Pfeiffer, R., *Ausgewählte Schriften*, Munich, 1960.
—— *History of Classical Scholarship I*, Oxford, 1968.
Redfield, J. M., *Nature and Culture in the Iliad*, Chicago, 1975.
Reeve, M. D., 'The Language of Achilles', *CQ* 23 (1973), 193–5.
Reinhardt, K., *Das Parisurteil*, Frankfurt, 1938.
—— *Tradition und Geist*, Göttingen, 1960.
—— *Die Ilias und ihr Dichter*, ed. U. Hölscher, Göttingen, 1961.
Robertson, D. S., 'The Food of Achilles', *CR* 54 (1940), 177–80.
Roemer, A., *Homerische Aufsätze*, Leipzig, 1914.
Rohde, E., *Psyche*, trans. Hillis, London, 1925.
Samter, E., *Homer* = *Volkskunde im altsprachlichen Unterricht*, I, Berlin, 1923.
Schadewaldt, W., *Ilias-studien*, Leipzig, 1938.
—— *Von Homers Welt und Werk*, 4th edn., Leipzig, 1965.
Scheliha, R. von, *Patroklos*, Bern, 1943.
Schmiel, R., 'Telemachus in Sparta', *TAPA* 103 (1972), 463–72.
Schmitt, R., *Dichtung und Dichtersprache in indogermanischer Zeit*, Wiesbaden, 1967.
—— ed., *Indogermanische Dichtersprache*, Darmstadt, 1968.
Schrade, H., *Der verborgene Gott*, Stuttgart, 1949.
—— *Götter und Menschen Homers*, Stuttgart, 1952.
Schwabl, H., 'Zur Selbständigkeit des Menschen bei Homer', *WS* 67 (1954), 45–64.
Scott, J. A., *The Unity of Homer*, Berkeley, 1921.
Segal, C., 'The Theme of the Mutilation of the Corpse in the Iliad' = *Mnemosyne*, Suppl. 17, Leiden, 1971.
Severyns, A., *Le Cycle épique dans l'école d'Aristarque*, Liège, 1928.
Shannon, R. S., 'The Arms of Achilles and Homeric Compositional Technique' = *Mnemosyne*, Suppl. 36, Leiden, 1975.
Silva Gadelica, trans. S. H. O'Grady, 2 vols., London, 1892.
Sittl, C., *Die Gebärden der Griechen und Römer*, Leipzig, 1892.
Smick, E. B., 'The Jordan of Jericho', *AOAT* 22 (1973) = *Essays C. H. Gordon*, 177–80.
Snell, B., *The Discovery of the Mind*, trans. Rosenmeyer, Berkeley, 1953.
Snodgrass, A. M., *The Dark Age of Greece*, Edinburgh, 1971.
Solmsen, F., *Kleine Schriften*, 2 vols., Hildesheim, 1968.
Spieker, R., 'Die Beschreibung des Olympus', *Hermes* 97 (1969), 136–61.
Spiess, H., *Menschenart und Heldentum in Homers Ilias*, Paderborn, 1913.
Starr, C. G., *The Origins of Greek Civilization*, New York, 1961.

210 BIBLIOGRAPHY

Stella, L. A., *Tradizione micenea e poesia dell'Iliade*, Roma, 1978.
Stinton, T. C. W., *Euripides and the Judgement of Paris*, London, 1965.
Strasburger, G., *Die kleinen Kämpfer der Ilias*, Diss. Frankfurt, 1954.
Strasburger, H., 'Homer und die Geschichtsschreibung', *SB Heidelberg*, 1972.
Táin Bó Cuailnge, Translated as *The Tain* by T. Kinsella, Oxford, 1969.
Thackeray, W. M., *The Letters and Private Papers of W. M. T.*, ed. G. N. Ray, London, 1945.
Theiler, W., *Untersuchungen zur antiken Literatur*, Berlin, 1970.
Trumpf, J., *Studien zur griechischen Lyrik*, Diss. Cologne, 1958.
Trypanis, C. A., *The Homeric Epics*, Warminster, 1977.
Tsagarakis, O., *The Nature and Background of Major Concepts of Divine Power in Homer*, Amsterdam, 1977.
Usener, H., *Kleine Schriften*, 4 vols., Leipzig, 1912–13.
Valk, M. H. A. L. H. van der, *Textual Criticism of the Odyssey*, Leiden, 1949.
Varley, H. P., I. and N. Morris, *The Samurai*, London, 1970.
Vidal-Naquet, P., 'Temps des dieux et temps des hommes', *Revue de l'histoire des religions* 157 (1960), 60–75.
Vivante, P., *The Homeric Imagination*, Indiana, 1970.
Völsunga Saga, ed. and trans. R. G. Finch, London, 1956.
Waele, F. J. M. de, *The Magic Staff or Rod*, Nijmegen, 1927.
Walcot, P., *Hesiod and the Near East*, Cardiff, 1966.
Webster, T. B. L., *From Mycenae to Homer*, 2nd edn., London, 1964.
Weil, S., *The Iliad: or, The Poem of Force*, trans. M. McCarthy, New York, n.d.
Whitman, C. H., *Homer and the Heroic Tradition*, Harvard, 1958.
Widsith, in *Anglo-Saxon Poetry*, trans. R. K. Gordon, London, 1926, 67–70.
Wilamowitz-Moellendorff, U. von, *Homerische Untersuchungen*, Berlin, 1884.
—— *Die Ilias und Homer*, Berlin, 1920.
—— *Der Glaube der Hellenen*, 2nd edn., Basel, 1955.
—— *Kleine Schriften*, IV, Berlin, 1962.
—— *Kleine Schriften*, V. 2, Berlin, 1937.
Willcock, M. M., 'Mythological Paradeigma in the *Iliad*', *CQ* 14 (1964), 141–54.
—— 'Some Aspects of the Gods in the *Iliad*', *BICS* 17 (1970), 1–10.

GENERAL INDEX

Achaeans, how characterized 4,
15–18
Achilles
his character 46, 50, 52–6, 68–9,
74–6, 84, 98, 122, 127–8,
134, 161, 187, 193–4
its unity 46, 70
character and plot 73–5
and heroism 55, 69, 74–6, 93,
99–100
and Agamemnon 52–3, 71, 157–8,
159–60
and Athena 147, 158–9
and Calypso 59
and Diomede 74
and the gods 163
and Hector 21, 59, 69, 84–5, 126,
138, 163
and Lycaon 16, 54–5, 116, 191
and Odysseus 15, 100–1
and Priam 19, 69, 88, 100, 191
and Zeus 88
his armour 36–7, 126
his cup 17–18, 88
his death 28, 93–5, 100–1, 128,
166–7, 191
his oath 11–12
fasts 15–16
raw flesh 20
Actions
symbolic 2–3, 24–30, 120; see also
scenes
of hospitality 27
of an oath 11–12, 26
of mourning 27
singing 97 n. 50
supplication 24–6
weaving 97–8
actions of cult 148–9; they express emotion 3, 16–18, 27,
46–7, 67–8, 128 n. 43, 149–50
actions of supernatural power
26–7, 29–30, 37–8
Agamemnon
his character 9, 11, 50, 52–5, 80,
82, 101, 106–7, 157–8
its unity 70–2

character and plot 73
and Zeus 9–10, 86, 169
see also Achilles
Analysis, nineteenth century xv,
30 n. 75, 48 n. 125, 55, 61–2,
64, 71–2, 110 n. 13, 117, 133,
137 n. 57
Andromache 2–3, 6–7, 18, 22, 61,
65, 97–8, 109–10, 120, 122,
129–30
Animals 40, 135, 151, 173, 177
Aphrodite 30 n. 76, 200–1
and Troy 5
and Helen 86–7, 156–7
Apollo 42, 82–3, 85, 130, 136, 150,
152, 154–5, 157, 170, 192,
199–200
Ares 34 f., 37, 185, 200
Argus, devoted dog 12, 111
Aristotle 34 n. 87, 36 n. 92, 166 n. 48
Armour 7–8, 30 ff., 33, 36, 129,
136–7, 165–6
arming scene 19, 36 f.
Assyria 16 n. 42, 32, 33 n. 89, 35 n.
90, 38 n. 96, 41 n. 105, 45–7,
95 n. 45, 161 n. 35, 162 n. 38
Athena 28, 37, 63–4, 78, 151, 158–
60, 163–4, 169

Baal 38 n. 96, 160
Beowulf 14 n. 34, 39 n. 98, 93 n. 35,
98
Bible, references xvii, 15, 27 n. 70,
32 n. 81, 34 n. 89, 38 n. 96,
40 n. 100, 41, 45 n. 115, 46 n.
117, 86 n. 12, 115 n. 25,
151 n. 16, 153–4, 157 n. 27,
171

Cath Maige Turedh 34 n. 87
Characterization, Chapter 2 passim
see under Psychology, and also
under Achilles, Agamemnon,
delicacy, Hector, Odysseus
Cid, Song of My 17, 103
Clothes, Symbolism of 3–4, 18, 21,
28–9, 115

Complexity
  heroic 72
  moral 99
  psychological 57–67, 78–80
  religious 171, 193
  of the gods 198–202
  of the plan of Zeus 170
  of vision of human life 203
Corpse
  importance of 44–9, 137–8, 160–1
  fate of 13, 19–21, 44, 91, 115–19,
      137–8
  Cúchulainn, see under *Táin Bó
      Cuailnge*

Darkness 41, 91, 94, 143, 162, 170–2
Dead, the 3, 38, 47, 99–100, 119, 147
  world of 160–2, 189
Death, Chapters 3 and 4 *passim*; 33,
      46, 105
  and life 44, 48, 55–6, 69, 76, 87,
      90, 95, 102, 177–8, 202–4
  and the hero, 33, 72–6, 87–95, 99,
      167, 191
  and the gods, 188
  and *kēres*, 43
  and character, 56
  and virtue, 93, 191
  men called to death, 42–3
  death of a girl, 142
  see also corpse; dead, the; life
Delicacy 57–8, 60, 62–4
Dionysus 21, 187
Divine background 163–6
Divine perspective 18, 43, 87–8, 106,
      128–30, 137, 163, 178, 201
Doloneia, the 13, 54

Eddas, the 20
Egypt 16 n. 42, 35 n. 90, 38 n. 96,
      86 n. 12, 95 n. 45
Enki and Ninhursag 175–7
Epic Cycle, the 114 n. 23, 159 n. 29,
      166–7; *see also under* Theban
      epics
Epigrams 141–3
Euripides 189, 196 n. 53
Eustathius 32 n. 79, 34 n. 87, 48 n.
      125, 61 n. 20, 109, 124, 132,
      135, 137, 194 n. 43

Fasting 15, 149; *see under* food
Feis Tige Bricrenn 15 n. 36, 39 n. 97

Fianagecht 25 n. 66
Finnegan, R. xvi
Food and drink, significance of
      14–17, 19, 88
  of the gods 59 n. 17, 187–8
  raw flesh 19–21, 34
Formulaic theory xv

Geriguiaguiatugo 174–5
Glory 3, 95–102
'God-like' 11 n. 28, 82 ff., 88–9,
      92–3, 168, 177, 187, 203
Gods, Chapters 5 and 6 *passim*
  alleged lack of *numen* 147 ff.,
      171–2
  all-pervasive 144, 163–5
  arbitrary 88–9, 169, 188
  call men to death 42
  deceive men 41, 169
  dignified 150–60; and undigni-
      fied 198–202
  ease of action 130, 153, 168–9,
      188–9, 191–2
  free from care 138–9
  give sceptre 9 ff.
  give weapons 32–3
  inscrutable 170–1
  intervention, in human form 166,
      172 ff.
  invidiously seen 189, 192, 196, 202
  lack virtue 93
  laugh 183–4
  live together 186–7
  love men 33, 85–8, 128, 138, 195,
      198
  manifest themselves 151
  men resemble 82 ff., 167–70; con-
      trast with 130–1, 153–5, 162,
      167–70, 187–9, 197, 199
  mythological and elemental 154,
      cf. 29
  nature responds to 40, 151
  watch men 82, Chapter 6 *passim*
  see also god-like; Paris, Judgement
      of; religion; and the names
      of individual gods

Hector
  and Achilles 21, 59, 69, 84–5, 126,
      138, 163; pursued by Achilles
      21–2, 112, 166, 181, 190,
      193; wears armour of Achilles
      36, 126

and Andromache 3, 7, 65, 93, 97, 109–10, 120–1
and glory 96–8
and the gods 43–4, 94, 128, 154, 169
and Hecuba 25
and Paris 6–9
and Patroclus 42, 45, 68
and women 6–7, 68, 92
and Zeus 86, 128, 138, 195
his spear 13
overconfident 5, 163
his death 1–3, 28, 84, 147
his corpse 47, 59, 69, 85, 100, 138, 182, 187
Helen 5–8, 31–2, 67, 77–8, 80, 86–7, 96–8, 111, 156, 163
Heroes
code of 74
and death 72–6, 90–5
disappearance not explained 170
and fear 93
food of 19
and glory 95–100
greatness of 35–9, 76 n. 49, 89–90, 158, 166, 177–8
loved by gods 85–8
not Berserkers 92
not weird 177
predominance in Greek mythology 32, 46–7, 81, 160, 177
resemble gods 82
see also under Achilles, death, god-like
Heroism
in Iliad and Odyssey 80, 100
complex 72
paradox of 92
viewed as suffering 101–2
and Achilles 55, 69, 74–6, 93, 99–100
Hesiod 170, 184–5, 186 n. 20
Hittites 26, 86 n. 12, 200 n. 63
Homosexuality, in Homer, non-existent 104 n. 4
Honour, marks of 14–15, 99

Iliad
poem of life and death 44, 95, 111, 138, 143, 162, 202
sophisticated conception 1
tragic 22, 108, 118, 138
small and large units 108, 127

characters and plot 73–6
and glory 100
and heroism 80, 87, 162
and suffering 102, 143
and the supernatural 39
and women 65
invents 'archaic' myths 185
see also divine perspective, naturalism, Odyssey, pathos
Irony 10, 23–4, 29, 53, 59 n. 17, 63, 66, 112 n. 18

Kēres 43
Kirchhoff, A. 61–2
Kirk, G. S. 15 n. 40, 25 n. 66, 51, 72 n. 39, 140, 147–8, 158, 173–8

Laughter 183–4
Life
see death
Homeric vision of 69, 102, 130, 138–9, 143

Madness, of fighting 21, 35
Maldon, Battle of 85 n. 9
Malory, Sir Thomas 94, 143
Marriage
true and false 6
sacred 40
human and divine 93
Menelaus 4–5, 54–5, 67, 70–1, 77–8, 84, 101, 123, 167
Miracles, see Naturalism and Objects, magical

Naturalism
literal, not Homeric 19, 141–2
fighting stylized 93
and death 90–5
and the supernatural 32, 39, 165–7
Nausicaa 22, 57–8, 61–3, 165
Near East, Ancient xvii, 9–10, 16 n. 42, 26 n. 68, 30 n. 76, 34, 35, 38, 41, 45–7, 85–6, 92 n. 35, 95 n. 45, 153 n. 22, 160, 161 n. 35, 162 n. 38, 175–7, 186, 197 n 54, 200 n. 63; see also Assyria, Bible, Egypt, Enki and Ninhursag, Hittites, Ugarit

Nibelunglied 4 n. 8, 14 n. 34, 15 n. 39, 20, 92 n. 35, 103
Njal, Saga of 39

Objects, Chapter 1 *passim*
magical 30 ff.
  girdle of Aphrodite 30
  aegis 30–1, 152
  in the *Odyssey* 31–2, 165–7
significant
  bed 12–13, 26 n. 69
  boundary stone 24
  bow 12
  breast 25
  chariot 26
  clothing 2–7, 18, 21, 28–9, 115
  corpses 44–9
  cup, 17, 18, 88
  hearth 25
  helmet 134–6
  plume 135
  rags 29
  sceptre 9–13, 26
  spear 13, 44
  tomb 23
  washing-places 21–2, 112
  weapons 7–8; embody energy 30–5; given by gods 32–3; and the warrior 36
  loss of significance 99–100
Odysseus
  character 15, 24–5, 28–9, 54, 62–3, 86, 101, 155–6
  and Achilles 15, 100–1
  and Calypso 56–7, 64
  and Circe 56
  and Helen 77
  and Nausicaa 57–8
Odyssey, its character, contrasted with the *Iliad* 12, 22, 24, 31–2, 42 n. 107, 56 ff., 67, 69, 76, 100–2, 110–11, 112 n. 18, 118–19, 127, 139, 164–5, 192, 203; *see also* 15 n. 40, 61–3, 79–80
Oral poetry xv f., 30 n. 75, 51

Page, D. L. 16, 59 n. 16, 149 n. 12
Parents, bereaved 108, 113, 123–7, 132, 134, 138
Paris 3–8, 23, 80, 82–4
  and Hector 5–9
  Judgement of 9, 66, 170, 195

Parry, A. xvi, 11 n. 28, 52 n. 5, 75 n. 48, 100 n. 56, 111
Pascal, Blaise 201–2
Pathos, Chapter 4 *passim*, 2, 18, 22, 84–5, 104 ff., 168, 195
  ascending scale 129–30
Patroclus 17–18, 27, 33, 42, 45, 67–8
  and the plot of the *Iliad*, 73, 87–8, 94, 136, 149, 161
Penelope 64, 78–9
Priam 16, 23, 113 n. 20, 117, 119, 126, 132, 153, 191
Psychology
  Homeric interest in, Chapter 2 *passim*, 3, 6, 16, 18, 19, 46, 139
  complex and inscrutable 57–67, 70 ff., 78–80
  unity defended 70 ff.
  psychology and plot 73–5
  unrealistic 76–7
  presentation of actions in the light of 3, 46–7
  gentleness 68–73
  see also actions of cult, characterization, delicacy, women

Redfield, J. M. 7 n. 19, 65, 74 n. 46, 145–7, 158, 160, 164 n. 42
Reinhardt, K. 13 n. 31, 56 n. 12, 70, 89 n. 22, 141, 185 n. 16, 195 n. 49, 199
Religion xvii, 38, 40–4, Chapters 5 and 6 *passim*
  a real religion 201–2
  atmosphere of divine scenes 151, 153, 158
  not monstrous 166, 172–8
  see also divine background, divine perspective, god-like, gods, and the names of individual gods

Saint-Simon, Duc de 121 n. 33
Sarpedon 14, 73, 84, 190, 195
Scenes: representative 1–8, 24, 44, 56, 69, 157; *see also* actions
Scholia on Homer xvi, 2 n. 5, 3 n. 7, 4 nn. 9 and 10, 6 n. 15, 7 n. 18, 8 nn. 21 and 22, 12 n. 30, 13 n. 31, 15 n. 37, 19 n. 50, 21 n. 57, 22 n. 60, 23 n. 62, 28 n. 72, 34 n. 87, 36 n. 92,

38 n. 96, 44 n. 112, 47 n. 120, 50, 52 n. 4, 54 n. 8, 60 nn. 18 and 19, 61 n. 20, 62 n. 22, 65, 66 n. 33, 68 n. 34, 75 n. 48, 100 n. 57, 103 n. 2, 104, 106, 107–10, 118, 122, 126–7, 133–4, 136 n. 55, 141 nn. 65 and 67, 183, 185, 194 n. 43, 195 n. 49, 196 n. 51; see also Eustathius

Shout
  of Agamemnon 29
  of Eris 29–30
  of gods 37–9
  of Achilles 38
Song, and destiny 96–8, 101–2, 143
Style
  of Achilles 75
  compressed 44
  lapidary 127, 141
  objective, Chapter 4, esp. 139
  restraint 121, 142–3
  style of divine scenes 150–9
    enjambement 152 n. 21
Suppliants 24
  slain in the *Iliad* 53–6, 91

Táin Bó Cuailnge 39 n. 97, 39 n. 98, 99
Taste, and literature 65
Thackeray, W. M. 110
Theban epics 14, 20, 104 n. 4, 167
Thetis 17–18, 24, 27–8, 190–1, 199
Trojans
  their character 4, 23
  and Priam 113 n. 20
Troy
  its fall, how represented 1, 28, 117

its lost happiness 22, 23–4, cf. 86, 112

Ugarit 27 n. 70, 33, 38 n. 96, 160, 200 n. 63

Virgil 103, 191 n. 36
Völsungasaga 41 n. 105, 92 n. 35, 93 n. 38

Weil, Simone 93 n. 38, 193 n. 41
Widsith 34 n. 87
Women
  world of 6–7, 22, 65, 92 and n. 33, 112
  psychology of 56–61, 65–8, 76
  hard to trust 79
  bereaved 120–4, 131–4, 138

Zeus
  arbitrary 89
  dignified and undignified 198–9
  inscrutable 169–70
  loves men 33, 86–8, 128, 138, 195–6
  reproached 196
  sublime 154
  view of men, 190
  watches men 87–8, Chapter 6 *passim*; looks away 131, 197
  Achilles resembles 88
  heroes resemble 82
  and Achilles 17
  and events 44, 170
  and Hector 129
  and Hera 40, 66, 184, 196–7, 200
  and Thetis 24–6, 190–1, 199
  the aegis 30–1, 152
  gives the sceptre 9

INDEX OF HOMERIC PASSAGES

This index lists passages discussed, not all those referred to in passing or as supporting evidence.

Iliad	page	*Iliad*	page
1. 1–5	118	343	14
7	11, 52	522	113
14	26	536–8	106
29–31	107		
43–52	150	5. 49 ff.	114
91	52	59 ff.	125
131	53	149–51	125–6
157	75	152–8	124
174	10	434–42	155, 199–200
193–200	146–7, 158–60	539 ff.	105
234–40	11	684–8	109
244	52	738	30
318 ff.	157–8	889–98	200
352	127		
413–17	128	6. 46–65	54
396–406	185	145–221	72
498 ff.	199	212–21	27
500–15	24	318–24	7–8
528–9	26	355–8	97–8
603	189, 192	390 ff.	7
		403	1
2. 100–9	9	416	161
326–30	42	431–9	65, 122
393	115	500	28
478	82		
698–709	132–3	7. 241	194
872	4, 115	423–31	48, 137
		8. 220 ff.	29
3. *init.*	3–4	252	30
1–9	4	384	28
30–7	83–4	491	13
125–8	97		
243–4	111	9. 33	74
299–301	26	186–9	98
395–420	5–6	379 ff.	99–100
413–20	86–7, 156	410–16	99
454	5	644 ff.	74
		10. 199	13
4. *init.*	196–7	372 ff.	54
1–4	180		
50–4	170	11. *init.*	29
156–82	71	72–7	198
237–9	122	82–3	203
257–62	14	99	105

Iliad	page		*Iliad*	page
11. (continued)			51	4, 135
120	113		194–6	126
130 ff.	53		200–8	129
159–62	120		300–3	108
164 ff.	22		397–400	194
241–3	133		421	161
262 ff.	105		437–42	135
328 ff.	125		446 ff.	190
336	202		591–6	171
383 ff.	23		629 ff.	42
391–3	120		645–7	170
604	85			
632	18		18. 71 ff.	27
814–18	108		79–82	163
			121–4	122
12. 310–21	14, 73, 92		205 ff.	37
			222–31	38
13. 1–7	131, 197		245	14
171–5	132		270–2	115
345–6	202		303–5	5
381	131			
428	132		19. 12 ff.	36
578–80	134		78 ff.	71
653–8	113		147	16
831	115		150 ff.	15–16
			295–302	68
14. 157 ff.	66		338–9	68
214–17	30			
347–51	40, 200		20. 48 ff.	37
384	31		56 ff.	184
501–2	123		200–42	72
			389–91	107, 141
15. 318	31		392	75
361–6	130, 202		408	126
495–6	122			
537–9	135		21. 15–20	157–8
610–14	128		94–6	55
650–2	114		110	93, 191
705–6	109		122–4	116
			201–4	117
16. 119–22	44		389–92	183
130–44	36		405	24
221 ff.	17–18		544 ff.	42
384 ff.	41			
430–3	181		22. 18–20	188
538–40	107		66 ff.	117
638–40	84, 137		79 ff.	25
775	106		86 ff.	116
786–95	152		153 ff.	21
793–800	136		166–70	181, 190
837	114		172	112
			208–13	154
17. 24–27	123			

Iliad   page
22. (continued)
    265   33
    335–6   116
    346   20
    371   47
    393–5   84–5
    401–4   138
    410   1
    445–6   109–10
    468   2, 120
    508–14   3, 121

23. 43   16
    222   123, 134
    581 ff.   26
    805–8   193–4
    890   71

24. 56–9   187
    93–102   17, 190–1
    166   68–9
    169–73   153
    207   20
    212   20
    234   19
    255–6   126
    258–9   82, 187
    349 ff.   23
    507 ff.   69
    520–1   119
    525   191
    541   55, 100
    621 ff.   16
    667   100
    723–7   129
    743   61

Odyssey
    i. 57   111
    153   97
    159–60   192
    198   64
    325   97
    353   98, 143

    ii. *init.*   12

    iii. 108–11   127
    371–82   151

    iv. 71 ff.   67
    219–30   31
    259–89   77

Odyssey   page
    v. 98–105   59–60, 62
    160–225   56–7
    203–20   60–1

    vi. *init.*   57–8, 63
    41–6   168, 189
    130–40   22
    141–85   25
    309   192

    vii. 142   25
    237   78
    263   57
    299–307   61–2

    viii. 73–110   63–4
    362–6   200
    461 ff.   57–8, 61
    577–8   98

    xi. 482–91   100–1
    618–20   196
    632–5   162

    xv. 125   97

    xvi. 157–63   151
    256 ff.   155

    xvii. 260 ff. 12
    290 ff.   12
    312   111

    xviii. 67   18–19
    366   29

    xix. 33–42   151
    269 ff.   64

    xx. 201–3   196

    xxi. 55   13
    82   13

    xxii. 1   29
    298   31

    xxiii. 177 ff. 13

    xxiv. 351   139

Hymn to Apollo
    182–6   192